RANDOM ACTS OF CULTURE

Clarke Mackey moves with panache from personal perspective into a bold interdisciplinary account of why art is the way it is in our present-day society, and how it could—and why it should—be otherwise.

— RUTH HOWARD, Artistic Director, Jumblies Theatre, Toronto

This is a pioneering book. Contemporary societies lack, and badly need, an understanding of that part of culture that people make for themselves. Clarke Mackey brings this often invisible realm and its history into clear view. His book will help everyone who wants to think about the future of culture.

— DAVID CAYLEY, producer of CBC Radio's *Ideas* and author of *The Rivers North of the Future: The Testament of Ivan Illich*

Clarke Mackey invites us to rediscover the artist we all carry within our adult, consumerist, alienated selves.

— GUSTAVO ESTEVA, Zapatista advisor, negotiator, and visionary, and author of *Grassroots Post-Modernism*

About the author

Clarke Mackey teaches in the Department of Film and Media at Queen's University, Canada. His feature films, television shows, and documentaries on social justice issues have won awards and garnered much critical praise. In the early 1980s, Mackey took a six-year sabbatical from his media career to work as a preschool teacher. It was during this time that he first developed his ideas about vernacular culture.

CLARKE
MACKEY

RANDOM
ACTS OF
CULTURE

RECLAIMING ART AND COMMUNITY
IN THE 21ST CENTURY

BETWEEN THE LINES
TORONTO

First published in 2010 by
Between the Lines
401 Richmond Street West, Studio 277
Toronto, Ontario M5V 3A8
Canada
1-800-718-7201
www.btlbooks.com

Library and Archives Canada Cataloguing in Publication

Mackey, Clarke
    Random acts of culture : reclaiming art and community in the
    21st century / Clarke Mackey.

Includes bibliographical references and index.
ISBN 978-1-897071-64-9

1. Art and society.   2. Popular culture.
3. Civilization, Modern—21st century.   I. Title.

HM621.M3267 2010   306.09'05   C2010-904971-3

Cover images: Bread and Puppet Theatre performance and puppet close-up, Spiral
Garden, and Watts Tower photos by Clarke Mackey; graffiti and yarn bombing photos
by Jennifer Tiberio; Glasgow May Day parade close-up photo by Joseph Tohill

Printed in Canada

 **Mixed Sources**
Product group from well-managed
forests, controlled sources and
recycled wood or fiber
www.fsc.org Cert no. SW-COC-000952
© 1996 Forest Stewardship Council
FSC

Between the Lines gratefully acknowledges assistance for its publishing
activities from the Canada Council for the Arts, the Ontario Arts Council,
the Government of Ontario through the Ontario Book Publishers Tax Credit
program and through the Ontario Book Initiative, and the Government of
Canada through the Canada Book Fund.

 Canada Council for the Arts   Conseil des Arts du Canada   Canada    ONTARIO ARTS COUNCIL CONSEIL DES ARTS DE L'ONTARIO

CONTENTS

LEARNING
FROM CHILDREN

■

*As a twelve-year-old I could draw like Raphael, but it has
taken me my whole life to learn to paint like a child.*

— PABLO PICASSO

Making culture is the way in which human beings construct meaning from the experience of their senses and describe the
mystery at the centre of existence. It is what we use to think about
difficult problems and to find joy in the wonder of everyday life. It
is how we attempt to achieve emotional catharsis, pass on wisdom
to our children, and learn the art of living and dying. Those who are
inclined to talk in scientific terms say that culture—like hunger, sexual desire, and verbal language—is part of our evolutionary inheri-
tance. It is "in the genes," so to speak. Medical professionals tell us
that participation in artistic activities has incontrovertible benefits
for physical and mental health, and that passive spectatorship has
few. They say that people who dance, sing, paint, dramatize, make
up stories, or compose poetry are more vital, happy, and live longer
than those who remain consumers. Studies show that in old age
these "amateurs" use fewer prescription drugs, go to the doctor less
often, and are more independent.

Still, despite the obvious benefits of culture-making, Western culture appears to be organized for other ends.

In the late 1970s I took a six-year sabbatical from my career as a Canadian filmmaker to work full-time with preschool children. At the time it seemed as though I was returning home after years of exile to a place where the inhabitants spoke a language I once knew but had mostly forgotten. The ways in which children exist in the world, in their bodies, in their imaginations, fascinated me. Children, all children, as far as I can tell, want to move, sing, paint, speak in rhymes, tell tall tales, imagine themselves as someone else, and fashion three-dimensional objects with magical powers. At its most basic this activity is what art is; and, like walking and talking, art comes naturally to human beings. No one teaches us; we are compelled to do it. Indeed, in my experience *teaching* art to young children—as opposed to providing materials and permission—can have disastrous results. Yet when they make art on their own, children have a sense of concentration and a passion that most adults envy.

Preschool children gravitate towards what teachers call dramatic play, often undertaken in a dress-up area or a corner of the yard outside. In private places, when they believe they are out of the earshot of adults, children create elaborate worlds out of the raw materials of their imaginative environment. The subtlety, wit, and narrative complexity of the co-operatively performed impromptu epics created by three-year-olds still astonish me. Surely theatre historians do not need to look to the ancient Greeks to uncover the origins of drama. They would be better off spending a morning at their local co-op preschool.

During that time when I was doing art, music, drama, and story-telling with children daily, my commonplace assumptions about art and culture were severely shaken. The preschool provided a radically different vantage point: now I could view, with new and

2

critical eyes, the dominant cultural order that I had invested my life in serving. I became particularly sceptical of the prevailing idea that art is made by the gifted few for consumption by the untalented many. Most people today agree that robbing preschoolers of the opportunity to explore perception and meaning through imaginative play has serious psychological consequences for the children's emotional and intellectual development. That is why paints, musical instruments, and dress-up areas are standard in day cares and nursery schools. Yet by the time most children reach school age they have been transformed into the consumers of culture rather than its makers. The chosen few get special training. Some of the untalented learn art appreciation. Most of the rest search for their cultural sustenance prepackaged on a thousand electronic screens.

Has this always been so? Why and how does it happen? What are its consequences for individuals and societies? My search for the answers to these questions launched me on a surprising journey that has lasted half a lifetime. Its roots go back as far as I can remember.

∎

In the late 1950s my urban parents rented a sprawling, yellow-brick farmhouse near the town of Bronte, Ontario. The house was situated on about a hundred acres of farmland. The backyard was littered with trash, including a derelict automobile and several old tables. The grounds included a decrepit barn filled with rusting machinery. Beyond the barn was a sizable creek at the bottom of a steep bank, with patches of bush hedging the back fields. I still remember the hours I spent bathed in the whispering, wind-blown grasses, warmed by dappled light filtering through the trees. It was my eight-year-old version of a spiritual awakening.

When my mother and father, three small children, and a tiny baby first landed there in our 1950 Ford sedan, we had very little money. (Later, when my father's salary improved, we moved back into the city.) At the beginning the children owned few toys, and the family was without a television. Later we acquired a cheap black and white TV set with rabbit ears that could get the Canadian Broadcasting Corporation on good days. We kids would dress up in homemade costumes and build junk structures that we could inhabit and destroy, often improvising elaborate narratives for days on end. These performances were a bricolage composed of fragments from our favourite books, movies, and television shows put through the blender of our collective imagination. Forts, schooners, castles—all were fashioned from overturned furniture, musty old blankets, and discarded lumber. The old car doubled as a submarine or a space-ship until it was towed away one day in some misguided attempt on the part of the landlord to improve the property.

We may have lived in the country, but we were far from isolated. On an adjoining farm were two girls who were close to us in age. Their father hired me—not yet ten—to pluck chickens, drive the tractor when they were bringing in the hay bales, and pick apples. I would often accompany him on the Saturday pilgrimage to his stall at the St. Lawrence Market in Toronto, where I would haggle with Italian ladies over the price of a capon. Our lane led out to the Queen Elizabeth Way, a busy four-lane highway filled at all hours with trucks and cars speeding past on their way south to Hamilton and the United States. Down behind the barn, a couple of miles away, unmistakably marking the horizon, was the Cities Service oil refinery, later purchased by British Petroleum. The machine whine and loud chugging that emanated from that plant, and the yellow flames and smoke that lit up the night sky, remain forever etched in my memory.

My father was a teacher and my mother an artist. They both saw themselves as very modern. They talked a great deal about creativity. We were surrounded by books and art-making. They plied their four kids with a seemingly unlimited supply of art materials. In the winter, when building forts outside became too difficult, I depicted my boyhood fantasies of adventure and war using an HB pencil on plain white typewriter paper. By the time we left the farm I had attempted several still lifes using my mother's oil paints.

Artists and their activities held an important place in my parents' hearts. When I was about ten years old, they took me to the Art Gallery of Toronto to see a Vincent Van Gogh exhibit. I remember being fascinated both by the expressive realism of the work and the prototypical tortured-artist stories that surrounded this post-impressionist painter.

At some point—I might have been thirteen—I asked the kind of question that many children innocently ask. "Who is the greatest artist in the world?" My mother hesitated before replying, "Well, I guess you would have to say Picasso." (She now denies any memory of this pivotal conversation.) Later that year we went to a Picasso exhibit. As I walked through the high-ceilinged Art Gallery's echoey halls and looked at the framed images on the walls, I found myself wondering, "What's the big deal?" Like many other people when they are first faced with modernism's great originator, I found Picasso's work confusing and unappealing. Many people thought he was a great artist, possibly the greatest, but I didn't get it. I can appreciate Picasso now, but at the time the unpleasant experience of exclusion left a major imprint on my childish consciousness. It was my first clear memory of feeling inadequate because I was not part of the cognoscenti. I have felt this way many times since.

Throughout elementary school my passion for singing drove me to join various school and church choirs. These were not pleasant experiences. On several occasions the choir directors and other children pointed out to me that I sang off-key. No one ever tried to work with me to correct this common problem. Instead they told me that I lacked musical talent. Later, when I was older and the music got more demanding, one choir leader actually told me to mouth the words and not sing out. I eventually stopped singing altogether.

Cinema finally claimed my artistic allegiance. With movies I could indulge in my passion for images, stories, imaginative worlds, sounds and music, and performance. This was the mid-1960s, a time of extraordinary innovation in the world of cinema. By that time my nomadic family had settled in the big city of Toronto and I discovered a film society that showed classic art films. Mainstream films never did excite me that much, but when I discovered Canadian and international art cinema I was hooked: Claude Jutra, Ingmar Bergman, Michelangelo Antonioni, and Orson Welles became my heroes.

The childhood pattern continued: watching and listening led to doing. Early experiments in feature filmmaking in my home city, films such as *Nobody Waved Goodbye* (1964) and *Winter Kept Us Warm* (1965), generated an exciting sense of possibility. Maybe I couldn't sing, but I believed I could tell stories on film, and people I knew were actually doing it. By the age of fourteen I had commandeered the family Super-8mm movie camera and was starting to create short films. The next year a family friend who worked for the Board of Education loaned me a 16mm Bolex camera. Using funds raised from a summer job, I purchased some film and started shooting a half-hour movie called *On Nothing Days* about the life of a teenage boy in the suburbs. I also talked my way onto a feature film shoot downtown as a production assistant.

I had my life all planned out. I was going to be a "great filmmaker." When I was seventeen, *On Nothing Days* was broadcast on national TV. At age twenty I completed my first feature, *The Only Thing You Know* (1971), about a young woman's first experiences with love and independence in downtown Toronto. It was well received by the critics and won some awards, but quickly disappeared from sight. For the next decade I patched together a living by occasionally directing films and television shows, teaching at a couple of universities on limited contracts, running filmmaking workshops in schools, community centres, and prisons, and editing other people's movies for wages. I was able to pay the rent this way, but I was beginning to question the choices I had made. Childless and living in the exclusively adult world of the film and television industry—a world crowded with ego, ambition, and avarice—I found my identity as an artist under siege.

The preschool detour started innocently enough. An ex-girl-friend studying sociology at the University of Toronto asked me to videotape children playing together in groups. She wanted to analyze their behaviour and interactions as part of a paper she was writing. The location was a parent co-operative preschool nursery in the basement of an old Anglican church close to campus. I went once with the camera and just observed, getting to know the kids. It was a friendly, relaxed place. On my next visit I rolled the Sony Portapak camera and recorded a couple of hours of group play at various locations in the nursery room. I don't remember how useful the tape was for my friend—I assume she wrote her paper—but the experience of visiting the school changed my life profoundly.

While I could not precisely articulate my motivations, I knew I wanted to reconnect with this way of being. I asked Elizabeth and Patricia, the two preschool teachers, if I could volunteer at the nursery.

Because I had learned to draw and paint as a child I ended up trying my hand at art activities. In the beginning I made a lot of mistakes—mostly having to do with behaving too much like a kid rather than like an adult—but eventually I began to learn how things worked. I also befriended some of the parents, most of whom were connected with the university. After a few months one of the teachers decided to leave the school. The parent board began looking around for a replacement, and someone asked me if I was interested in applying. After some discussion the board agreed to hire me.

Right from the start I knew that I was there because I wanted to learn something from the kids, not the other way around. If the children gained something from their interactions with me—or more precisely from the environment I hoped to provide for them—so much the better. I was there because I wanted to get as close as any adult could to the homeland of childhood. Memories of the farm, the drawings, the impromptu dramas, came flooding back. It was here that the ideas that inform this book took shape.

■

Most people think about art, culture, and entertainment based on a set of largely unconscious and thus unexamined assumptions. There are many variations, but, put crudely, both art works and popular entertainment are seen as commodities, perhaps of a special kind, created in advance by trained professionals and purchased by the consumer-spectator. The role of the consumer in this system is to select appropriately from a range of choices those works that are most interesting or enjoyable. The media, and critics in particular, play a crucial role in guiding purchasing choices and influencing the kind of work that cultural producers create; ownership and copyright are always central issues because economic exchange is a central feature of producer-consumer relationship. In this version of reality, popular artists and entertainers are said to have a special gift that compels them to speak for their community and historical moment and even, in certain remarkable circumstances, "for all time."

These unexamined assumptions, like so many others in Western society, are surprisingly anti-historical. For most of human existence—whether you measure that as one million years (the beginning of humanoids) or fifty thousand years (from the time when modern homo sapiens first appeared)—art, culture, and entertainment were organized differently. While people have always told stories, sung and danced, spoken in rhymes, and adorned their bodies and dwellings with beautiful and rare things, they did not, before the modern age, think of these things as products for sale.

Evidence of this history can be found in the etymology of the words that people use to describe these activities. The English word "art," in the sense that we use it today as "fine art," distinct from craft, did not appear in the language until the middle of the eighteenth century. In large parts of the world today, it is not a word that people think much about or have a clear concept of. Translators find it difficult to render the word "art" into many non-Western languages. In more traditional communities, there is seldom any reason to disembed a special category of imaginative activities and objects from ordinary life and give them special status. Culture, the more inclusive term, is even more recent. British thinker Raymond Williams said, famously, that culture is "one of the two or three most complicated words in the English language" because of the complex array of conflicting meanings that find a home in its two syllables.

So it is too with the words "popular" and "folk." Popular is supposed to mean "of the people" and refers to the common, everyday culture of the majorities, to distinguish it from the more refined high culture of the elites. It is an interesting distinction, but the word has migrated far from its original meaning. The term "popular culture" is now often used as a synonym for mass culture—pop music, Hollywood movies, commercial television, video games. The elision of "popular" with "commercial" papers over an array of interesting contradictions. For one thing, the makers of pop culture today, while they poach freely from street, playground, and kitchen culture, constitute a powerful elite. Their claim to speak for the majority—sometimes legitimized by a new generation of hip academics—is deeply tainted with self-interest. One of my principal arguments here is that if you want to find out how most ordinary people make meaning, you should not be looking at the mass culture they consume, but rather at how that mass culture is either ignored or remade in everyday life. A new word needs to be found to describe genuine popular culture in its many forms.

"Folk" is also a term that seeks to hide a troublesome dialectic. Folk culture is commonly defined as ethnic and historical. It is something that our grandparents or elders did, perhaps back in the old country or on the farm here in North America. Many in the educated urban middle class find folk culture quaint and vaguely embarrassing; others are attracted to its exotic aesthetics. It is central to the idea of folk culture that it should not change. Indeed, there are those who argue that people who tamper with folk traditions by modernizing and hybridizing are considered, at best, crass turncoats and, at worst, thieves of someone else's identity. Folk culture is not a term you would normally use to describe the everyday activities of modern city dwellers.

The poverty of these words eventually forced me to look elsewhere for a way of talking about imaginative activities engaged in by "ordinary" people: family stories and celebrations, dinner parties, gardening, home movies, letter writing, street dancing, living-room sing-arounds, homemade art and clothing, community sport.

All of these activities are clearly aesthetic, but they tend to be excluded from the term "art" by the reigning assumptions of our time.

I finally found what I was looking for in a small book of essays by Ivan Illich. In *Shadow Work*, Illich endeavoured to make a distinction between subsistence activities embedded in social life, "unpaid activities which provide and improve livelihood," which he called "vernacular work," and the unpaid labour performed by people (mostly women) to support modern consumer culture, which he called the "shadow economy." As Illich explained:

> Vernacular is a Latin term that we use in English only for the language that we have acquired without paid teachers. In Rome, it was used from 500 B.C. to 600 A.D. to designate any value that was homebred, homemade, derived from the commons, and that a person could protect and defend though he neither bought nor sold it on the market.

The main contrast between one and the other is that "this simple term"—vernacular—is "totally refractory to any analysis utilizing concepts developed in formal economics." The term can thus be used to make a distinction "between the expansion of the shadow economy and its inverse—the expansion of the vernacular domain."

Expanding on how Illich uses it, I propose to use the word "vernacular" to describe a set of imaginative activities that go back to the beginnings of human life and are still active today, but are seldom included in discussions of modern culture. Most of us make a distinction between mass culture and "high" or serious art. I insist that a third category is necessary to describe creative activities that take place outside of the consumer marketplace and the world of trained professionals. I call this third category "vernacular culture."

What follows is an account of my attempt to understand the historical forces that have shaped people's aesthetic practices and my search for vernacular culture at the beginning of the new century. I am guided on this journey by my realization that the cultural, the political, and the social are all connected in a web of relations and representations that inhabit our most intimate and unconscious selves. They influence and define our deepest feelings and aspirations. They constantly reveal themselves in the smallest details of everyday life.

■

I first imagined writing this book almost thirty years ago. It has taken me an unconscionably long time to complete. The idea weathered much neglect, an ongoing long-term relationship, two children, the making of a couple of feature films, and a university teaching position. On several occasions I tried to push the whole thing out of my life. But the tyrant plagues me still. My original reluctance to carry through was based, I realize now, on certain deep fears, including the fear of being marginalized from the world of ideas I am so privileged to be part of. Blank stares and funny looks greeted me whenever I mustered up the courage to mention vernacular culture. The idea apparently did not resonate with how most people experienced the world.

But recently certain important things have changed. We live in an apocalyptic time. The dire consequences of our reckless two-hundred-year-long experiment in industrial capitalism can no longer be ignored. We have entered a period that James Howard Kunstler calls "the Long Emergency" and economist Nicholas Stern describes as "the greatest market failure in history." Old assumptions have lost their currency, particularly when it comes to culture and art.

The people who fight over the ungainly but fashionable term "postmodern" seem to be planting new crops in the old fields. I now find ideas that I once thought forbidden being uttered aloud in undergraduate classrooms. The time has come for these seedlings I have been incubating to accept their uncertain fate in the dangerous but fertile ground of public debate.

Modernity and Western culture have been under attack from many quarters in recent years. Imperialism, colonialism, ethnocentrism, elitism, violence, alienation, inequality, and climate change— these describe some of the serious negative consequences of the industrial age. Amidst the clamour of voices it is sometimes difficult to recognize and celebrate the genuine achievements of the West: individualism and the rejection of xenophobia and provincialism, democratic ideals and the affirmation of equality, human health and well-being, and the highly original works of Shakespeare, Beethoven, Rembrandt, and Bergman, to name but a few. It is absurd to think that it might be possible to go back to a simpler time, before modernity, in order to escape from the sins of the Western world. As Canadian composer R. Murray Schafer once said to me, "It is not a question of going back. Progress is an invention of the modern age; so is regress." Even if a return to the past were imaginable, I for one would advise against it. We have gained much wisdom from the experiment of modernity. As I see it, there is neither progress nor regress, just change.

While describing the past and the present, I want to propose a possible future that is not an extension of the past, but an act of imagination—not as some sort of self-fulfilling prediction, but as a way of seeing our age with new eyes. Taking our starting point from children everywhere, I suggest a playful, emotionally committed recovery of the pleasures of vernacular culture in the ruins of the industrial age. But the recovery I suggest is neither innocent nor nostalgic. Vernacular culture, by definition, is a moving target. It is always local and improvised. It is necessarily extremely diverse. The changes I hope for will provide more opportunities for people to realize their full humanity in all its many forms: artistically, politically, spiritually. I have no doubt that individual identity, democratic ideals, pluralism, literacy, and electronic technology will all play major roles in this process, but the results cannot be predicted. As the children at the nursery school showed me long ago, openness to surprise is our most potent tool.

BEDTIME
STORIES

■

It is hotter than it should be for early June. Mother leaves the office early on Friday to drive her seven-year-old son to piano lessons. The driveway and parking lot of the school are packed with idling, air-conditioned cars. The boy is surly when he sits down in the back seat. She has just turned the radio off, and he immediately dons the iPod earphones and provides only the most perfunctory answers to her questions about school today. When they arrive at the church to meet the piano teacher, she can see that her son is not happy to be there, but she soldiers on. The teacher is paid for a new technique book and then the mother heads off to take her daughter shopping. Her son will have to get home on his own.

The daughter may be twelve, but she wants to be sixteen. Fighting between mother and daughter over clothes has become almost a daily occurrence. At the mall the girl heads for The Gap and mother follows, feeling like her slave. The daughter tries on miniskirts and tight, midriff-revealing tops. The naked sexuality of it is obvious to everyone, including the girl, but she wants to fit in and her mother recognizes her need to do that.

Because no one had time to cook, Mom, Dad, and the kids end up going out to a cheap restaurant for supper. The adults know the food is not healthy, but no one could face even boiling an egg after the hellish week that they have been through. Eating in a restaurant that serves healthy food would be just too expensive. The family is trying to save for a trip to Disney World. After dinner the kids want to watch TV. There's a new show on that is supposed to be really great. Mother nixes that in favour of an early bedtime.

How is she going to get the kids to sleep? Even in the embrace of commodities and their stresses it is sometimes possible to tap into a different layer of existence. What about resorting to one of the oldest and most intimate rituals in the human life world: the bedtime story?

Being told a story at the threshold of unconsciousness is one of the most serene and healing joys of life, for adults as well as children. Most of us harbour primal memories of the ritual from our own childhoods. Parents are well aware of the pleasures involved in bringing stories to the darkened bedrooms of their children. Grownups even occasionally share tales with each other before sleep.

When a seven-year-old asks for a bedtime story, adults have a few choices. They could choose to read from a book. They could recite a well-known tale from memory. They could tell a true story from the family's past. Or they could make something up. Because teller and listener are face to face, they can test the waters and negotiate a solution that is satisfactory to both. If the adult reads from a book, the child may want to change the name of the main character to her name or that of someone she knows. This implicitly acknowledges the pleasures of identification, and recognizes the specificity of this moment and the relationship between the two of them.

If tellers recall a story from memory, they will almost certainly change it from one recounting to the next. Certain details will get emphasized and others will fall away. New elements will get added. This is not just because of faulty memory. As they tell the story, they can see and hear the reactions of the listener. People embellish the parts of a story that excite their listeners and themselves, and leave out the boring bits.

If they tell a story about themselves, they are sharing parts of their own pasts, reclaiming the past and making it part of the child's mythology. My daughter used to request stories about when I was "bad" as a child. (I actually had quite a bit of material to draw from, though she never heard the worst bits.) A story made up from scratch, even if not consciously thought through, will almost certainly take its themes from issues that are close to the surface of awareness between adult and child.

This is a moment of intimacy between two people who love each other. The requirement of skill or virtuosity in the teller is negligible. Storytellers certainly don't want to be boring, but they are seldom judged harshly by their listeners for being bad performers. (There are exceptions. I know a very kind man who used to sing lullabies to his tiny daughter. When she was four, the kid had heard enough. "I'll go to sleep, I promise," she pleaded. "Just don't sing to me." I guess some basic level of competence is necessary.)

In addition, there is nothing commercial about this event. It would be absurd to even imagine the requirement that children pay their parents to tell stories, and no one I know would ever consider sending out a royalty cheque for the bedtime use of published material.

The telling of a bedtime story is a simple example of everyday vernacular culture. It has roots going back to the very beginnings of human existence, and it demonstrates four key characteristics that mark it as being distinct from the everyday commercial culture that we all know so well.

1) You Have to Be There

Commercial culture is made up of objects—paintings, texts, musical scores, moving images—that have exchange value and can be stored and repeated. The same can be said of performing arts such as dance and theatre, which might at first seem ephemeral. In most cases performances are notated and repeated (like Shakespeare's plays or Balanchine's ballet choreography). Vernacular activities often include objects, but they are objects that possess little in the way of exchange value. Vernacular culture is something that people do, usually together with others, on special occasions. The "others" and "together" are more important than the "something."

The concept of vernacular culture is closer to being a verb than a noun: it is about process rather than product. As such, it is highly context-dependent. If vernacular objects are moved, or performances are repeated, they tend to lose a significant part of their original meaning. Imagine trying to repeat your family's Christmas dinner every night for a week and charging admission. More to the point, imagine videotaping Christmas dinner and playing it back next year in lieu of roasting another turkey. Not just the smells and tastes are lost; the whole experience is transformed.

That is why in museums artifacts like masks and pottery from traditional cultures, taken from their original context, can sometimes seem lifeless and without aura. Unlike Western art, which is made to be exhibited, these objects, despite the aesthetic value ascribed to them by curators, are little more than the leftovers from someone else's dinner. Like the bedtime story, vernacular events are site-specific, time-specific, one-offs.

2) *Never the Same Way Twice*

In a culture dominated by texts—musical scores, published versions of plays—some interpretive variation is desirable at the moment of performance. The very slight variations introduced by different performers in new contexts can take on an importance that may even seem excessive at times. For example, the difference between how two different musicians interpret the Bach *Sonatas for Unaccompanied Violin* arouses debate and controversy in various reviews and listener reactions, yet the changes are so subtle that untrained listeners barely notice. But to tamper with the text itself is another matter. In 1958 pianist Glenn Gould recorded Mozart's *Piano Concerto in C Minor*. He made certain "improvements" to the maestro's work by ignoring Mozart's expression and tempo markings, adding additional ornamentation, and rewriting the left-hand part. Most critics and listeners were outraged.

This precision in repetition has reached near-perfection with the development of mechanical reproduction. We can now listen to a precise, mechanically reproduced performance of Gould playing Mozart (controversially), even though the performer has been dead for decades. In this context, copyright and claims of authorship obviously become very important for both texts and recordings.

The world of the vernacular introduces a different set of expectations. Rituals are by definition concerned with repetition. Traditional stories and songs important to a social group are constantly repeated, often over many generations. Yet these kinds of repetitions are of a different order from those common in commercial culture.

Researchers who have studied well-established oral storytelling traditions among non-literate people in Eastern Europe and other places say that the underlying structure of traditional stories remains intact from one telling to another, even from one generation of tellers to another, but each individual retelling is seldom word-for-word identical. Narrative elements are rephrased and new details added, while others are taken away. When asked about this lack of precision, oral storytellers don't really understand what the questioner means by literal accuracy. For them it is still the same story in all the ways that matter.

In the world of vernacular culture, repetition with constant variation is the norm, much like the jazz musician riffing on a familiar tune. In the example of the bedtime story, variation adds variety and updates the details for the specific audience and moment. Vernacular culture is flexible and context-driven. Concepts of copyright and individual authorship are beside the point.

3) Anybody Can Do It

One of the great achievements of Western culture is how it empowers spectators to experience works at a critical distance, sitting safely in a theatre seat or on the couch in the family room. Spectators respond internally to what the artist offers and, in the case of a live performance, applaud as required at the end. The rich internal experience of art at a distance is something that educated people in the Western world defend with passion. For some it is the prerequisite of civilization and democracy. But the pleasures of pure spectatorship are foreign to the vernacular world. While there are usually divisions of labour in vernacular culture, all present are expected to participate. Completely passive spectators are not trusted.

Take traditional country dancing. This is not the now more familiar country and western line dancing but, rather, an older style of group dancing that originated in the United Kingdom in the eighteenth and nineteenth centuries among the farming classes. The most common North American variant, with some significant alterations, is square dancing. In the last three decades, however, another variation, called contra dancing, has gained considerable popularity in North America, particularly in parts of New England among the educated, urban, middle class.

English, Scottish, and Irish contra and country dancing all share certain features. First, the dances consist of a small number of "figures," or steps, done with a partner and combined in different sequences. Most of us can remember "do-si-dos" and "ladies' chains" from high-school square-dance class. Even the most uncoordinated neophyte can pick up these steps fairly quickly. The dance leader or "caller" first teaches the order of the figures and makes sure that all of the dancers practise what they are supposed to do. The music is preferably supplied by a live band, rather than from a recording, so that the caller can adjust tempo and dance length. Live bands can also "read" the dancers and change tunes when necessary in response to group energy. When the dance begins, the caller yells out the steps just before they are required. Elaborate patterns based on one set of couples moving towards the front of the room and another towards the back make the whole thing look quite complicated, while retaining the relative simplicity of each individual's contribution. Experienced dancers can add flourishes and extra steps without altering the flow of the patterns and without interfering with the less experienced dancers. Because of the simplicity and flexibility of contra dances—the precarious balance of conformity and individuality—people of various ages and skill levels can participate equally.

Vernacular activities are structured for maximum participation of all present. Because of this, virtuosity, when it exists, is deemphasized. Individual flourishes and improvisations are encouraged as long as they don't alter the flow of the performance (and sometimes even when they do), but the important message of country dancing is community and relationship rather than skill and performance. This emphasis distinguishes it from commercial culture, in which virtuosity is a highly valued commodity. People are only willing to pay high ticket prices if they are convinced that they are about to experience a work, a performance, of unique genius.

4) Not for Sale

As the example of the bedtime story demonstrates, vernacular performances are neither repeatable nor transportable. They encourage participation and de-emphasize virtuosity. As such, they are useless as commodities. You would never think of paying your lover for the meal he cooked for you, as if you were getting it in a restaurant. Official society tends to value things primarily in economic terms. This is why vernacular culture is seldom acknowledged in contemporary cultural discourse. We know that Picasso's paintings have extraordinary monetary value, even if we've never seen them or don't like them. Their monetary value, representative of their relative significance and influence, makes us pay attention. Vernacular activities, when noticed at all, are generally praised along with motherhood and multiculturalism; but their monetary value is negligible. Some folk-art works and roots music recordings are sold, to be sure, but by that point they are the decontextualized traces of past experiences. In modern society, vernacular culture in the form of dinner parties, jokes, family traditions, homemade memorial services, gossiping about the outrageous behaviour of a friend, singing Christmas carols, and telling bedtime stories is still alive but in varying states of health. These activities remain popular despite (or maybe because of) their resistance to commerce.

■

The vast vernacular ocean, the physical and cultural commons in which human life subsists, has always been viewed by entrepreneurs and corporations as a wild frontier to be tamed, a resource to be mined for gold. The tactics are various, but the goals are simple: observe, mass-produce, and market back society's subsistence activities for a profit. This commodification has been carried out with nearly all of the things that people once did for themselves within families and communities. Child-rearing; food growing and preparation; care of the sick and the dying; the making of shelter, furniture, and clothing; emotional support and spiritual renewal; music and dancing; artistic expression and imaginative play; gossip, news, conversation, political negotiation, storytelling—all have been turned into commodities for sale or services provided by professionals.

Of course, the territory is never completely conquered. People everywhere still find ways of living outside the embrace of money. But investors want a reasonable return on their investments and, with that goal, the commercial economy must continue to expand. More and more people, further and further from the centres of power, are compelled to earn wages in order to be able to pay for things that their ancestors once fashioned for themselves. For most, the marginalized and dispossessed majority, this introduces a new form of indignity. Before, they lived without money; now, they are poor, eligible for the pity and charity of the social minorities.

The failure of consumer society, however, demands that we question the logic of the market and the cultural forms it has spawned. What was once marginal or old fashioned now gains a new relevance. There are important lessons to be learned from those who choose to resist the assumptions of our time.

SNAPSHOTS
FROM THE EDGE

■

It's insane to imagine that this [close to] a mall, in this time, in this place, people could look at one another in ways that are not instrumental, where they would just somehow take pleasure in one another.

—JUTTA MASON

In the cities of Europe and North America it seems as if all aspects of human relationships are cradled in the buying and selling of merchandise and services. Children compete for the latest toys. Spouses anticipate their furniture purchases and vacations. Lovers go out for dinner and a show. Friends have "a coffee." For those of us living in the big cities at the beginning of the twenty-first century the vernacular is in retreat. Even so, reactions against the prevailing tide continue to assert themselves—a conspiracy hatched in the private world of family and close friends, far from the watchful eye of marketers and surveillance cameras. Others courageously claim public space. These acts of vernacular culture are seldom recognized for what they are.

The modest examples that follow are recent and most originate in Canada, where I live. Some I experienced directly; others were gleaned from the back pages of newspapers or Sunday morning radio documentaries. Despite great variation, they are united in the ways in which they assert a more convivial, human-centred world view and refute basic assumptions so dear to the hearts of economists and stockholders in the globalized economy.

■

One afternoon in early May 2007 in the Glebe neighbourhood of Ottawa, Willem Grant, ten, and his sister Alise, eight, started drawing a hopscotch pattern on the sidewalk in front of their home. Within minutes other kids came along and spontaneously added to the game. In the end, a dozen children drew over two thousand chalked squares extending all the way around the block and beyond. People all over the neighbourhood enjoyed the fun. Adults from a local high-rise building came out to see the collectively created project. A ninety-year-old woman recalled playing hopscotch as a girl in Toronto.

Suddenly this innocent springtime game was cut short when a city maintenance truck arrived and spent an hour power-washing all the chalk off of the sidewalks. The workers did not wash the dust out of the gutters or clean up any of the other debris on the street. Their cleanup focused exclusively on the hopscotch game. Alise characterized the maintenance workers' actions as "brutal."

It turned out that a local resident had phoned the authorities to express displeasure about "graffiti" on the street. The city had recently passed a tough anti-graffiti bylaw, and its employees were responding, as required, to a public complaint. Within hours other chalk drawings, poems, and squares labelled as "random acts of hopscotch" started appearing all over the city. A spontaneously formed group called the Ottawa Community Chalk Network created a trail of hopscotch squares and drawings four blocks long that led to the front door of city hall. One city councillor, Clive Doucet, said he would introduce an amendment to the anti-graffiti bylaw to exempt chalk drawings. "For generations now, we've made [the streets] basically exclusive right of ways for cars," he said. "And I think now, finally . . . people are suddenly realizing: Maybe we should be thinking of our streets as public spaces for people as well as cars."

Later city officials released a statement expressing their regret about removing the sidewalk chalk. They said that in future they would act more thoughtfully, adding that a heavy rain would have eventually washed the markings away.

■

In affluent Japan homelessness was largely unheard of until the economic boom went sour in the early 1990s. Corporate restructuring and layoffs to deal with the downturn left thousands of people without jobs or supports. In 2005 estimates of the number of homeless people living in Japan's larger cities ranged from twenty-five thousand to fifty thousand. For these individuals, mostly middle-aged men who seek refuge from the weather along urban riverbanks and in small parks, the dream of middle-class gentility is just a bad joke.

Unlike many of the homeless in North American cities, these Japanese street people are seldom associated with crime, drug use, or prostitution. To keep out of the cold and wet, thousands of them have fashioned small shelters out of scrounged materials: wood, corrugated metal, blankets, shipping pallets, temple ornaments, blue tarps, cardboard, and thick manga comic books retrieved from wastepaper bins. These structures are built to be disassembled quickly, because police raids are frequent. One year in Osaka hundreds of police and public employees clashed with homeless squatters to clear the parks for the springtime flower festivals.

Tokyo-based artist and architecture school graduate Kyohei Sakaguchi began documenting and photographing this squatter architecture in the early 2000s. His images show neat, aesthetically pleasing, imaginative structures. One has a tiny dog house attached to the side; another boasts a beautiful container garden of bonsai shrubs and trimmed camellias. Hinged doors and bamboo blinds are common. One structure has a second story; another was built under a bridge and incorporates a piece of playground equipment. There is a cardboard house, lashed together with rope, in the shape of a car. It is placed on a simple warehouse dolly so that it can be wheeled around as required to keep ahead of the law.

Itsuo Nakamura lives in one of the houses that Sakaguchi photographed. A former camera engineer, Nakamura is sixty years old and single. His simple house, on the bank of the Sumida River in central Tokyo, is a six-by-four-foot masterpiece of improvisation. The walls and roof are made of cardboard and tarpaulins attached to wooden supports with tape and string. He owns a small oil stove for cooking and heat and a single shelf for food and the paperback thrillers he loves to read. On the roof is a small solar panel to power his miniature TV and radio-cassette player. He says, "A day of sunshine in the summer gives me enough to watch TV for six or seven hours."

"I don't want to idealize the situation homeless people find themselves in," says Sakaguchi, "but in a world where most of us live in mass-produced, concrete boxes, Zero Yen Houses are precious works of art. They deserve to be recognized."

Sakaguchi carries on the work of architectural historian Bernard Rudofsky, who wrote two books on informal architecture four decades ago: *Architecture Without Architects* (1964) and *The Prodi-*

gious Builders (1977). It was Rudofsky who first coined the term "vernacular architecture," which is now widely used. Like Rudofsky, Sakaguchi wants to celebrate everyday human ingenuity and aesthetic sensibility; unlike Rudofsky, he has more urgent political concerns. For Sakaguchi, the structures and the context of their construction are the reverse of the overconsumption and resource depletion that plague the newly globalized economy. He believes that people can learn from these untutored builders about how to live in a way that is more sensitive to the natural world. He says, "These homes embody simplicity, functionality, and are at one with their environment, like the tea house of Rikyu Sen." A famous sixteenth-century tea master, Rikyu Sen preached frugality through the tea ceremony.

Because the squatters have almost nothing they are forced to live along communal lines, sharing house-building tips and skills. In some cases they earn small amounts of money working as day labourers. Itsuo Nakamura could probably afford a cheap room in a slum house. "But I prefer it here," he says. "Here I have no worries." Okawara, another street-dweller, who like most Japanese takes off his shoes before entering his canvas and wood house, says he also prefers his current situation: "It sometimes gets cold, but I like the view of the river."

■

Every summer since 1984, artists, educators, therapists, and community workers at the Bloorview MacMillan Children's Centre in Toronto have been carrying out an extraordinary experiment in the marriage of contemporary vernacular culture with the helping professions. Sometimes one and sometimes two day camps integrate children from the local community with children who are physically and mentally challenged. At one site all of the activities take place around a large garden laid out in a spiral. At another, the Cosmic Bird Feeder, the garden is in the shape of a big star. At each site, art, ceremony, storytelling, and play dramatize a narrative that unfolds over the whole summer. As the organizers put it, this is a "collaborative process between children, artists and the natural world." Children and adults plant, tend, water, and harvest all the plants and vegetables that grow there. Participants also make masks, puppets, and costumes, bake bread and cookies, and tell collective stories called "true stewies." They create ceremonies and parades, sing and make up songs, and play percussion instruments. Everyone embraces a spirit of committed playfulness.

The *Spiral Garden Resource Book* describes the "mythopoetics" of one summer's epic, revealing how play—with its reliance on metaphor, ambiguity, and spontaneity—is the defining model for all activities. The season started with a musical, costumed procession to the institution's kitchen to gather scraps for the compost. When they returned, the children were confronted with "Jahungalali," the spirit of the compost, angered because he wasn't invited on the procession. The garden's main antagonist, the mischievous Crow, devised a new way of luring Cosmic Bird away from its responsibility to care for Cosmic Egg. A wooden cruise liner, complete with figurehead, promised to take Bird deep into the starry Milky Way. The garden's scarecrow was transformed into Creature, the agent that must foil Crow's deception. With the help of magic symbols and glyphs created by the children, Creature lured Crow away from the precious egg and ruined his plan.

Later, a real dead snake, killed by a lawn mower, was buried near the back edge of the yard in an elaborate ceremony that involved an elongated coffin and a rousing rendition of "When the Snakes Go Marching In." Shortly after that, Mulla Tooki Lulu, a whirling dervish, made an appearance and inspired a rash of dervish puppets. Stories of how these characters arrived at the garden were collected by a scribe and an assistant. After that, wooden spirit houses were built, possibly to house the rather naughty Naka Clowns that were populating the site. The summer climaxed with a ceremony to inaugurate the prayer wheel at the centre of the garden. That wheel would hold Cosmic Egg, carefully wrapped and placed in a cradle that allowed it to spin—necessary for its successful incubation.

Jan Mackie, the co-ordinator of Cosmic Bird Feeder at the time, told me that everything the group did was "a reaction to consumerism, to fragmentation, to disconnectedness to the earth." The garden staff, she said, included people who were very creative, and they wanted "to do something else with their art besides hang it somewhere." They felt the need both to integrate the able-bodied children and the children with disabilities, and to integrate the object-making, the activities, the art, with story.

> You make puppets, but then you take them off and you animate them and they become characters, or you take something from woodworking and you take it to painting and you take it to another level and then you can take it to where there's fabrics and beads and shells and things, and you can take it further. Then it can become a box or some other object that becomes part of the story.

While the garden staff directed the flow of the narrative, it would be wrong to say that they made it up. The staff took their cues from the children's own imaginative creations and enthusiasms. No one had any idea, at the beginning of that summer, where things would end up. The story evolved based on the particular group of kids and their collective state of mind over time.

■

Ron Grimes, Professor of Religion and Society at Wilfrid Laurier University in Waterloo, Ontario, is one of the founders of an academic discipline called ritual studies. In this capacity he has written a number of academic articles and books about rituals of all kinds. But unlike a lot of other academics, he has put his ideas to the test at something called the ritual lab. This is a class he undertakes with university students; the goal is to work collectively to "invent" new rites of passage and other kinds of rituals and celebrations. Grimes is well aware of the dangers and contradictions inherent in such an activity; yet he chooses to attempt it anyway. His philosophy and methods are instructive for anyone wanting to reimagine personal or family traditions.

While Grimes admits that there are many ways of inventing or reinventing ritual, he recognizes that lots of them "will result in failure, will result in self deception." He is adamant that the task cannot be done by sitting down at a desk or computer and working it out or setting it down in advance in your head, in the way that you would write a poem or a play. Or, as he says, you can't "sit down with a committee and say, alright, now I'm going to invent myself a myth or a ritual. It doesn't work." The impetus must come from elsewhere. One big problem, he says, is that "we have a culture that is intensely interested in the self" and "tends to be narcissistic," which raises "a lot of possibilities for self-indulgence"—which in turn makes him somewhat hesitant to even attempt to develop new rituals.

Nevertheless, he argues, it is possible for individuals and groups to do so; he believes that although people cannot invent symbols, they can prepare themselves to allow symbols to emerge. "You can prepare a group to do certain kinds of things that will resonate, and people, in the midst of it, will sense that something important, if not sacred, has gone on." As an example he mentions the case of someone going to their grandmother's funeral: "As often happens, they aren't able to do the work they need to do at the funeral and so on. It often leaves a person immobilized and in chaos." Grimes says to them, "What do you *need* to do to be able to bury your grandmother?" He is not looking for "a verbal answer." He is looking for them to find out what they need to do to be able to bury their grandmother.

To teach people to respond, to follow, Grimes uses a variety of exercises "to learn the difference between simply acting arbitrarily on the one hand and responding on the other. Or acting from a plan on the one hand or responding on the other." Part of what he tries to do is to undermine the usual way in which people go about constructing or revising a rite. The usual pattern is to move from conception to action, which, he argues, leads to a "split human being, doing things to illustrate ideas. As long as you're doing things to illustrate ideas, it's the surest way to have a dead rite on your hands."

Grimes is not opposed to thinking and criticism—"I insist that whatever we do be subject to criticism and evaluation"—but that part of things should come at the end. The first step is to get the participants to stop talking, get them going "without thinking about what they're doing." He starts the students off by having them do something other than talking—walking, "honking" on a musical instrument they don't know how to play, maybe just breathing—any physical activity that helps them to be comfortable with "leading with their hands and feet rather than leading with their brains."

In part you have to teach people simply how to move randomly. Literally sometimes we just walk, just walk around the room, just walk, walk and walk and walk and walk. Or breathe. It doesn't make any difference.

Some will want to talk about it as following your unconscious; some will interpret that as "following the spirit"; some will interpret it as following the sense of the group. So, what I try to suggest is that as long as you refrain from naming it in some fashion, the more you will learn. Now, I'm not resistant to any of those terms, but particularly when I'm in the lab situation itself, I'm resistant to all of them.

The other part of it is to be able to wait it out. "You wait on your muscles and your bones, you wait on your unconscious, you wait on God, I don't know what it is you wait on," he says. "But you simply wait, and often you go down a hundred wrong paths." What finally happens is that people discover what it is they need to do, and that they need to do it over and over again. They might need to bow to the floor, or walk to the park, and they will have to repeat that action over and over, perhaps a hundred times. The workshops he gives are different from most workshops because of the seemingly endless repetition built into them.

At first they're bored. We are a culture that doesn't know what to do with repetition. We think that repetition is boring. I pound this over and over again, that monotony is not necessarily boredom. Boredom is a particular cultural reaction to monotony. So eventually what happens is that they discover some other sides of monotony, some other sides of simply repeating something over and over.

In a process such as this, so far from the instrumentality of modern life, even the failures must be pretty interesting.

■

What does an emerging, postmodern vernacular culture look like? Perhaps no other example I can give epitomizes it better than recent developments in Dufferin Grove Park in Toronto. There are over five million people living in the Greater Toronto Area. It is widely regarded as a city of immigrants. Over 50 per cent of the population are visible minorities compared to a white Anglo-Saxon norm. The area around Dufferin Grove Park in the central west part of the city has a greater population of first- and second-generation immigrants than do other parts of the city. Right across the street is a large, enclosed shopping mall.

In 1995, in this ordinary, mid-sized park, a group of neighbourhood mothers formed an organization called the Friends of Dufferin Grove Park and decided to build a wood-fired public bread oven. They were quite clear about their reasons for doing so. They wanted to increase "neighbourliness" in the park, and they had found that public cooking fires, originally campfires, provide a "strong tonic" for achieving this aim. Jutta Mason, one of the mothers and widely regarded as the chief custodian of the oven, puts it this way:

> There was no big plan, just the idea that a park could be a place where people find out who their neighbours are. If their neighbours are younger or older or richer or poorer or different-looking, or with different manners, so much the better. The fabric of neighbourhood life is meant to be textured and colourful!

The oven, which supplies large quantities of delicious bread and pizza to everyone in the park, winter and summer, is a "story magnet."

People who came to Canada from all over the world gather around and start talking about how public food was cooked and eaten in their places of origin. Strangers feel more inclined to talk to each other.

The oven has generated many spinoff activities. First, partly to supply the oven with fresh materials and partly to improve the area around the oven, volunteers planted vegetable and flower gardens. A community puppet theatre company took over an old field house. Musicians started performing in the park on summer weekends. Street fairs, a powwow, ball hockey, women's soccer, pizza day, and Friday suppers were added to the list. An outdoor theatre festival is held each June. A rink house used for skating and hockey in the winter becomes a shelter during the other seasons. Art and drama classes for kids, craft fairs, storytelling, and bicycle repair clinics are now regular events. A popular farmers market, based in the park, now supplies local produce to the community every Thursday.

It is surprising how all of this takes place. First, the Friends of Dufferin Grove Park is not a formal organization. It does not run the park or have annual general meetings or elect a board of directors. It is an ad hoc group of volunteers who contribute their time to make the park a better place to be. The daily operations of the park are supervised and maintained, as always, by the city's employees. Most of the musicians, dancers, and actors who perform in the park are paid for what they do out of the park's budget or from special grants. Pizza and other food are available at a reasonable charge—pizza is $2 a slice and the Friday meal costs $5. The people who make this food are paid by the City Parks Department. (Vernacular culture does sometimes include money, but the goal is to recover costs, not make a profit.) Despite all these links to the municipal bureaucracy, the activities at Dufferin Grove Park are the opposite of a planned, top-down, "community-building" exercise run by professional social workers. According to Mason:

> It's about the piece-meal, eccentric doings of ordinary people when they cook over fire in a park. What happens when people are not prevented from cooking and being together in this way, is as powerful as a law of physics. It can be midwife'd, but it can't be planned.

One of those eccentric doings happened spontaneously one year in June at the kickoff event for the annual Dufferin Mall Summer Concert series. It was a thoroughly rainy day, and the opening concert eventually had to be called off. The scheduled performers—a Portuguese cultural group, a Georgian choir called Darbazi, and a salsa group—arrived at the park in any case because for a while in the late morning it looked as though the rain might clear up. Then the rain began to fall steadily.

"We had the pizza oven fired up already," Mason recounts, "so we thought we might as well make the performers some lunch while we waited out the rain." Her volunteer "youth crew" helped to put pizzas in the oven, and then, "when the sky really opened," all of the gathered crowd, including the musicians, "jammed into the rink house and pizzas were passed from hand to hand because no one could get near the pizza table. The Darbazi choir formed a little circle and began singing, with a background of the drumming of the rain on the pavement outside the open doors." A couple of members of the youth crew donned Parks Department yellow raincoats and went out to the oven and cooked another round of pizzas.

Members of the Portuguese group decided to do their dance in the rink house, and they somehow managed to find enough space to perform. "They had an old man who plays a squeezebox and an even older woman who sang in a strange, exotic keening voice, and all the others in the group, some of them teenagers and young children, lined up across from one another and danced, and sang at the same time. They had bright red scarves and sashes that flashed when they twirled."

Despite the falling rain, some neighbourhood people joined the crowd, lining up outside the rink house, standing under their umbrellas and peering through the windows to see the dancers. "There was no room inside but it didn't matter—the dancers were dancing and singing for each other." The other performers joined in with their acts too. "The sound bounced back off the walls and was somehow further amplified by the torrents of rain," Mason says. When one group finished their piece, another one would start up. "It was so extraordinary and so beautiful I thought I could die right then."

■

In 1997 a ten-year-old boy, Bardia Bryan Zargham, looked out the window of a subway car leaving the King station in downtown Toronto. What he saw on the wall of the tunnel left a deep mark on his consciousness. It was graffiti: colourful, audacious, illegal, painted quickly and dangerously on city property. Two years later he announced to his mother that he had become a graffiti writer. His parents had moved to Canada from Iran in 1983. His mother was a hairdresser. His father worked as a mechanic. They had divorced a year and a half after Bardia's birth. The boy lived most of the time with his mother in various apartments in the northern suburbs of the city.

Illegal or not, Bardia conducted his chosen vocation with extra-ordinary single-mindedness. His friends remember finding him sleeping in the high-school hall some mornings after a long night of "bombing." He was, by all accounts, a stylish boy who loved Green Day, rap, and hoodies. His friends Centre, Focus, Johnny, Chop, Fan, K.T., Order, Large, and Guillotine all expressed a great deal of respect for him. He didn't do drugs, despite their availability and popularity with his crowd, and he only drank socially. He worked very hard at his craft, perfecting his technical skills with spray cans. He could paint long, ruler-straight lines with Zen efficiency and add 3-D effects in seconds. His choice of colours was always related to the colour and texture of the background.

Like most graffiti writers, he had a tag, or nickname, that he would paint repeatedly in bubble letters, sometimes as many as fifty or a hundred times a night in dangerous, very public places, like the sides of buildings or overpasses. He had to scale fire escapes and jump across the tops of buildings to do his work, constantly dodging the cops. The size, location, and danger associated with the bombs were directly related to his prestige. His tag was "Alpha."

The other graffiti artists who knew Alpha are, when asked, quite articulate about what they are doing and why. It is illegal, yes, and a kind of vandalism, they agree. But they point out that everywhere you look you see imposing and copious advertising messages paid for by corporations. They ask, why can't individual citizens respond to those, in a similar way, at the same locations?

On February 1, 2005, Alpha noticed a parked freight car in the railway yards at Christie and Dupont. A freight car is by far the most prized and perfect canvas for the adventurous bomber. Alpha had to borrow a friend's spray cans because he didn't have his own with him. While working on a very large version of his tag in bubble letters, Alpha was struck by a passing train. He died a few hours later.

Over one hundred teenagers, most of them unknown to his parents, attended his funeral, travelling by public transit to the suburban mosque. Over the next few months "R.I.P. Alpha" appeared in locations all over the city. He had become a kind of underground celebrity. Alpha's friends now come to visit his mother and comfort her. They have now become "her boys."

■

Contrast Alpha's story with another a mere two years later. In the summer of 2007 graffiti became legitimate. The Yves Laroche Gallery in Montreal mounted a high-profile show featuring local artists who normally work illegally on the street at night. At the show's opening, over two hundred of the city's most sophisticated and well-heeled art lovers showed up. The curator, twenty-four-year-old Ximena Becerra, was responding to trends elsewhere in the world. In Britain the work of graffiti artist Banksy was selling like Picasso's art a century earlier, with famous Hollywood stars paying over $600,000 for a single painting. The work at the Montreal show also sold well. When asked to explain this trend, gallery owner Laroche said, "Our clients used to have white hair. Now, they're between 25 and 45—graphic designers, computer programers and tattoo artists."

Differing approaches to graffiti—from Alpha's in Toronto to the Laroche gallery in Montreal—reveal interesting tensions between vernacular and commercial culture. Context is key. Alpha's wall writing, his vandalism, occurred at the grassroots, and its aim was entirely social. It made no sense economically. For the Montreal gallery clients, work with similar origins is captured, recontextualized, and transformed into a commodity to be sold for economic gain. Ironically, the artist seldom benefits much from this transformation, although graffiti artists are usually poor enough that any cash is better than none. Without begrudging the artists or the gallery agents their daily bread, I want to consider the implications of this difference on human relationships and aesthetic meaning. This kind of consideration necessarily requires a long view of human cultural activities.

THE
VERNACULAR OCEAN

■

The historian's home is on the island of writing. . . .
Beyond the island's shores, memories do not become
words. Where no words are left behind, the historian
finds no foundations for his reconstructions. In the
absence of words, artifacts are silent. We have often
felt frustrated, but we accept that prehistory cannot
be read. No bridge can be built to span this chasm.

— IVAN ILLICH AND BARRY SANDERS

In 1951 a group of archeologists under the direction of Dr. Ralph Solecki began excavating a limestone cave in Iraq. Until then, the Shanidar Cave in the Zagros Mountain highlands had been inhabited by Kurdish farmers. After nine years of laborious digging on the site, a team of researchers from the Musée de l'Homme in Paris uncovered the skeletons of seven adults and one child who they believe had occupied the cave about sixty thousand years earlier. Four of the skeletons appear to have come from bodies deliberately buried. One of these burials, in particular, became famous. According to evidence found at the Shanidar IV site, a middle-aged man died in the spring. Based on the orderly distribution of pollen grains in the soil around the body, anthropologists speculated that he was laid out on a bed of woody horsetail and covered with yarrow, cornflowers, St. Barnaby's thistle, groundsel, grape hyacinths, and a kind of mallow. Most importantly, the distribution of the pollen grains indicated that the flowers were intentionally arranged in simple patterns above and beside the body. The researchers also found out that many of the sort of flowers found in the Shanidar IV burial had been used, until very recently, as local herbal medicines in the region.

Archeology, normally a tedious, slogging science with few epiphanies, can sometimes inspire extraordinary moments of compassion: moments when human beings briefly stand at the precipice of time and look over the edge at the deep mysteries of the past. This must have been one such moment. It takes only a little imagination to visualize the scene, however long ago, where a loved one is put to rest while family and friends roam the fields around the cave and bring back bunches of white, yellow, red, blue, and purple wild flowers, which they combine in a sensitive, ritualized floral arrangement. Our distant ancestors, it appears, had a distinct sense of beauty and feelings for each other similar to you and me. This discovery led famous archeologist Richard Leakey to speculate that our Neanderthal ancestors had a "keen self awareness and concern for the human spirit." At least one novel—*Clan of the Cave Bear* by Jean M. Auel—was inspired by the Shanidar cave discoveries.

Almost forty years later, however, University of Michigan archeozoologist Jeffrey D. Sommer, writing in the *Cambridge Archaeological Review*, threw doubt on the discovery. He made a plausible argument that the so-called "flower burial" at the Shanidar Cave was created by the burrowing behaviour of the Persian jird, a small rodent native to Iraq. The jird, it seems, has a habit of storing, in its burrows, nesting material and food, including seeds, flower heads, leaves, and other vegetal material. Excavators noted many such burrows right next to the burial; and 70 per cent of all the rodent bone recovered from Shanidar Cave was from the Persian jird. Suddenly the beautiful narrative of aggrieved family and friends engaged in the ritual burial of a loved one is thrown in doubt by the speculations of a sober scientist.

The Persian jird theory does not "prove" that our ancestors were *not* emotional aesthetes; it simply proposes an alternative explanation for the pollen grain distribution. Which story do you prefer? Personally, I still prefer the first narrative and am quite prepared to accept that our ancestors were compassionate artists, whether or not the pollen grains, in this particular instance, were left by rodents. No one has provided any irrevocable evidence to disprove my belief. If, however, you credit art and emotional sensitivity to recent cultural evolution and the rise of civilization, the new theory may provide some comfort.

This story illustrates the difficulties that arise when anyone tries to write about any past that existed before the invention of writing. History, by definition, is a systematic account of the past beginning only a few thousand years ago, when the ancestors of modern accountants in the ancient civilization of Sumer began keeping track of sheep herds by scratching marks on clay tablets. Most of what we call history is actually the record of certain literate societies—civilizations—over the last three thousand years. Everything else—the vast majority of human experience—is said to be "prehistory," or outside of history, and is thus open to large helpings of speculation.

Nonetheless, hundreds of people and dozens of books are involved in passionate debates and sometimes deeply personal conflicts over rival accounts of prehistory. Why? Because even though "no bridge can be built to span this chasm," how we imagine our origins has a significant impact on our behaviour in the present. All origin myths are about who we think we are right now, because they set out to establish a description of "human nature."

The modern origin myth really begins in the West with Thomas Hobbes, who in 1651 wrote famously, just at the very beginning of the capitalist revolution in Europe, about the time:

> Where every man is enemy to every man, the same consequent to the time wherein men live without other security, than their own strength, and their own invention shall furnish them withall. In such a condition, there is no place for Industry; because the fruit thereof is uncertain; and consequently no Culture of the Earth; . . . no Knowledge of the face of the Earth; no account of Time; no Arts; no Letters; no Society; and which is worst of all, continuall feare, and danger of violent death; and the life of man, solitary, poore, nasty, brutish and short.

Not everyone agreed with him. The other side of the argument came in 1672, when fellow Englishman John Dryden coined the term "noble savage." Decades later Jean-Jacques Rousseau made the noble savage famous when his *Discourse on Arts and Letters* (1750) won a prize at the Academy of Dijon. Rousseau argued that when man lived in a "state of nature," before civilization and society, he was basically good, and that it was the advancement of art and science that had corrupted humanity with wars and inequality. Rousseau developed these ideas further in his *Discourse on Inequality* (1754), in which he attempted to answer the question, "What is the origin of inequality among men?" His answer, in a word, was civilization.

Hobbes and Rousseau influenced generations of origin myth-makers that followed. We can hear the ghost of Hobbes even in the most recent speculations about prehistory in Ronald Wright's widely read *A Short History of Progress* (2004). Wright provides archeological evidence at the beginning of the book to support his view that our early ancestors engaged in genocidal warfare with other humanoids.

> If it turns out that the Neanderthals disappeared because they were an evolutionary dead end, we can merely shrug and blame natural selection for their fate. But if they were in fact a variant or race of modern man, then we must admit to ourselves that their death may have been the first genocide. Or, worse, *not* the first—merely the first of which evidence survives. It may follow from this that we are descended from a million years of ruthless victories, genetically predisposed by the sins of our fathers to do likewise again and again.

In addition, Wright cites Paul Martin, Tim Flannery, and others to make the case that early humans were responsible for mass species extinctions and environmental devastation long before the beginnings of agriculture. He even makes the case that agriculture may have been an adaption to deal with the loss of game and habitat brought on by profligate hunting.

> The *perfection* of hunting spelled the *end* of hunting as a way of life. Easy meat meant more babies. More babies meant more hunters. More hunters, sooner or later, meant less game. Most of the great human migrations across the world at this time must have been driven by want, as we bankrupted the land with our moveable feasts.

Rousseau's arguments get fresh treatment in Oxford-trained anthropologist Hugh Brody's book *The Other Side of Eden: Hunters, Farmers and the Shaping of the World* (2000). Here Brody argues that our foraging ancestors were natural ecologists, husbanding resources skilfully, and that their "material well-being depends on knowing, rather than changing, the environment."

> Hunter-gatherers are not passive harvesters but are engaged in the complicated business of maintaining the world around them to ensure that its produce is bountiful. But the central preoccupation of hunter-gatherer economic and spiritual systems is the maintenance of the natural world as it is. The assumption held deep within this point of view is that the place where a people lives is ideal: therefore change is for the worse.

Early people, in Brody's view, also found ways of avoiding conflict by practising population control through birth spacing and occasional infanticide: "In this world of egalitarian individualists, hunter-gatherer populations have relatively small and scattered populations. The need for mobility and the availability of resources appear to encourage hunter-gatherers to limit their numbers."

For Brody it was a minority of agriculturalists in the Tigris-Euphrates valley who had the monopoly on violent warfare and ecological devastation. In this view, the ecological devastation of their homelands drove early farmers to form armies and begin a long history of conquest that Brody believes continues into the twenty-first century.

> The conquest of hunter-gatherers by farmers in the Old World may not have been all that different from the advance of European agricultural frontiers in the New World. The European discovery of Australia, North American and southern Africa was, for the most part, an encounter between agriculturalists and hunter-gatherers.

These samples give a taste of the passionate debates that exist around prehistory and of what is at stake there for the meaning of the present human narrative; but most parties do agree on certain key events. This provisional, accepted view begins with the idea that human-like beings existed for about a million years, beginning in the great plains of Central Africa, as one evolutionary branch of a common ancestor who also led to apes and chimpanzees. There were various versions of this humanoid creature, over this time, but *Homo sapiens* (sometimes called Cro-Magnon)—modern humans— appear in the fossil record about fifty thousand years ago. As far as genetic makeup goes, Cro-Magnon people were identical to you and me. If a time machine could be fashioned to make an exchange of newborns, the Cro-Magnon baby, nurtured in a North American suburb, could turn out to be a good computer programmer, while our twenty-first-century baby, raised in the African savannah, would undoubtedly become skilled at hunting, gathering, and telling the stories of her people.

As some archeologists remind us, this imaginary baby exchange has interesting implications. *Homo sapiens* evolved to prosper by hunting and gathering on the plains and in the forests of Africa, Asia, and Europe. They have *not* evolved to live in modern cities. Some of the problems of modern life, these archeologists believe, stem from this contradiction. What is certain is that for 85 per cent of the time that *Homo sapiens* have lived on this earth, they were hunter-gatherers (and some still are).

What does archeology tell us about the art and culture of pre-civilization? Here again, the evidence is sparse and controversial, but swings strongly in favour of the idea that early humans decorated their bodies, homes, and tools beyond the functional. The remains of early musical instruments have been found, and much has been made of the cave paintings at Lascaux and elsewhere because they provide material evidence of an artistic impulse. There is likewise no reason to think that storytelling, singing, and dancing were not also staples of human existence from the very beginning. These activities exist in all known human groups past and present for which there are reliable reports.

What is also certain is that these cultural activities were organized in a very different way from art and culture in the modern Western world. But what exactly are these differences and how important are they? To answer this question we are forced to rely, once again, on conventional historical sources: the writings of literate travellers who set out into the vast ocean of vernacular life and returned with thoughtful reports, riddled as they may be with the preconceptions of their own time and place.

FORAGING

FUNDAMENTALS

■

Beyond the story of the lineages of Noah are those
for whom Genesis is not the creation: the humans
who live by hunting rather than by agriculture.
The wild and the unclean; the shadow populations
of the Bible story. Archeology and anthropology
have their own creation stories. According to these,
hunting peoples have a claim to the earth that reaches
back a hundred times further than that of the farmers
whom the biblical God created and cursed.

— HUGH BRODY

Social anthropologist Richard Lee, in an article read by
thousands of undergraduates since it was first published in 1969,
writes about "Eating Christmas in the Kalahari." In this story Lee
tells us about the time he was doing research on the hunting and
gathering subsistence economy of a group in Southern Africa called
the !Kung Bushmen or San people. After living in their midst for
over a year, he wanted to show his appreciation for their co-operation
by slaughtering the "largest, meatiest ox that money could buy"
and offering it as a Christmas feast to the 150 men, women, and
children in the group. He found the perfect animal in a local herd

and asked the herdsman to keep it well fed until Christmas day.

As rumours of his plan spread, Lee received distressing comments from the !Kung. They referred to his ox as a "bag of bones." They asked him, "Are you too blind to tell the difference between a proper cow and old wreck?" Lee could see that the animal was fine, yet the comments persisted. Distressed, he consulted his !Kung friends. Everyone he spoke with agreed that it was going to be a hungry celebration, with no dancing, and that everyone would go home without "enough meat to quiet the rumbling in their stomachs." Lee was so disheartened that he told his wife he was considering leaving town rather than face the disaster that seemed sure to come.

Upsetting as it was, Lee decided to go ahead with the feast as planned. The ox, of course, was as fat and ample as he had expected. All present ate their fill, had great trance dances, and went home satisfied. They laughed at the elaborate practical joke they had played on the unsuspecting anthropologist.

Lee, upset and confused, was determined to find out what had happened. When he cross-examined a number of his more trusted informants he was told that he should stop being so sensitive: this is how the bushmen always treat each other. Anyone killing a large animal has his success ridiculed and downplayed, even though everyone will share the meat. Lee was still unsatisfied. He approached his closest friend, Tomazo, and asked him why a man who had gone to all that trouble to track and kill an animal and provide food for everyone, including the children, should be subject to insult.

He was surprised by the cryptic answer he got: "Arrogance."

"Arrogance?" he asked.

"Yes, when a young man kills much meat he comes to think of himself as a chief or a big man, and he thinks of the rest of us as his servants or inferiors," he was told. "We can't accept this. We refuse one who boasts, for someday his pride will make him kill somebody. So we always speak of his meat as worthless. This way we cool his heart and make him gentle."

It was then that Lee finally realized what had happened.

I had known for a long time that in situations of social conflict with Bushmen I held all the cards. I was the only source of tobacco in a thousand square miles, and I was not incapable of cutting an individual off for noncooperation. Though my boycott never lasted longer than a few days, it was an indication of my strength. People resented my presence at the water hole, yet simultaneously dreaded my leaving. In short I was a perfect target for the charge of arrogance and for the Bushmen tactic of enforcing humility.

The significance of this story is twofold. It speaks to the kinds of misunderstandings that plague all intercultural encounters, especially ones that involve inequality and power, and the canny realism of people who live without the comforts of membership in Western consumer culture. But, on another level—and this is Lee's main point—it confronts us with an example of a hunter-gatherer group that is "aggressively egalitarian." When community membership is a matter of life and death, and envy and social conflict can threaten everyone, it makes sense that social mechanisms will be invented to keep these emotions in check. Lee did not recognize what was going on at first because he came from a world in which envy and inequality were a matter of course. Experiences like Lee's—stumbling and puzzlement at the border between two contrasting world views—shine a revealing light on our own unspoken certainties.

The Western popular imagination has long believed that Hobbes's description of the stone age was basically accurate: human beings who lived in prehistoric conditions, it was understood, had no time for anything but the most rudimentary of cultural practices because they spent all their time trying to find enough food just to keep from going hungry. Food was scarce, and life was hard. In the 1960s and 1970s Richard Lee was part of a group of anthropologists—including Marshall Sahlins, James Woodburn, Lorna Marshall, and Colin Turnbull—who began to dismantle these popular myths. While there are wide variations in cultural practices and beliefs amongst foragers, these researchers also found many striking commonalities.

In a dramatic series of studies these anthropologists showed that virtually all hunter-gatherer groups, including those in the resource-poor far north or in the Kalahari Desert, worked the equivalent of two or three days a week at finding and preparing food, as opposed to spending all their time at food-gathering. Their lifestyles afforded foragers much more free time than most people in modern industrial society have. Sahlins, in a classic essay on the subject, called these groups "the original affluent society." Other researchers found that, while there was often anxiety about and preoccupation with food, most hunter-gatherers ate a well-balanced and nutritious diet. The researchers were also surprised to learn that, in many cases, when offered a chance to become agriculturalists or herdsmen, hunter-gatherers refused.

Different lifestyles breed different ways of looking at the world. Anthropologists observed that, compared to either modern farmers or city dwellers, hunter-gatherers had significantly different attitudes to interpersonal relations and to ecological and religious consciousness. Not only did they conserve the animal and plant life in their environments, usually by moving to a new location when availability went below a certain level, thus allowing land and wildlife to regenerate, but they also made the study of animals and plants their lifelong pursuit. Observers have repeatedly commented on the encyclopedic knowledge of local plants and animals that is commonplace for the average forager.

For these societies, the modern industrial idea that individuals can successfully "go it alone" against the pressures of family and peers to fulfil their unique dreams and aspirations is unknown. Membership in the group is everything. The opposite is nothing less than death. Anthropologist Lorna Marshall, writing about the !Kung in the 1970s, describes how one band behaved:

> Separation and loneliness are unbearable to them. I believe their wanting to belong and be near is actually visible in the way families cluster together in an encampment and in the way they sit huddled together, often touching someone, shoulder against shoulder, ankle across ankle. Security and comfort for them lie in their belonging to their group, free from the threat of rejection and hostility.

Marshall, however, points out, "Their security and comfort must be achieved side-by-side with self interest and much jealous watchfulness." In other words, like the members of all human societies, these people also have tendencies towards exclusion, unfairness, and inequality. Everyone has to work hard to maintain the cohesiveness of the group, sometimes through strategies like the one described by Lee around the killing of the ox. When conflicts cannot be solved by other means, the last resort is for some members of the group to head off and form their own band.

Most observers agree that, unlike almost all agriculturally based societies, including our own, forager groups are genuinely egalitarian. Recent commentators have tried to qualify this finding. In *Guns, Germs, and Steel*, for instance, Jared Diamond states: "The

55

term 'egalitarian' should not be taken to mean that all band members are equal in prestige and contribute equally to decisions. Rather, the term merely means that any band 'leadership' is informal and acquired through qualities such as personality, strength, intelligence, and fighting skills."

Still, the evidence suggests that in most cases foraging communities have no permanent leaders. While decisions are usually made by consensus, some people wield more influence. As Lee indicates, "In group discussions these people may speak out more than others, may be deferred to by others, and one gets the feeling that their opinions hold a bit more weight than the opinions of other discussants." Anyone who appears to be ambitious for power or personal gain, however, is immediately ignored. Of the influential people, "None is arrogant, overbearing, boastful, or aloof. In !Kung terms these traits absolutely disqualify a person as leader and may engender even stronger forms of ostracism." All of this is particularly impressive given that the men in these societies have hunting weapons that they could use at any time against the others to establish themselves as the "alpha male."

The discussion of egalitarianism becomes more contentious when we talk about gender relations. Much feminist scholarship maintains that inequality between men and women is as old as prehistory, and that only modernity has opened the possibility for greater gender equity. The question becomes complicated given that in almost all traditional societies women do certain things and men do others. But a division of labour does not necessarily mean inequality, as a close analysis of the anthropological record reveals. Eleanor Leacock and Karen Endicott, for example, both argue, based on different sets of evidence, that women in most hunter-gatherer bands have higher status and more personal freedom than do women in most farming, herding, and industrial societies—as demonstrated in a greater freedom of movement and greater involvement in group decision-making. Even though men might be physically stronger and wield dangerous hunting weapons, these societies offer little evidence of domestic violence or coercion, especially when compared with agrarian societies. Leacock, who specializes in the historical study of the Montagnais-Naskapi people of Central Canada in the seventeenth century, cites a revealing passage in the *Jesuit Relations*, a series of reports by French Catholic missionaries trying to convert the "savages" in the New World wilderness. In his report Father Paul Le Jeune noted that "Disputes and quarrels among spouses were virtually nonexistent." That was because "each sex carried out its own activities without 'meddling' in those of the other." Le Jeune found it difficult to accept how the Montagnais "imagine that they ought, by right of birth, to enjoy the liberty of wild ass colts, rendering no homage to anyone whatsoever." In this society women had "great power," and men were not inclined to make their wives "obey" them or even to be sexually faithful to them. According to Leacock, Le Jeune "lectured the Indians on this failing, reporting in one instance, 'I told him then that he was the master, and that in France women do not rule their husbands.'" Just as faulty for Le Jeune was the tendency of the women to join men in "sharp and ribald joking and teasing." Le Jeune complained, "Their language has the foul odor of the sewers." However much it might be assumed to be otherwise, male "savages" apparently did not feel superior to women.

"Indian giver" is a pejorative term used to describe someone who appears to give a gift freely but then wants it back. The label originated in the Puritan colony of Massachusetts in the eighteenth century. When Thomas Hutchinson published the history of the colony in 1764, he wrote, "An Indian gift is a proverbial expression signifying a present for which an equivalent return is expected."

But this behaviour, which the colonists thought uncivilized and unfair, is actually at the core of hunter-gatherer social relations. An elaborate system of reciprocal sharing and gift-giving not only redistributes food and other necessities among all members of the group, but is the social glue that keeps the band together. The sharing of food, particularly meat, among all members is one of the most fundamental principles on which forager social relations are based.

When Marshall tried to talk to the !Kung about this practice, she found: "The idea of eating alone and not sharing is shocking to the !Kung. It makes them shriek with an uneasy laughter." In addition to sharing meat and other food, people are always giving each other gifts and expecting gifts in return. Many of these gifts are not immediately useful: bead necklaces and other body adornments, musical instruments, wooden bowls, or dance rattles. They give "to measure up to what is expected, to make friendly gestures, to win favor, to repay past favors and obligations, to enmesh others in future obligation . . . and also out of genuine generosity and friendliness." Then, too, as Marshall says, "The !Kung, with their highly developed powers of observation and visual memory, to keep track of the commonest objects, know the ownership, and remember the history of the gifts." If an appropriate return gift is not rendered in a reasonable length of time it is permissible to ask for it. Stealing is virtually unknown, not because of some higher ethical ideal, but simply because the group is small and there is little privacy. Any thief would be caught and ostracized. Envy is softened through constant exchange.

Hard as it may be for inhabitants of the post-industrial urban landscape to imagine, the forager regime of group membership and reciprocal obligations includes a deep respect for individual decisions. While individuals face a great deal of powerful social pressure to conform, numerous examples exist of people making unpopular decisions and being tolerated. Indeed, according to anthropologists, this happens in the vast majority of cases in which there is serious disagreement. These societies deal with conflict through focused, passionate, and often lengthy discussion. Compromises are common and forgiveness is expected. Gift-giving and joking relationships go a long way towards mitigating jealousy and social tensions. This is not to say that members never resort to physical force. Murder and blood vengeance are also facts of life in most hunter-gatherer societies. But murders are committed by individuals in fits of rage. Unlike agricultural societies, force is never used by those in power to subdue those weaker or lower in social status. Murderers are never heroes, and violence is always seen as a deeply unfortunate outcome of conflict. When !Kung men encounter someone they have never met, they commonly put down their weapons at a distance and approach unarmed, engaging the other in discussion. Police, armies, and wars are as foreign to hunter-gatherers as are private automobiles.

Nor is this to say that hunter-gatherer societies are perfect. Like all human societies, drudgery, disagreements, and unhappiness are commonplace. Food is sometimes a source of great anxiety. People die from infectious diseases more often than they do in Western societies. In some complex hunter-gatherer cultures, like the Northwest Coast American Indian cultures, social hierarchy and even slavery are evident in the historical record. But I think it is possible to join anthropologist Tim Ingold in calling the forager consciousness "a radically alternative mode of relatedness."

■

While foragers usually decorate their tools, homes, and bodies with attractive designs, and while they own small things that are beautiful and loved, but have no practical value, it is reasonable to say that foragers are most sophisticated in the relational arts: talking, story-telling, music-making, dancing, and ritual performance. Marshall describes the art of conversation in one !Kung settlement:

> The !Kung are the most loquacious people I know. Conversation in a !Kung encampment is a constant sound like the sound of a brook, and as low and lapping, except for shrieks of laughter. People cluster together in little groups during the day, talking, perhaps making artifacts at the same time. At night, families talk late by their fires, or visit at other family fires with their children between their knees or in their arms if the wind is cold.

The people tell old stories, daydream about future hunts, gossip, or discuss gift-giving.

> While a person speaks, the listeners are in vibrant response, repeating the phrases and interposing a contrapuntal "eh." "Yesterday," "eh," "at Deboragu," "eh," "I saw Old/Xashe." "You saw Old/Xashe," "eh, eh." "He said that he had seen the great python under the bank." "EH!" "The python!" "He wants us," "eh, eh, eh." "to help him catch it." The "ehs" overlap and coincide with the phrase, and the people so often all talk at once that one wonders how anyone knows what the speaker has said.

The conversations include sexual jokes and insults. Later in the day other activities come into play along with the talk: "Individual singing of lyrical songs accompanied by the //gwashi (pluriarc), snatches of ritual music, the playing of rhythmical games, of the ritual curing dances occupy the evenings as well, but mostly the evening hours are spent in talk."

While modern society cherishes a scientific view of facts and empirical truths, foragers tend to see truth as "dialogically" established. "In oral culture," as Brody explains, "the transacting of an agreement, the confirming of a piece of information, occurs between the one who tells and those who listen."

> A chief is accepted as a chief because his or her accounts are upheld by all who have heard them, and are recognized as consistent with the stories of other and neighbouring chiefs; acceptance by those who listen and are witnesses legitimizes the authority of that chief, and the story is "true." Expertise in relating histories is matched by expertise in listening and assenting to them. The tests of validity are in the relationship of narrator to listener, and in the accumulation of these relationships over long periods of time.

As in all oral traditions, stories and songs abound. Some of them come from a distant past, others are recent or impromptu. Songs, for example, can be used for social communication: "The !Kung say that a song composed specifically about someone's behaviour and sung to express disapproval, perhaps from the deepest shadow of the encampment at night, is a very effective means of bringing people who deviate back into the pattern of approved behaviour." Other songs and stories are part of a cycle about the distant past when the gods walked upon the earth and animals were still people (what the Australian Aborigines call "Dreamtime"). The central characters are often morally ambivalent tricksters and shape-shifters. These stories, in the !Kung tradition, are told almost exclusively by the elders. Some people appear to be better storytellers than others, but, according to folklorist Megan Biesele, almost everyone over forty-five is confident telling stories from the evolving cycle. These stories are not meant for children. They are usually bawdy, sometimes horrific, and often ridiculous. Biesele notes:

> Though there is a keen enthusiasm for the performance of stories, their contents themselves are looked upon with scorn. The stories are heard with anything but awed reverence. Instead, amused indignation greets the outrageous or bumbling adventures of the long-ago people. !Kung have no explanation for why their ancestors related to them so many absurdities. "Hey! The doings of the ancient times are foul, I tell you!" was how Ti!kai n!a ended one of her stories.

62 In addition, listeners and tellers make no distinction between truth and fiction. In the worlds of the stories, both seem to exist at the same time.

For foragers, "Nature is pervasively animated with moral, mystical, and mythological significance. . . . Animals feed both the stomach and the mind and beguile the heart." Male and female shamans are common in these societies. Healing and transcendence are the goals, and altered states of consciousness are the vehicles. The most recent view of the many upper paleolithic cave paintings found in Southern Europe is that they were painted between twenty-five thousand and fifteen thousand years ago by shamans in their search for transcendence. While the !Kung sometimes use hallucinogenic drugs, other methods are more important in bringing these altered states of consciousness into existence: drumming, singing, dancing, and physical exhaustion. Trance dancing aimed at achieving something called "!kia" is a regular practice. In one community studied by Richard Katz, about half the men and one-third of the women were involved in trance dancing, usually once or twice a week: "The entire village comes to such dances, including children and old persons. The women gather around the fire, singing !kia songs and rhythmically clapping their hands. The men dance in a circle around the women, some working themselves up into a !kia state."

Most dances last from dusk to dawn. According to the !Kung, when in !kia, people can cure illness, handle fire, and see with X-ray vision. Their spirits can travel great distances, viewing the land from above. The practice has similarities to modern performance art, with lots of audience participation. Some commentators suggest that besides its other functions, the transcendence of the shamans is a road to difficult social change, fuelled by intuition. Brody suggests, "Shamanism prepares the brain to work at its fullest, widest potential. There is a profound and intelligent uncertainty. . . . The analogue nature of myth mirrors a sense that the world itself defies digital ways of speaking." He contrasts the ontologically ambiguous world view of the shaman with the three great "religions of the book," which he sees as "digital," in the sense that clear distinctions are established between good and evil, true and false, and other oppositions. Genesis, Brody says, "is the starting point of an intellectual and religious heritage in which conflict between two opposing forces defines what human beings should and should not do."

■

In the 1950s a perceptive young British anthropologist named Colin Turnbull lived for three years among the BaMbuti pygmies in the Ituri rainforest in Central Africa. His account of daily life, hunting parties, love affairs, coming of age rituals, and the non-pygmy tribes who tried to assert their authority has become a classic example of what Clifford Geertz calls, in anthropological circles, "thick description." Turnbull, clad in his khakis and still habituated to his afternoon tea, became a close friend and confidant to several pygmies. Never comfortable with the scientific arrogance of much of the ethnographic writing of the time, Turnbull wrote a moving, first-person account of his encounter with a culture profoundly unlike his own. His book *The Forest People: A Study of the Pygmies of the Congo* quickly became a best-seller when it came out in 1961 and is still one of the most eloquent descriptions of hunter-gatherer consciousness that exists—especially notable for its emotion as well as the implied insights into our own society's flaws. Recently, like the writings of so many other anthropologists who achieved fame outside their field, Turnbull's work has been the target of debunkers who have accused him of being a hopeless romantic. In Turnbull's case, however, his most enthusiastic critic, a next-generation anthropologist named Roy Robert Grinker, did a dramatic about-face and became a sympathetic biographer instead.

At the centre of *The Forest People* is an extended description of a ceremony that Turnbull witnessed in 1957. The community undertook this ceremony, called the "molimo," at irregular intervals. Before the molimo began, the camp was closed to outsiders. Every family had to contribute food or firewood. Then, as night fell, and for every night over the next two months, the women and children went inside the huts and pretended to sleep. The men sat around the *kumamolimo* (the hearth) and gazed into the fire, with the collected food in a basket nearby. "But first the men must sing, for this is the real work of the molimo, as they say; to eat and to sing, to eat and to sing."

Turnbull, a classically trained musician, recorded and analyzed some of these songs. Like so many other hunter-gatherer singing traditions, the songs are cyclical rather than linear. A melody or harmonic pattern is repeated with improvised variations, ad infinitum. The rhythm is usually a simple four-four time, but the offbeats are constantly being emphasized in a complex pattern over several bars. When sung as a round, the music has the effect of a pulsation or throbbing. Each singer improvises harmonic variations on the melody, creating a rich polyphonic texture. In many cases the variations involve melodic inversion similar to the fugues composed by Bach and other baroque composers in the Western tradition.

Another common song form is the call and response. For the molimo, the men around the fire called out a fragment of melody and, deep in the forest, a bass, animal-like voice responded. This was the "animal of the forest." As the musical dialogue continued, the sounds coming from the forest moved closer. Eventually several men danced into the clearing carrying two long objects dripping with water from having just been made to "drink" in the stream. Turnbull was distressed to discover that these revered spiritual objects, the voice of molimo, were actually metal drain pipes stolen from roadside construction gangs. The pygmies, by singing and blowing into these pipes, were able to produce a remarkable number of beautiful and profane sounds. The pipes stayed by the fire for some time and were anointed with hot ashes as the singing continued. Eventually they travelled, still sounding, around the whole camp and then disappeared back into the forest on the backs of the dancers.

The men would then eat from the prepared pots of food. "I was told, however, that everyone had to eat, just as no adult male was allowed to sleep but had to sing while molimo singing was in progress. Apparently one of the greatest crimes a Pygmy male can commit, if not the greatest, is to be found asleep while the molimo is singing." Then the singing resumed and the younger men danced around the fire. A few hours before dawn people would drift off to sleep, the oldest leaving the fire first. While that appeared to be the end of the event, it was not. The molimo trumpets would return at dawn, carried by the teenage boys, making raucous noise and waking everyone. The older people complained loudly, but no-one came out of the huts. The charade that it was the animal of the forest was sustained by common agreement.

For a month I sat every evening at the Kumamolimo; listening, watching, and feeling—above all, feeling. If I still had little idea of what was going on, at least I felt that air of importance and expectancy. Every evening, when the women shut themselves up, pretending that they were afraid to see "the animal of the forest"; every evening when the men gathered around the fire, pretending they thought that the women thought the drainpipes were animals; every evening, when the trumpet drainpipes imitated leopards and elephants and buffalos—every evening, when all this make-believe was going on, I felt that something very real and very great was going on beneath it, something that everyone took for granted, and about which only I was ignorant.

But the surprises were not over. A few weeks later a very old woman arrived in the camp with her husband. She stayed with several girls in a hut near the fire. Turnbull thought he could hear them practising molimo songs. One night, when he expected the women to retire to their huts as was customary, he noticed that they instead stayed around the fire with the men. The old woman and a beautiful young girl named Kondabate were at the centre of the action.

After a while the men started singing again, but gently, and then with a shock I realized that the women were singing as well, the sacred songs of the molimo. And they were not just joining in, they were leading the singing. Songs that I thought only the men knew and were allowed to sing—all of a sudden the women were showing that they not only knew them but could sing them with just as much intensity.

Then the two women, the old and the young, danced together. "Their movements were perfectly coordinated, even to the twitching of their heads; as they sank down close to the ground they might have been one person." What followed was a remarkable, elaborate chorus line in which the molimo fire was repeatedly destroyed by the old woman and repaired by the men.

Each time the old woman made a more determined effort to stamp the fire out of existence. And each time the strangely beautiful and exciting erotic dance of the men gave it new life. Finally the old women conceded defeat and retreated among the others. Shortly afterward all the women disappeared, and the men rearranged themselves at the Kumamolimo without making any mention of what had happened.

It was still not over. The singing started again, and this time the old woman came out alone and began to dance once more. She took a long roll of twine and knotted a loop around each man's neck until they were all tied together.

Moke spoke—I am not sure whether it was for my benefit or because it was his place to say what he did. He said, "This woman has tied us up. She has bound the men, bound the hunt, and bound the molimo. We can do nothing." Then Manyalibo said that we had to admit we had been bound, and that we should give the woman something as a token of our defeat; then she would let us go. A certain quantity of food and cigarettes was agreed upon, and the old woman solemnly went among us again, untying each man. Nobody attempted to loose himself, but as each man was untied he began to sing once more—the molimo was free. The old woman received her gifts and went back to Cephu's camp, where she and her husband were staying. The couple stayed for another week or two, but she danced only once again. Before she left us she went to every man, giving him her hand to touch as though it were some kind of blessing.

Turnbull admits that, like the pygmies themselves, he can't explain the meaning of this performance, so full of intensity and make-believe.

There is an old legend that once it was the women who "owned" the molimo, but that the men stole it from them and ever since the women have been forbidden to see it. Perhaps this is a way of reminding the men of the origin of the molimo. There is another old legend which tells that it was a woman who stole fire from the chimpanzees or, in yet another version, from the great forest spirit. Perhaps the dance had been an imitation of this. I do not understand it by any means, but somehow it makes sense.

What Turnbull reported seeing in 1957 was not a ritual in the sense of a repeated and repeatable performance. Each performance of the molimo was unique. If he had gone back a few years later and been lucky enough to witness the molimo again, he would have seen something that had similarities to the earlier event, but many things would have been new. I have no idea if the molimo is still practised in Africa today, but Turnbull's description, filled as it is with his own preconceptions and emotions, provides evidence of a collective vernacular performance that is context-specific, unrepeatable, improvised, leaderless, and beyond commerce of any sort (unless we see the exchange of tobacco with the old woman as an economic transaction). It also contains an amazing dramatization of gender conflict and difference that demonstrates great wisdom.

For me this story is revealing not because it shows how we can "reconnect with our inner shamans," as the new-age magazine *Shaman* might suggest. I view with great sadness the attempts to sell primitive spirituality as one more consumer product to deeply alienated upper-middle-class North Americans. But I do believe that the experiences described by these anthropologists provide a fresh vantage point for looking at the assumptions that guide our own artistic and cultural pursuits. In particular, they show us how much art activities are about relationships, not material objects. **69**

THE FOLK AND
THEIR OBSERVERS

■

*Popular culture is one of history's losers: shattered by the
far-reaching cultural revolution between the end of the
Middle Ages and the contemporary age. Like all losers, it
has left few traces. Moreover, the few traces it did leave
were often distorted or mutilated by the triumphant
winners, much as the Roman emperor Augustus systemati-
cally tarnished the glory of Anthony, his hapless rival. This
mutilation was easily accomplished, what is more, since
popular culture was essentially oral, and its adversaries
wielded the formidable weapon of writing.*

— ROBERT MUCHEMBLED

Most historians consider the slow shift, beginning about
ten thousand years ago, from foraging to agriculture to be the
trigger for radical changes in human relations and consciousness—changes that were more far-reaching than those found in any
subsequent global transformation, including the Industrial Revolution or the digital age. Probably the most important new cultural
element wrought by the neolithic revolution was social stratifica-
tion. By the time the written record begins, about four thousand
years ago, kings, queens, nobles, and courtiers headed an elaborate

bureaucracy that was needed to manage the large majority of peasants and slaves who not only built the great cities—the walls, buildings, and other structures—but also kept them going.

With new social structures came different cultural forms, particularly among the upper classes. But it is here that the historical record contains a serious bias. The culture of the elite minority is well known to historians because it was the members of this group who invented writing and handed down their view of the world (Plato and Aristotle are perfect examples of this). But what about the culture of the majority from antiquity to industrialization? How did the peasants, slaves, miners, soldiers, and sailors tell stories, and dance, and make music and art? We assume that they did these things, and the shreds of existing evidence suggest that they did, but we know remarkably little about it. The vast majority of peasants and slaves could neither read nor write. They left no written records of their activities.

Historians who want to understand the vernacular culture of the majority in past agricultural communities are forced to rely on what they can find in marriage contracts, court transcripts, parish records, letters and diaries, memoirs, and literature as well as "parahistoric" evidence such as demography, architecture, clothing, and records of food consumption. They also have the observations, reports, and transcriptions from those few literate souls who chose to visit the common people and record their experiences. Homer and Hesiod, Magellan and Tasman, Bougainville and Cook, the *Jesuit Relations*, and even Samuel Johnson and James Boswell's trip to the Western Islands of Scotland in 1773—they all provide second-hand descriptions of everyday life among those still living in vernacular's embrace. Later, as the Satanic Mills were rising across Western Europe and the old culture of the vulgar classes was disappearing, people like the Grimm brothers and Francis Child began collecting and preserving folk stories and songs from these fading traditions. These reports, observations, and collections are often filled with contempt, misunderstanding, and naïveté, yet they are all we have if we want to decipher the beliefs, hopes, and passions of our peasant ancestors.

One of the jobs of modern historians who are concerned with agricultural people's culture is learning how to sift through this thin gruel of textual evidence for the tiny nuggets of reality hidden in the mix. It requires solving a puzzle that is missing most of its pieces; yet that is what a small army of historians has been doing over the last century. The picture that emerges, even with all the local variations, of medieval France, pre-Columbian Peru, or ancient China, is remarkable because of the deep similarities it unveils.

One great early witness was Father Jean de Brébeuf, a devout, compassionate Jesuit who lived a good deal of his adult life among the Wyandot people (known to the French as the Huron) deep in the woods of New France, now Canada. Before Brébeuf was captured, tortured, and killed by the Huron's long-time enemies, the Iroquois, in 1649, he sent back to France some of the most carefully observed descriptions of life "among the savages" that have ever been recorded. With these reports, published in English as *The Jesuit Relations and Allied Documents*, modern anthropologists have been able to reconstruct a rich and nuanced description of a group of people living on the threshold between hunting-gathering and farming.

While Brébeuf was a gifted writer who obviously loved the people he lived among, he wrote his reports for his superiors in France. They were documents promoting the work he was doing, intended to keep the money coming so that the conversions to Christianity could continue. As a result, we hear many apologies for the strange and un-Christian practices of his charges—the people never washed, they acted like gluttons, and they belched at meals—and clearly reveal the European values of both writer and intended readers. But the descriptions are detailed enough that the emotions, passions, and aspirations of these long dead people cut through the writer's apparent piety.

At one point in the *Relations* of 1636, Brébeuf says of the Huron, "They exercise hospitality among themselves gratuitously." He describes a tradition of feasting called "Ononharoia."

> I blush to say that they engage in [feasts] often whole days and whole nights, for they must, by the end, empty the pot. . . . A feast is a matter of importance, they cry, driving away those who arrive after the eating has begun and when the distributor has filled everyone's bowl, in which there is usually enough to keep one eating from morning until night. . . . Such indeed is the kingdom which the devil has usurped over these poor beings. May it please our Lord to have pity on them and to deliver them from this tyranny.

The most magnificent of the feasts, he wrote, were the ones they called "Atouronta aochien," or singing feasts. They would last up to twenty-four hours and the cooks would use some thirty or forty kettles for the food, with as many as thirty deer eaten. Some eight or nine villages might be invited, "or even the whole country."

> The largest cabin of the village is chosen to receive the company. *They do not hesitate to inconvenience themselves for each other on these occasions.* . . . When the company is assembled, they sometimes begin to sing before eating, though occasionally they eat first in order to sing more heartily. . . . During these songs and dances, some will make motions of striking down

their enemies, as if in sport. Most commonly their cries are hen, hen, or hééééé, or else wiiiiiiii.

One of the most heart-wrenching passages in the 1636 *Relations* is Brébeuf's description of the magnificent "Feast of the Dead." He is uncharacteristically positive about this event. Written as a first-person narrative, it contains much less of the paternalistic commentary apparent elsewhere.

> Twelve years or thereabouts having elapsed, the elders and notables of the country assemble to decide on a definite time to hold the feast that will be convenient for the whole country and the foreign nations that may be invited. . . . Once the decision is taken, preparations are made to transport all the bodies [of those who have died in the intervening years] to the village where a common grave is located, each family seeing to its dead with a care and reflection that can hardly be described. . . .
>
> Still, it seems to me that what our Indians do on this occasion touches us still more and makes us see more closely and apprehend more vividly our wretched state. For, having opened the graves, they display before you all these corpses, and they leave them thus exposed in a public place long enough for the spectators to learn, once and for all, what they will be someday.

The cleaned bones of the dead were hung in bags in the long-houses and the people feasted among them. Special songs were sung, and contests of skill took place among the men and women. Later all the bones were gathered and a pilgrimage to the common grave began. Dressed in special robes and jewellery, the people walked with their "souls." They sang "haéé, haéé," and "repeated this cry of the souls along the way. According to them, this cry greatly consoles them. Without it, this burden of souls would weigh very heavily on their backs and cause them a pain in the sides for the rest of their lives." Brébeuf reports:

> I admired the tenderness of one woman . . . toward her dead father and children. She combed the hair of her father and handled his bones, one after the other, with such affection as if she wished to restore him to life. . . . As for the children, she put beaded bracelets on their arms and bathed their bones with her tears. The others could scarcely tear her away, but they insisted, as it was time to depart.

According to Brébeuf, two thousand people converged at the designated burial site and climbed up onto an enormous scaffolding that covered a long pit. Over a thousand gifts to the dead were displayed and announced. The process took hours to complete.

> At seven o'clock, they took the whole bodies down into the pit. We had the greatest difficulty in getting near. Nothing has ever depicted for me so well the confusion there is among the damned. On all sides you could have seen them unloading the decayed bodies, and on all sides was heard a horrible din of confused voices of people speaking without making themselves understood.

The bags of bones were hung on the scaffolding above the pit, apparently with the goal of dropping them in later. All night, the congregation stayed at the site, lighting fires for warmth. Before dawn some bones fell in, apparently by accident, setting off a chain reaction. Everyone crowded the scaffolding to dump in the rest of the bones. Brébeuf and his colleagues, resting not far away, rushed to the site.

As we drew near, we saw nothing less than the image of hell. The large space was quite full of fires and flames, and the air resounded in all directions with the confused voices of these barbarians. Eventually, the noise ceased and they began to sing, but in tones so sorrowful and lugubrious that it represented to us the horrible sadness and the abyss of despair into which these unhappy souls are forever plunged.

For a moment, while reading this moving description from four-hundred years past, we can reconstruct in our imaginations the extraordinary social power of this participatory ritual of mourning among these New World farmers.

■

The material life of agricultural workers was, and often still is, a grim affair. Farmers—who until the end of the nineteenth century formed 90 per cent of the total European population—have almost always been ill treated and mercilessly exploited. When people say that life is better in the modern world, they are usually comparing it, however vaguely, to life on the farm in previous centuries. Ironically, agriculture provided a more stable and abundant food source than foraging, but a less nourishing one—malnutrition came with the tilling of the fields, not with hunting. Agriculture was also more labour-intensive. Marshall Sahlins points out, "The neolithic saw no particular improvement over the paleolithic in the amount of time required per capita for the production of subsistence; probably, with the advent of agriculture, people had to work harder."

Diseases, many caused by close proximity to domesticated animals, were plentiful and deadly. Life expectancy was short. In Europe cold was always a problem, as well as insecurity about famines and political upheavals. State-sponsored wars and personal violence were familiar parts of daily life. The great historian Johan Huizinga tried to capture the spirit of this time in the opening passage of his book *The Autumn of the Middle Ages*:

> When the world was half a thousand years younger all events had much sharper outlines than now. The distance between sadness and joy, between good and bad fortune, seem to be much greater than for us; every experience had that degree of directness and absoluteness that joy and sadness still have in the mind of a child. Every event, every deed was defined in given and expressive forms and was in accord with the solemnity of a tight, invariable life style. The great events of human life—birth, marriage, death—by virtue of the sacraments, basked in the radiance of the divine mystery. But even the lesser events—a journey, a labour, a visit—were accompanied by a multitude of blessings, ceremonies, sayings, and conventions.
>
> There was less relief available for misfortune and for sickness; they came in a more fearful and more painful way. Sickness contrasted more strongly with health. The cutting cold and the dreaded darkness of winter were more concrete evils. Honor and wealth were enjoyed more fervently and greedily because they contrasted still more than now with lamentable poverty. A fur-lined robe of office, a bright fire in the oven, drink and jest, and a soft bed still possessed that high value for enjoyment that perhaps the English novel, in describing the joy of life, has affirmed over the longest period of time. In short, all things in life had about them something glitteringly and cruelly public. The lepers, shaking their rattles and holding processions, put their deformities openly on display. Every estate, order, and craft could be recognized by its dress. The notables, never

appearing without the ostentatious display of their weapons and liveried servants, inspired awe and envy. The administration of justice, the sales of goods, weddings and funerals—all announced themselves through processions, shouts, lamentations and music. The lover carried the emblem of his lady, the member the insignia of his fraternity, the party the colors and coat of arms of its lord.

People born into this way of life developed deep networks of affiliation as a defence against physical and psychological insecurities. The village was the centre of social life, and the surrounding area—the villages that local people could walk to—constituted the farthest reaches of the knowable universe. Similar to forager societies, membership in the group was of paramount importance. Mexican activist Gustavo Esteva articulated this attitude to life well in talking about people living in the community of Chicahuaxtla, a small Triqui village in the state of Oaxaca, in 1998. For anyone living there, he said, membership, indeed existence, in this community "is the first layer of your consciousness."

You really *are* San Andrés de Chichauxtla. It is not that you belong to Chicahuaxtla. It is not that you are a member of the community of Chicahuaxtla. You are Chicahuaxtla. You are that community. You *know* that you are that community and they know that you are that community.

These networks of affiliation—and not the nuclear family, as we would have it today—were the locations of the deepest emotional bonds. Instead of relying on the vicissitudes of adolescent sensuality, adults arranged marriages for their children to strengthen these ties. In this gendered world of different tools and different work for men and women, women were the people closest to the body—the ones who preserved the collective memory of the group, the ones who knew and saw things men did not notice, the ones who transformed "the raw into the cooked." Because of this they were more often than not the most respected and feared healers. Not surprisingly, then, when the Christian church decided to take more control over the souls of the peasantry in the late Middle Ages, the authorities found it necessary to silence or kill these wise women and create a myth about "witches."

■

Consumer time moves relentlessly and radically forward, always improving and upgrading the past. Tradition is distrusted. By contrast, agricultural time revolves in a circle, always returning, like the seasons, to where it started. Tradition is the reference point. Emotional life in the peasant village follows the same pattern. Passions and sorrows are linked to the necessity of reaping and sowing.

The medieval European annual cycle contained six major festivals: May celebrations, connected to sexual licence and fertility; Midsummer's Eve, also known as St. John's Day on the Christian calendar; the Harvest Feast, loosely associated with the Feast of the Ascension of Our Lady; Hallowe'en and All Souls' Day, a celebration of the ancestors; the Twelve Days of Christmas around the winter solstice, a very different festival from the one we celebrate in the modern era; and, starting in the new year, carnival and Lent. While most of these festivals had Christian associations, they were all pre-Christian in their origin and timing.

In recent years much has been written about the political and social significance of carnival in particular, but all of these seasonal festivals, as well as most weddings and funerals, followed similar patterns. According to cultural historian Peter Burke, carnival in Europe had three phases: processions, competitions, and performances. Its major themes were food, sex, and violence. Cross-dressing, "misrule," and the inversion of social class were *de rigueur*.

For another historian, Robert Muchembled, these "dense time cycles" addressed four central preoccupations: fertility, emotional discharge, active participation of social groups, and the redefinition of society. The fertility theme was obvious. During the May festival, for example, adolescents disappeared into the woods "where they spend the night in pastimes," after which they were said to have been "mayed." At other festivals, offerings were made to the mother goddess—the Virgin Mary was often a useful stand-in—and men wore long-nosed masks and other phallic substitutes. Emotional discharge came with overeating, excessive drinking, competitions, and arguments. Murders and injuries increased during carnival time. All elements of carnival—processions, competitions, performances—involved the participation of everyone in a guild or other social group. And while many have argued that all this misrule and emotional release provided a safety valve ultimately serving to reinforce inequality and the status quo, Muchembled and others contend that the carnivalesque in seasonal festivals also opened up the potential for dialogue and societal change. For example, the content of what was said or mimed about the lords and the clergy seldom went unnoticed by their targets, most of whom inevitably attended these events along with the commoners.

Whatever their significance in the lives of individuals, these celebrations returned annually for centuries.

Their more or less regular recurrence (every six to eight weeks) marked the rhythm of the peasant's year. At the end of winter the curve of work began to rise, and it peaked at the harvest . . .

to decline after then until the low point of winter's worst weather was reached. The great festive cycles provided a series of plateaux, of chances to adapt, along this bell curve. Such pauses were necessary because any change represented a danger and had to be accompanied by purifying rites to make the transition from the old to the new.

From Muchembled's perspective, these events had a common sequence: emotional discharge, followed by a longer period of joy and laughter during which "the seriousness of fear and suffering" was overcome, and, finally, a return to the renewed order with redefined limits. These activities were clearly the art and culture of their time and place and served many of the same functions that art and culture play in today's society; yet their form was significantly different.

■

For those nurtured in the arms of literacy, the structure and process of the verbal arts in the oral tradition are almost impossible to grasp. Perhaps the closest thing we have in modern society is the joke. We are all familiar with how the collective store of jokes and joke forms gets recycled, reused, and constantly revised over decades by thousands of anonymous users, who mostly learn the jokes by ear. (How email circulation of jokes changes the process is hard to tell.) Something like this is at work in the transmission and performance of songs and stories in non-literate cultures, although on a much more sophisticated level.

Jacob Grimm was one of the first modern intellectuals to try to understand the specifics of oral transmission. Along with his brother Wilhelm, he set out to record and publish the stories told by German "volk" at the beginning of the nineteenth century. They collected as many stories as they could, but, uncomfortable with direct contact with the peasantry, often transcribed these gems of rural folklore from middle-class women who remembered stories told to them by their peasant caregivers. In his introduction to what became known as *Grimm's Fairy Tales* (first published in 1812), Jacob pointed out that the original authors of these tales were unknown. The stories were created through a communal process: "*das volk dichtet*" (the people create). How this process actually worked, however, was not revealed for another century.

In the early 1930s Milman Parry, a graduate student of classics at Harvard University, set out to solve the "Homer problem" that had long dominated discussions of the ancient Greek texts. How had the author of *The Iliad* and *The Odyssey*, scholars asked, composed such great works, seemingly out of nothing, at the very beginning of the European literary tradition? Parry's hypothesis was that both poems were actually verbatim transcriptions of performances by singers working in an even more archaic Greek oral tradition. To prove his theories he travelled to the Balkans to record performances by illiterate bards singing in Serbo-Croatian and Albanian.

During that trip Parry and his team recorded 12,500 different stories, including sound recordings made on more than 3,500 individual 12-inch aluminum discs. Some of the stories were so long that they had to be sung in instalments over several days. Parry wrote:

> I was able to obtain in the few weeks of the summer a number of the sorts of texts I sought, e.g. several recitations of the same poem by the same singer; recitation of the same poem from uncle to nephew; several recitations of the same poem from the same region and from neighboring regions; versions from uncontaminated traditions of certain of the more famous poems

which have been printed in other versions over the period of a hundred years that the poetry has been noted; a poem composed immediately after an event; and so on.

Parry died in an accident shortly after his return to the United States, and it was left to his young assistant, Albert Lord, to continue the research. Lord returned to Yugoslavia in 1950 to record more epics, including some from the same storytellers whom he and Parry had met almost twenty years earlier. What Parry and Lord discovered is that, rather than memorize a story word for word as we might do in literate society, these bards assimilate, over many years, a large number of stock words, phrases, and story structures that they recall and combine in endless permutations. For the oral storyteller there is no "original" from which variations spring. Every iteration is a variation. Every performance is a new creation.

The performers themselves saw it differently. One storyteller named Zogic insisted to Lord that he could repeat a story exactly. "If I were to live for twenty years, I would sing the song which I sang for you here today just the same twenty years from now, word for word." When two verbatim transcriptions were compared, however, this exactitude was not found. The versions were recognizable variants on the story, but the actual words and structures of the lines were different. Lord observes: "Was Zogic lying to us? No, because he was singing the story as he conceived it . . . and to him 'word for word and line for line' are simply an emphatic way of saying 'like.' As I have said, *singers do not know what words and lines are*."

Bards construct their narratives from sound and rhythm. Words and lines are literary concepts. The bards' memories, however, are prodigious. On an earlier occasion Parry and Lord did an experiment with Avdo Mededovic, their favourite singer. They invited another singer, Mumin Vlahovljak, to show up with a story that Avdo claimed he had never heard before.

> Without telling Avdo that he would be asked to sing the song himself when Mumin had finished, Parry set Mumin to singing, but he made sure that Avdo was in the room and listening. When the song came to an end, Avdo was asked his opinion of it and whether he could now sing it himself. He replied that it was a good song and that Mumin had sung it well, but that he thought he might sing it better. The song was a long one of several thousand lines [several *hours* in duration]. Avdo began and as he sang, the song lengthened, the ornamentation and richness accumulated, and the human touches of character, touches that distinguished Avdo from other singers, imparted a depth of feeling that had been missing in Mumin's version.   **85**

When someone is steeped in a tradition and has no recourse to written texts, that person's memory is acute; patterns and details are discerned with what literate people consider to be superhuman accuracy. Also, as in any human group, many people are competent but some are more competent than others.

The real strengths of the oral tradition, however, reveal themselves in the role of the listeners. Each performance of a song or story may be different partly because of the mood of the singer, or partly because of faulty memory, but mostly it is because the *context* of each performance is different. Each time the story is shared the listeners are different, or, if they are the same listeners, the historical moment has changed. Unlike the disciplined, contemplative silence of today's audiences, peasant listeners—like their forager ancestors—were active responders. Their interjections and body language had enormous influence on the direction and emphasis of the performer. It is in this way that it can be said that "*das volk dichtet.*"

Then too, because performers are aware of their debt to tradition, the traditional songs and stories become somewhat impersonal—there are few if any references to "me" or to the narrator by name; and because the people who hear the songs and stories are aware that the performer is following tradition, they do not pass on the name of the singer or storyteller. That is why the folk songs and folk tales become anonymous. As Burke puts it, "The individual may invent, but in an oral culture . . . 'the community selects.'" Innovations or variations that appeal to the audience "will be imitated and so pass into the common stock of tradition." Specific performances that do not strike a chord or catch on will perish. "Thus successive audiences exercise a 'preventative censorship' and decide whether a given song or story will survive, and in what form it will survive. It is in this sense (apart from their encouragement during the performance) that the people participate in the creation and transformation of popular culture, just as they participate in the creation and transformation of their native language."

This kind of context-dependent flexibility is difficult or impossible to achieve in our bookish world, which is so full of exact copies. Actors working on stage will tell you how audiences can influence their performances from night to night, but in most cases these actors are working from a text that someone else at some other time has authored. They are expected to repeat the words precisely from memory.

While the performances and feats of memory associated with oral culture are almost completely lost to the modern world, another sort of impromptu verbal performance does seem to have survived modernity and urbanization and remains as strong today in most communities as it did in ancient times: gossip. Largely viewed as an

ethically questionable guilty pleasure in literate society, gossip remains an essential form of storytelling in human groups of all kinds.

John Berger, in his collection of stories about French peasants
called *Pig Earth*, emphasizes the importance of gossip to one community in the French Alps in the 1980s. In the village most daily
happenings are recounted each evening. The stories told combine
"the sharpest observation" with "lifelong mutual familiarities."

> Sometimes there is a moral judgement implicit in the story, but
> this judgement—whether just or unjust—remains a detail: the
> story *as a whole* is told with some tolerance because it involves
> those with whom the story-teller and listener are going to go
> on living. Very few stories are narrated either to idealize or
> condemn; rather they testify to the always slightly surprising
> range of the possible. Although concerned with everyday events,
> they are mystery stories.

The stories told do not just invite comment, they create it; the act
of remaining silent is a comment in itself. Spiteful and bigoted
responses become stories that are told and, in turn, become the
subject of further comment.

> Indeed the function of this *gossip* which, in fact, is close, oral,
> daily history, is to allow the whole village to define itself. The
> life of a village, as distinct from its physical and geographical
> attributes, is perhaps the sum of all the social and personal rela-
> tionships existing within it, plus the social and economic rela-
> tions—usually oppressive—which link the village to the rest of
> the world. But one could say something similar about the life
> of a large town. What distinguishes the life of a village is that
> it is also *a living portrait of itself*: a communal portrait, in that

everybody is portrayed and everybody portrays. As with the carvings on the capitols in a Romanesque church, there is an identity of spirit between what is shown and how it is shown— as if the portrayed were also the carvers. Every village's portrait of itself is constructed, however, not out of stone, but out of words, spoken and remembered: out of opinions, stories, eye-witness reports, legends, comments and hearsay. And it is a continuous portrait; work on it never stops.

And continuous also is the work of gossip in the daily lives of billions of people in cities and countries around the world: a commonplace narrative form of utmost complexity and subtlety whose influence in local cultures is seldom acknowledged, especially in the technology-saturated West.

THE POSTMAN AND
THE TILE SETTER

■

*To the peasant the empirical is naive. He works
with the never entirely predictable, the emergent.
What is visible is usually a sign for him of the state of
the invisible. He touches surfaces to form in his own
mind a better picture of what lies behind them. Above
all, he is aware of following and modifying processes
which are beyond him, or anybody, to start or stop: he is
always aware of being within a process himself.*

— JOHN BERGER

Ferdinand Cheval, born in 1836, grew up as a peasant in
the small village of Hauterives, in the Department of Drôme, not
far from the French city of Lyon. He received little in the way of
formal schooling. In his teens he apprenticed briefly as a baker's
assistant. After that he travelled to Algeria to work for a few months.
Eventually he returned to Hauterives, married, and became the
area's *facteur* (postman). His thirty-two-kilometre route consisted
of steep climbs, rocky terrain, and poor access. The area had once
been an ancient seabed, and the landscape is rich with fossils and
porous limestone sculpted by time and the elements. In bad weather
Facteur Cheval would seek refuge in barns or at the hearths of

friendly farmhouses. According to his autobiography, beginning at the age of twenty-eight he was plagued by a recurring dream. In this dream he built a rock palace: "a chateau of grottoes." On his lonely walks delivering mail across the French countryside, "in a trance-like state," he would think about this dream palace.

> What can a man do when walking everlastingly through the same setting, except to dream? I build in my dreams a palace passing all imagination, everything that the genius of a simple man can conceive—with gardens, grottoes, towers, castles, museums and statues: all so beautiful and graphic that the picture of it was to live in my mind for at least ten years. . . .
>
> When I had almost forgotten my dream, and it was the last thing I was thinking about, it was my foot which brought it all back to me. My foot caught on something which almost made me fall: I wanted to know what it was: it was a stone of such strange shape that I put it in my pocket to admire at leisure. The next day, passing through the same place, I found some more, which were even more beautiful. I arranged them together there and then on the spot and was amazed. . . . I searched the ravines, the hillside, the most barren and desolate places. . . . I found tufa which had been petrified by water and which was wonderful.

Cheval began collecting rocks in his pockets, but after his wife tired of mending his pants he turned to baskets strapped on his back and later to a wheelbarrow for carrying the stones home. It was then that he began to actually build the palace he had only imagined. "I said to myself: since nature wants to make sculpture, I will make the masonry and architecture for it." The year was 1879. He was forty-three. Cheval acknowledged, with humility, that he had no training in the visual arts, architecture, or sculpture. Apart from his brief experience in Africa he had never travelled. Yet he began the long process of constructing a structure of cement, wire, and stone, in the yard beside his house, twenty-six by fourteen metres (about eighty by forty feet). What he lacked in training and experience he made up for with determination and faith. It took him two decades just to build the outer walls. He would often rise at two or three in the morning and work until dawn, continuing to haul rocks many kilometres by wheelbarrow.

By all accounts Cheval worked intuitively, without a coherent plan, often taking cues from the rocks he found on the valleys and river bottoms near the village. He was often surprised by his creations and wondered how he could have been responsible for them. The Ideal Palace still stands today in Hauterives and is open to visitors. As you walk towards it from the east you face, on the right, the four high columns of what Cheval called the "Hindu Temple" and an imposing staircase up to the second level. On the left are three stone giants, all with fingers pointing skyward: Caesar, Archimedes, and Vercingetorix (defender of Gaul). Between them are the druid goddess Veleda and her Egyptian counterpart Isis. In the centre Cheval placed his wheelbarrow, tools, pails, water cans, and trowels, along with an inscription in French: "1906, I am the faithful companion of the intelligent worker. . . . Now his work is done, he can enjoy the peace that follows labour, whilst here, I, his humble friend, have pride of place." The surfaces of the Palace bear dozens of similar inscriptions. Some are religious sayings from various traditions—Buddhist, Christian, Jewish, Islam, Hindu—but most are Cheval's invention. As you walk around the north end you are faced with a strange and delicate cascade of river stones and animal shapes—stag, roe-deer, fawn, crocodile. This is no doubt where Cheval elaborated his exploration of nature's ancient sculptures.

The west wall is a collection of images that juxtapose religious and secular images: another Hindu Temple, a Swiss chalet, the White House, the Maison Carrée d'Alger, and a medieval castle. This is also the entrance to the gallery: an internal labyrinth filled with frescoes and reliefs of animals, trees, and humans. On the ceiling of the central crypt, Cheval inscribed in a circle, "Here I wanted to sleep."

Most people in his village thought he was a madman. They called him an "architect of the useless." This did not deter him. "I would be the first to agree with those who call me insane," he said. "The tongues started to wag in my hometown and surrounding district. They quickly made up their minds that 'there's a poor mad fool filling up his garden with stones.' I was laughed at, disapproved of and criticized but, as this kind of mental alienation was neither contagious nor dangerous, they didn't see much point in fetching the doctor and so I was free to give myself up to my passion in spite of it all." No one has recorded how his wife felt.

Eventually people outside the village began to recognize the unique achievement that was the Ideal Palace. In the last few years of Facteur Cheval's life, and for years after his death, professional artists made the pilgrimage from Paris to see this supreme example of "art *brut*." André Breton, one of the founders of surrealism, described Cheval as the "uncontested master of medianimic architecture and sculpture." Salvador Dali was impressed, and even Picasso paid a visit.

Originally Cheval planned to have himself and his wife buried inside the Palace. Whether it was local authorities refusing to allow it, or his own recognition that the bodies might detract from the playful quality of the work, he chose instead to create an elaborate tomb for himself in the Hauterives cemetery. It took him another ten years to complete that work. He then sat down and began writing his autobiography. He died two days after it was completed in 1924. He was eighty-eight years old.

■

The Los Angeles suburb of Watts is known to the world for a series of race riots in the summer of 1965. It is also recognized by some as the home of the Watts Towers, built by an eccentric Italian construction worker named Simon Rodia in the middle of the last century. Unlike Facteur Cheval, this working-class artist never left any kind of autobiography. Indeed, it is very likely that he did not know how to read or write. Most of the information we have about him comes from local, and often contradictory, oral histories.

When Sabato Rodia was born, in the last quarter of the nineteenth century, his roots sank deep in ancient peasant soil. His homeland, the Kingdom of the Two Sicilies, had been annexed to Italy less than twenty years earlier. It was a rural society filled with Etruscan frescoes, medieval castles, and beautiful Romanesque cathedrals, cupolas, and campaniles: layer after layer of civilization going back five thousand years. But Sabato's life, like the lives of so many others born in Campania, was to unfold in ways inconceivable to his feudal ancestors. At the age of twelve he turned away from his family's small farm in Ribottoli at the foot of Mount Vesuvius and, like so many others, plunged off the edge of time and emerged in the New World.

Sabato and his brother worked in quarries and on railway construction in the United States, finally settling in Northern California at the turn of the century. He married and fathered two children. (Other reports noted two marriages and three children.) Like many other immigrants, he earned his living as a construction worker. Sabato's marriage eventually fell apart, and he set off for Los Angeles alone. He was plagued by an inner tyrant. The year was 1921. He was forty-two years old.

After purchasing a small house on a wedge-shaped lot in Watts, Sabato—or Simon, as his neighbours called him—built a fence around his yard and began erecting structures out of steel rods, wire mesh, and concrete. The structures towered fifty to one hundred feet above the sidewalk. By day he helped to construct the buildings that housed the burgeoning new city; by night he created his towers. For thirty-three years he worked alone, in his spare time, with only a window washer's seat and some tile-setter's tools. He was a heavy drinker. Neighbours described how, late into the night, he would hang from his seat, high above the pavement, singing Italian operas along with his beloved Caruso playing on the Victrola below.

Inlaid into every foot of the towers and walls are thousands of rocks, tiles, shells, bits of glass from pop bottles, and even a pair of women's boots. Some of the tiles are extremely rare and must have been salvaged from local demolition jobs. The rocks came from Northern California, and the seventy-eight thousand shells from a beach miles away from Watts. Rodia, too poor to own a car, travelled by trolley and train to gather his materials. He fashioned nine major structures, each one different, but all unified by a consistent design. By all accounts, Rodia never planned his work in advance. He effectively made the towers up as he went along, by painstaking trial and error.

Sometime in the Watts period, Rodia passionately embraced evangelical Christianity. He started preaching about "true freedom, freedom of the spirit and soul," in a Mexican tent-revival church. At the base of one tower Rodia created a circular gathering place for his friends and neighbours. He called the towers *Nuestro Pueblo* (Our town). As a citizen of the immigrant, working-class community of Watts, Rodia witnessed many distressing events around his home. At the beginning of the Second World War his Japanese neighbours were shipped off to internment camps, and their land was handed over to the legions of new workers needed for the defence industry. At the end of the war these new workers, mostly unskilled blacks, were laid off. The seeds were sown for the powerful explosion of frustration and anger that would occur two decades later. In his seventies Rodia witnessed the beginnings of television and the rise of the consumer society. Close to his seventy-fifth birthday, in 1954, he declared the towers finished. He deeded the property to a Latino neighbour and moved north to be close to his sister. He never saw the towers again.

■

Whatever else might be said about the mainstream European tradition of secular art, one thing is certain: except for a very few exceptions, the tradition was invented, and continues to be created, by professional artists and critics—men and women who claim membership in the social class that holds political and economic power. This is not to say that artists of peasant or working-class origins do not exist. There are, of course, examples of this. Except for rare instances like those I describe here, these individuals, if they are serious, abandon their class origins to succeed in the profession, which requires years of schooling and a redefining of aesthetic judgement. This requirement was not always necessary, as Berger points out in his article "The Primitive and the Professional."

> The category of the professional artist, as distinct from the master craftsman, was not clear until the 17th century. (And in some places, especially in Eastern Europe, not until the 19th century.) The distinction between profession and craft is at first

difficult to make, yet it is of great importance. The craftsman survives so long as the standards for judging his work are shared by different classes. The professional appears when it is necessary for the craftsman to leave his class and "emigrate" to the ruling class, whose standards of judgement are different.

One way of understanding this distinction is to look at the terms used by critics to describe art originating from the working classes. The first word used was "primitive." Recently, other terms, designating various subcategories, have circulated: folk art, art *brut*, outsider art, marginal art, naive art. This terminology bespeaks both fascination and exclusion. Specifically, all the terms differentiate what they describe from "art" in the general sense: the work of serious "world class" professional artists and the network of galleries, grants, and critics that support them. Why primitive art works are fascinating is precisely because they have been made by people who refused to go through the class transformation necessary for their art to be taken seriously. It is the improbability of this refusal that is so fascinating. "The primitive begins alone; he inherits no practice," Berger says.

Because of this the term primitive may at first appear justified. He does not use the pictorial grammar of the tradition—hence he is ungrammatical. He has not learnt the technical skills which have evolved with the conventions—hence he is clumsy. When he discovers on his own a solution to a pictorial problem, he often uses it many times—hence he is naive. But then one has to ask: why does he refuse the tradition? And the answer is only partly that he was born away from the tradition. The effort necessary to begin painting or sculpting, in the social context in which he finds himself, is so great that it could well include vis-

iting the museums. But it never does, at least not in the beginning. Why? Because he knows already that his own lived experience which is forcing him to make art has no place in that
tradition. How does he know this without having visited the
museums? He knows it because his whole experience is one of
being excluded from the exercise of power in his society, and he
realises from the compulsion he now feels, that art too is a kind
of power. The will of primitives derives from faith in their
own experience and a profound skepticism about society as
they have found it. This is true even of such an amiable artist
as Grandma Moses.

I hope I have now made clearer why the "clumsiness" of
primitive art is the precondition of its eloquence. What it is
saying could never be said with readymade skills. For what it is
saying was never meant, according to the cultural class system,
to be said.

Despite the politics of production and reception of visual art in
the industrial world, works like the Ideal Palace and Watts Towers
do get made. These exceptions to the norm share many of the characteristics of vernacular culture. Both are profoundly "site-specific."
Facteur Cheval's Palace could not have been imagined or constructed without the stones of Drôme, which provided both inspiration and building materials. Rodia's walls and towers were made
from the castoff bed frames, ceramic tiles, shells, bottles, china,
licence plates, scrap metal, and used rebar of middle twentieth-
century Los Angeles. Both were "improvised" in the sense that
their creators had no predetermined plan, no blueprint, from
which they worked. The projects evolved over an extended time
period: coincidentally, both of them took almost the same length
of time to complete—thirty-three years. Professional virtuosity

as we normally define it was absent; neither of the artists received training in sculpture, architecture, or visual art of any kind, nor did they draw their inspiration from current trends in the art world. Yet, skill and aesthetic judgement are obviously evident in large quantities. In the case of the Watts Towers, the maker moved on, like Shakespeare, caring little for posterity, preservation, or "authorship." Finally, neither of the makers, by all accounts, ever thought about the possibility that their work might have "market value."

Still, if we are interested in developing a critical approach to vernacular activities, we need to consider other points. To begin, we can examine the aesthetics of these works. One of the most obvious features is that, even though both structures are essentially architectural, they lack rectangular shapes. Curves and progressively changing forms are the norm. Nature is the model, as Berger puts it, "not as a depository of fixed appearances, not as the source of all taxonomy, but as an example of continual metamorphosis." As in nature, the physical process by which they were created is inscribed on all the surfaces. They are meant to be experienced viscerally, with the whole body, rather than with the mind. In this, Cheval and Rodia have something in common with modernist sculptor Henry Moore and architect Antonio Gaudi. But whereas Moore's sculptures and Gaudi's buildings are meant to be viewed initially from a distance, making a statement through their hierarchy of forms and textures, the Ideal Palace and Watts Towers can best be experienced from the inside out. As Berger says about Facteur Cheval's creation, "The Palace is about the experience of being inside itself. You do not look at it any more than you look at a forest. You enter it or you pass it by." I experienced this myself on visits to each of these sites. I had the curious feeling that there was no coherent exterior that I could retain in memory. What I remember seeing instead, as I travelled through the labyrinth, was a narrative of small images, unfolding like a movie.

Both works also imply that something invisible exists just below the surface. In Cheval's Palace, the stones are arranged and mortared into place in such a way that they propose mysterious life forms yet to be. Rodia's towers are covered in a complex arrangement of tiles, shells, and multicoloured glass fragments that shimmer in the Southern California light in such a way that they suggest constant organic metamorphosis—what art critic Kenneth Scambray calls "polyphonic luminosity." This experience of light extends to the structures themselves: "The elongated, arched buttresses that criss-cross the site and that also form the round circles on the towers cast a network of changing shadows across the site."

These works are also produced and received within a certain social context. How do these works fit into the communities in which they were created? This is an important issue in any critical assessment of the manifestations of the vernacular imagination. Here I need to introduce another pair of terms: "appropriate" and "proportion." For the sake of this discussion, "appropriate" means "suitable or proper" and "proportion" means "a correct or ideal relationship in size, degree, etc. between one thing and another." The key relationship here is the one between the work and the community. In both cases they involve judgements of value.

At first glance it would appear that neither the Ideal Palace nor the Watts Towers passes the test. There is considerable evidence that many, perhaps most, residents of Hauterives neither valued nor approved of the Facteur's activities during his lifetime. While built in the garden adjoining his house, Cheval's creation looms above the other buildings and contrasts sharply with the humble architecture of the village. The contrast between the community and the work is even more pronounced in the case of Rodia's towers. Rodia lived at the end of a small suburban street in a city and a state that Irwin Thompson once described as being at "the edge of history," a place that was aggressively modern and future-focused. His neighbours were all modest working-class Mexicans, Italians, Japanese, and African-Americans. Rodia's outrageous behaviour must have been a strain and a worry for them, and his hundred-foot towers must have looked incongruous and dangerous. Stories were told of how some neighbours encouraged their children to vandalize the towers. That may have been one of the reasons that Rodia walked away in 1954.

But any evaluation of the appropriateness or proportionality of the vernacular in the age of mass media and industrialization should never be oversimplified. The medieval peasant was at the centre of his society. A network of obligations and traditions tied communities together. Vernacular activities were shared by all, and their appropriateness and proportionality were constantly being tested and renegotiated. By the time Facteur Cheval was born, at the height of the Industrial Revolution, the feudal world of his ancestors was rapidly disappearing, even in Drôme. While the Ideal Palace can be seen on one level as a response, an opposition, to the inhuman rigours of industrial consciousness, it could not have been possible without the combination of universal education and mass media associated with modernity. Cheval was able to create images of foreign lands and quote from the texts of exotic religions because he read regularly from encyclopedic magazines published in France at the end of the nineteenth century. The humble postman, we might say, had developed a global consciousness through reading. This consciousness, however, did not in any sense imply acceptance or celebration of the dream of industrial progress. On the contrary, Facteur Cheval was actively opposed to much that modernism had to offer.

Unlike the postman, Simon Rodia left his home and peasant roots before he was a teenager. For the rest of his life, he submitted his body to the boiler room of that great experiment in unbridled capitalism, the United States of America. At home in California, during his free time, he laboured for three decades on a monument to his old peasant consciousness built from the detritus of the new world. There is considerable evidence that Rodia was vocal in his criticism of the emerging world of television and consumer culture. Like the Ideal Palace, Watts Towers is a powerful, intuitive critique of the modern world and its follies. In making that critique it appears to challenge the conventional attitudes of the surrounding community.

Still, these kinds of things are never quite so simple. After Rodia left Los Angeles to live in a squalid boarding house in Northern California, the towers took on an eerie, lonely quality. They whistled in high winds. People were afraid they were going to collapse. Eventually the city's Building Department decided that demolition was necessary, and only the courageous efforts of a local citizens' committee kept the towers standing. Some three weeks after Rodia's death, in 1965, the people of Watts rioted, and thirty-six people were killed. Anything symbolizing white power and privilege was attacked. But Simon Rodia's Watts Towers were left unharmed. They stand today, restored and strengthened at great cost to the municipality. Perhaps they were not as inappropriate as they first appeared to be.

SOCIAL MAJORITIES
AND SOCIAL MINORITIES

■

*The computer has become the storehouse, the
"memory" of modern urban information: in peasant
cultures the equivalent storehouse is an oral tradition
handed down through generations; yet the real difference
between them is this: the computer supplies, very swiftly,
the exact answer to a complex question; the oral tradition
supplies an ambiguous answer—sometimes even in
the form of a riddle—to a common practical question.
Truth is a certainty. Truth is an uncertainty.*

*Peasants are thought of as being traditionalists
when placed in historical time; but they are far more
accustomed to living with change in cyclical time.*

*A closeness to what is unpredictable, invisible,
uncontrollable and cyclic predisposes the mind to a
religious interpretation of the world. The peasant does not
believe that Progress is pushing back the frontiers of
the unknown, because he does not accept the strategic
diagram implied by such a statement. In his experience
the unknown is constant and central: knowledge
surrounds it but will never eliminate it.*

— JOHN BERGER

Many trees have been felled and much ink has flowed in the publication of books and articles analyzing the history of the past two centuries, including the evolution of industrial capitalism and modernity. Most commentators see the contemporary world—the end product of the Enlightenment—as "the true, the good, and the inevitable." An outspoken few see it as nothing less than a catastrophe for people and the natural environment.

Modernity—a constellation of ideas and practices including representative democracy, individualism, secularism, wage labour, scientific medicine, compulsory education, transnational corporations, and electronic media—claims and asserts universal application. The left and right in the West agree that modernity is both a description and a prescription for the whole world. People on the right see economic globalization as the most recent version of this new gospel; most on the left favour a more humane and equitable version of globalization that includes education, health care, and democracy, but globalization nonetheless. The *facts* of the modern age do not necessarily match either ideal, but for those engaged in debates about the future, how the facts get described is just as various. What most people do agree on is that we experience modernity differently depending on where we are born and who our parents are.

What are these facts? According to United Nations population statistics for 2005, the "developed world" accounts for slightly more than 1 billion of the world's 6.5 billion people, or about 16 per cent. Of the other 5.5 billion, only a small fraction can afford a computer, a car, and a flush toilet. If we include the elites in Africa, South America, and Asia we can safely say that about 20 per cent of the people in the world today experience modernity primarily as a "good."

What about the other 80 per cent? For these, the vast majority of the world's population, the benefits of a modernization based on the dictates of the developed world are less obvious. An increasingly large number have entered the international labour force as factory workers, agricultural workers, miners, domestics, or sex-trade workers, servicing the ever-expanding international economy. A majority of these people work in inhuman conditions for very low pay. The last few decades have also been a time of unprecedented migration. These migrations are sometimes chosen—fuelled by hopes, reasonable and naive, for a more secure life—but are more often forced on people by violence and starvation. People thus uprooted and exiled often wonder what, if anything, they have gained from the modern experiment.

Others—between 20 per cent and 40 per cent of the world's population—are neither workers nor consumers in the new world system. These people have lived subsistence lifestyles for generations, or they have become redundant migrants in the cities of the South or, increasingly, the homeless and the unemployable in the world's richest metropolises. For these "marginals"—like the Tutsis of Rwanda, who were killed in the thousands in a racist war that originated in the colonial policies of Belgium, a war fuelled by poverty and quietly ignored by a docile United Nations—modernity has little of substance to promise them.

Here I want to look at local cultures in the modern world not from the standpoint of the elites at the industrial centre—something I have been trained to do from childhood—but rather through the eyes of those who stand outside the dominant system. I want to look at today's cultures from the viewpoint of that other 80 per cent.

Such an approach faces enormous pitfalls. To take this position forces one to confront the unexamined sacred cows of Western culture. The most widespread and difficult of these is the belief that, for whatever their faults, universal education and the electronic media of radio, television, and the Internet are ultimately forces of good for underdeveloped communities because they bring to these communities the liberating ideas and aspirations of the developed world.

Even as nuanced a commentator as Arjun Appadurai, whose book *Modernity at Large* did so much to shine the spotlight on non-Western "postelectronic" cultures (his term), focuses much of his attention on how non-Western communities use mainstream electronic media. With globalization, Appadurai suggests, comes a new role for the imagination. While he acknowledges that, for individuals and groups in the developing world, consumer society can be oppressive, he thinks Hollywood action films, American sitcoms, CNN, and fantasy games offer "new resources and disciplines for the construction of imagined selves and imagined worlds" and "tend to interrogate, subvert, and transform other contextual literacies."

> Electronic media give a new twist to the environment within which the modern and the global often appear as flip sides of the same coin. Always carrying the sense of distance between viewer and event, these media nevertheless compel the transformation of everyday discourse. At the same time, they are resources for experiments with self-making in all sorts of societies, for all sorts of persons. They allow scripts for possible lives to be imbricated with the glamour of film stars and fantastic film plots and yet also to be tied to the plausibility of news shows, documentaries, and other black-and-white forms of telemediation and printed text. Because of the sheer multiplicity of the forms in which they appear (cinema, television, computers, and telephones) and because of the rapid way in which they move through daily life routines, electronic media

provide resources for self-imagining as an everyday social project.

While Appadurai's warning about the complexity of local reactions to mass culture as it moves outside North America is apt, his faith in the abilities of ordinary people to fashion empowering new identities by patching together pieces from the lives of the stars, action films, and TV talk shows is wishful thinking. A diet of mass-produced junk culture provides about as much nutrition for the alienated soul as a daily Big Mac has for the starving body.

Another closely associated sacred cow is the widely held assumption that the rest of the world both envies and desires the lifestyle of the well-heeled American or European. Is it not the case, mainstream media and daily gossip ask, that if the starving South Asian peasant could have a microwave oven and a cell phone, he would greedily embrace them and all that they represent? Are the benefits of these things not obvious to all? The answer is never so simple.

It is precisely these unexamined assumptions that Mexican thinker Gustavo Esteva and South Asian scholar Madhu Suri Prakash challenge in their book *Grassroots Post-Modernism: Remaking the Soil of Cultures*. They start with the idea that modernism is so prevalent today that it is inaccurate to speak about any contemporary society as pre-modern, yet what remains is a sleeping giant. The moral economy of the forager and peasant societies, even in the disembedded, dismembered circumstances of the new century, is still at work in the day-to-day lives—and the vernacular imagination—of social majorities. Esteva and Prakash provide many examples of marginal, traditional societies that have evolved organically in strikingly original ways. These examples are not carbon copies of the past, nor do they resemble in any way the conventional ideals of Western modernity. To describe these new communities, they reluctantly borrowed, with some irony, the term "postmodern." Esteva tried to explain this choice of the term in a conversation we had in 1998.

> Of course, we all know that the scholars have spoiled the word, and you cannot be innocent in using the word postmodern. But still I want to use it. This condition of being postmodern, for me, is to go *beyond* modernity, *after* modernity and, in many senses, against modernity. You must take into consideration that half of Mexican peasants have been at least once in their lives in the U.S. The life in the U.S. or the life in Mexico City, they know what it is like. What we are saying is that these people, who can be seen from the outside as traditional people— that can be seen with a folkloric eye—they have in fact experienced modernity, they know what modernity is, and after experiencing modernity they have said, "No thanks, we don't want to stay there."

While acknowledging that the worlds of these "common people" are heterogeneous, Esteva and Prakash attempt to make comparisons between them and *homo economicus*: those who are committed participants in consumer culture. The first comparison has to do with attitudes to time and space. Urban professionals, according to Esteva and Prakash, cannot live without their watches. Managing time is the main ingredient of a successful life. Yet, for "the people of the villages" in Mexico and India, for example, mastering space is much more important: their community, their home, their land. Because of their relaxed attitude to time, common people often have conflicts with the emissaries of the developed world they encounter. Misunderstandings abound when appointments and deadlines are missed.

This fundamental difference has important implications when it comes to planning. "What is a plan?" Esteva asked in our conversation. "It is the conviction that by doing this or that I will really control the future, I will master the future. Well, we know that we cannot master the future. Because of that we have no plans." It is having no plans that encourages improvisation. A mechanic in a small village who has to deal with a model of a car that he has never seen before will have to improvise a repair, Esteva says. It may not be the perfect repair, or even the best repair for that particular car, but at least the car will get the driver to the next city.

> The principle of improvisation means that you really know the field, and then you improvise in a very creative way in a different kind of relation with the thing, you have a dialogue with the thing. You are talking with the thing, with nature, with a plant, with whatever you are dealing with. You are improvising.

That kind of improvisation—the necessity to improvise—leads to a different kind of relation to the future. "What I see in homo economicus," Esteva says, "is that they are never here."

> They are in transit from the past to the future. They are going to one place. They are studying to get a diploma, then the diploma will be to have a job, and the job will be to have some money to satisfy some economic goals. And whenever they have an economic goal satisfied they have the next. They are all the time going from here to there. They are not here in this place, where we are right now. The common people are here all the time. They have an attitude about the future that implies that they have hopes but not expectations. About the future I know nothing, except that I don't know if the future will exist for me

or not. I know that both the future and the past are only ideologies, and the only thing that I have is my present.

People with hopes instead of expectations behave in interesting ways. Social majorities often engage creatively in local forms of resistance against powerful global forces that threaten their livelihood. A few of these examples are well known—Nobel laureate Rigoberta Menchú in Guatemala, the Zapatistas in Mexico, and the Chipko and Narmada resistance battles in India, for instance—but many, many others seldom get reported in the Western media. Unlike the militant Marxist guerrilla warfare common in the Third World in the 1950s and 1960s, these resistance groups usually eschew violence and show little interest in seizing state power.

Yvonne Dion-Buffalo and John Mohawk suggest that colonized people have three choices: they can become good subjects, bad subjects, or non-subjects. It is precisely the last of these three that characterizes most of the stories in *Grassroots Post-Modernism*. Rather than demanding something—land, resources, rights—from the state and the elites, thus legitimizing those in power, these resistance movements simply ignore the state and take power into their own hands, thereby "disrobing the emperor." A well-known example of this tactic is the Salt Satyagraha led by Mahatma Gandhi in 1930. At that time, colonial British law decreed that all salt in India had to be purchased from centralized manufacturers, and those purchases were heavily taxed. Gandhi suggested that people start making their own salt and ignore the oppressive law. The British were horrified to discover that millions of Indians followed Gandhi's example; there were not enough jails to hold the violators.

Whereas the myth of the individual self is at the centre of modern life, the social majorities are attempting to retrieve or remake cultural commons that are linked to community and place. As Esteva and Prakash point out: "The individual self is cut out of the cloth of modern beliefs. Produced by industrial technologies, this cloth bears no resemblance to the fabric of traditional commons and community."

Yet these cultural commons are not conventionally traditional. They often involve new technologies such as local video, radio broadcasts, and the World Wide Web, in addition to storytelling and communal festivals. But they are fundamentally different from the mass culture of television, radio, and magazines that is so prevalent in the "global village," especially in regard to how history is told and remembered.

There are two irreconcilably different ways and kinds of remembering worlds or events. In fact there is such heteronomy between these two sets of experiences that we do not think that we can use the same word, "memory," to refer to them. If we want to keep the word for our memory as modern men and women, we need to use another to speak of that collective way of remembering that occurs when people's lives are living memories: continually changing, shared with neighbours, friends and relatives, with a past and future that constitute a "commons" and not a "private collection." The remembering that is a part of the "memory" of a village story-teller, telling thousands of times the same story and every time with a difference, is critical for the remembering without which there can be no community. In contrast there is the remembering of a student, digging into her "memory" to present the important facts on the final exam in order to get the best grade, her personal ticket to upward mobility. Unlike the first, the second "liberates" persons from their communities, promising progress and upward mobility for the individual self, "free" to belong to the community of his/her own choice—which means, in fact, having no community.

For those people enclosed in "the prison of the individual self," holding the spoils of an industrial education, medicated with the drugs of scientific medicine, comforted by the sentimentality of mass culture, and connected to the world through electronics, the dances of the "social majorities" can be witnessed, can be examined, can even be purchased, but it becomes increasingly hard to hear the music they dance to. It is as if one is watching their movements from behind soundproof glass.

■

The critical tools and approach of Gustavo Esteva and Madhu Prakash can be used to comprehend another cultural narrative that is still unfolding in the heart of North America's most powerful nation and partly defines its character: the history of African-American music. Well-documented accounts of African-American music—both sacred church music and its secular cousin, the blues—describe conditions and characteristics that Esteva and Prakash would recognize: forced migration, slavery and servitude, marginality, diffusion of high and low culture, technology, and cultural evolution.

Before 1750 few, if any, Europeans had attempted to bring Christianity to the thousands of African slaves working in the American colonies. There were even those who suggested that the blacks were not human. This situation changed in the second half of the century during a religious revival that became known as the Great Awakening, a movement including whites as well as blacks. The preachers who went to convert the African "heathen," however, were not prepared for the enthusiasm with which this new religion was embraced. The doctrines of the Bible were transformed in the crucible of African ancestral religions and practices into a new, syncretic belief system. In some cases, for example, the Yoruba creator-god Obatala became the vengeful god of the Old Testament. (In one Yoruba story, Obatala gets drunk before making human beings, which is why we have so many imperfections.) Christ became identified with the Yoruba storm-god Shango. The traditions of group singing, trance dancing, spirit possession, and shamanism practised in Africa were incorporated into the Christian service. Take, for example, a letter written by Samuel Davies, a preacher working in Virginia in 1755, to friends back in London:

> The books were all very acceptable, but none more so than the Psalms and Hymns, which enable them [the slaves] to gratify their particular taste for psalmody. Sundry of them have lodged all night in my kitchen, and sometimes when I have awaked about two or three o'clock in the morning, a torrent of sacred harmony has poured into my chamber and carried my mind away to heaven. In this seraphic exercise some of them spend almost the whole night. I wish, Sir, that you and other benefactors could hear some of these sacred concerts. I am persuaded it would please you more than an Oratorio or a St. Cecilia's day. . . . I cannot but observe that the Negros, above all the Human Species that I ever knew, have an Ear for Musick, and a kind of extatic Delight in Psalmody; and there are no Books they learn so soon or take so much pleasure in, as those used in that heavenly Part of divine Worship.

One of the interesting things about Davies's account is the implication that the slaves could read text and even music from books. This flies in the face of other reports that African slaves were illiterate. It suggests that perhaps some slaves, at least, taught themselves to read, even in the absence of schooling.

The African-American tradition of worship through song and dance evolved further during the Second Awakening of the nineteenth century—the time of the great outdoor camp meetings attended by both blacks and whites. Most forms of so-called "white gospel" singing known today in the American South, as well as the African-American spirituals, refined themselves during this fertile time of temporary white-black integration. The whites who attended these meetings were profoundly impressed by the "deep melodious organ-like music welling from a thousand African throats" and would often sit silently and just listen. Not all the whites, however, approved of the rapturous performances coming from the black side of the camp. In 1819 John F. Watson wrote a pamphlet titled "Methodist Error, or Friendly Christian Advice to Those Methodists Who Indulge in Extravagant Religious Emotions and Bodily Exercises." In it he scolded his counterparts for letting impressionable white congregations witness such godless behaviour. His writing revealed a distinct distain for musical improvisation.

> Here ought to be considered, too, a most exceptional error, which has the tolerance, at least, of the rulers of our camp meetings. In the blacks' quarter, the colored people get together, and sing for hours together, short songs of disjointed affirmations, pledges or prayers, lengthened out with long repetition *choruses*. These are all sung in the merry chorus-manner of the southern harvest field. . . . From this cause I have known in some camp meetings, from 50 to 60 people crowd in one tent, after the public devotions had closed, and there continue the whole

night, singing tune after tune (though with occasional episodes of prayer) scarce one of which were in our hymn books. Some of this from their nature (having very long repetition choruses and short scraps of matter) are actually composed as sung, and are indeed almost endless.

For a brief period after the Civil War, things got better for the freed slaves. For about a decade African-Americans had an increased sense of confidence and even participated to some degree in local and federal politics. But the promise of freedom was quickly dashed. By 1877 the Union army had withdrawn from the South and the "anti-negro crusade" had begun in full force. The racism of the Ku Klux Klan, which was so chillingly celebrated in the world's first movie blockbuster, *Birth of a Nation* (originally titled *The Clansman*) in 1916, continued unabated until well into the 1960s. During this second period of oppression, the black churches all over the U.S. South became "centres of resistance, of education and of community." The tradition of singing worship also evolved, with the old spirituals being left behind in favour of "black gospel."

The distinction between artistic culture as a collection of objects—paintings, songs, plays, dances, books—and artistic culture as social process comes into play here. If we approach this music by looking only at its artifacts—songs transcribed and published—the tradition seems incomprehensible. The coherence and meaning of the African-American religious song tradition only become apparent in the repeated and constantly evolving performance process.

Musicologist Christopher Small uses the phrase "rituals of survival and resistance" to describe this music. He argues that the slaves' version of Christianity was fundamentally different from that of their white owners.

The slaves' problem was not sin—that was a luxury only white folk could afford—but the suffering that was inflicted upon them through what they knew was a monstrous injustice and absurdity. Their problem was to keep from submitting to existential despair, and they solved it, not once and for all, but over and over again every day of their lives, with a faith in a god who was not, could not be, the god of the masters, and in his promise of ultimate justice and freedom, not just in the next world but in this.

They were able to solve this problem, despite the constant fragmentation of communities due to the demands of the slave economy, because they inherited African traditions that were flexible, decentralized, and "depended neither on written sources nor on the presence of specialists, and were thus open to endless re-creation not just by a few but by all."

How they chose and radically reworked their source material is a prime example of this procedure. Many of the songs sung in African-American churches are European and American Protestant hymns, but they are rendered almost unrecognizable through the performance process. Even today African-American congregations love to slow a tune down, "almost to immobility." They elaborately ornament each note of the melody. Anyone familiar with the music of Ray Charles will recognize the characteristics of this "surge" style. "Long metre" singing was something that observers noticed people doing in New England and even in the Scottish islands in the eighteenth and nineteenth centuries, but it never reached the sublime perfection of that in the African-American tradition. In other cases the lines of a hymn are separated by spaces in which the congregation is expected to interject refrains and spontaneous responses. Equally common is the practice of taking a single phrase or call and response and repeating it with variations and additions, sometimes for very long periods. Often as the preacher finishes speaking the congregation surges into a spontaneous chorus, echoing a key phrase from the sermon. Some of the spirituals collected over the years no doubt began life as an on-the-spot response to a particularly inspiring preacher.

Another unique aspect of this music is the interaction between song leader and congregation. Most performances involve active, creative participation by the entire gathering. Small notes a pattern "of improvised hymnody," often with the leader singing a couplet and the congregation responding with a "Glory, Hallelujah!" or "Roll, Jordan, roll." They might answer the leader's question—"Oh brethren, will you meet me/In Canaan's happy land?"—with "By the grace of God we'll meet you/In Canaan's happy land."

But it is not only the words that are improvised. Harmony in the African-American tradition is also an open-ended affair, with each singer expected to contribute individually. William Francis Allan, the editor of *Slave Songs of the United States*, written in 1867 during the Second Great Awakening, put it this way:

> There is no singing in *parts*, as we understand it, and yet no two appear to be singing the same thing—the leading singer starts the words of each verse, often improvising, and the others, who "base" him, as it is called, strike in with the refrain, or even join the solo, when the words are familiar. When the "base" begins, the leader often stops, leaving the rest of his words to be guessed at, or it may be that they are taken up by one of the other singers. And the "basers" themselves seem to follow their own whims, beginning where they please and leaving off when they please, striking an octave above or below (in case they have pitched the song too low or two high) or hitting some other

note that chords, so as to produce the effect of marvelous complication and variety. And what makes it all the harder to unravel the thread of melody out of this strange network is that, like birds, they seem not infrequently to strike sounds that cannot be precisely represented by the gamut [notation] and abound in strides from one note to another, and turns and cadences not in articulated notes.

All of these practices, complete with their emotional intensity and religious feeling, explore, affirm, and celebrate both community and individuality. For those who are oppressed and who recognize that consumer treasures and the pleasures of the wealthy are beyond their grasp, what is morally right tends to be those things that strengthen and preserve their own community. The democratic nature of these proceedings, with the creative participation of all concerned, is nothing if not an affirmation of group feeling.

■

The blues, in many ways, is the mirror image of sacred music. It is almost all secular and, in terms of content, bitingly realistic. The blues expressed, in its initial forms, harsh truths of the life of its practitioners and audiences: sex, drugs, criminality, infidelity, poverty. No doubt it evolved from earlier forms of secular music heard and practised in slave communities: "work songs, songs of praise, of ridicule and satire (of both white folks and fellow slaves), songs of longing and distress at parting, songs of complaint and of flattery."

Classic blues, as developed in the Mississippi Delta in the first three decades of the twentieth century, has a deceptively simple structure when looked at from the perspective of Western art music. A series of twelve bars in four-four time is repeated ad infinitum until the song is finished. The chord progression is nearly always the same: four bars in the tonic, two in the sub-dominant, two more in the tonic, then a progression of dominant, subdominant, tonic, and dominant again. This simple, repeated harmonic pattern has led some classically trained musicologists to view the blues as being devoid of musical interest, although they might acknowledge that it has sociological interest. But three important musical innovations make this form extremely interesting.

The first innovation is the "swing" rhythm. To "swing" means to lengthen the first eighth note in every pair, in what poets call a "trochaic" pattern. Swinging also means that, rather than emphasizing the first beat of each bar, which is typical in Western concert music, the musicians give a greater emphasis to the second and fourth beat of each measure (the so-called "back beat" in rock drumming). The extent of these alterations and syncopations is left to the performer and is constantly readjusted from one iteration to the next. Subtle variation is the norm. The result is a complex, forward-moving, and expressive rhythmic pattern that never sounds "square." It is also not uncommon for solo performers to add beats, bars, and rhythmic flourishes according to the feelings of the moment. A perfect example of this can be found in the 1936–37 recordings of iconic bluesman Robert Johnson, who extemporaneously adds whole bars to extend certain moments for emotional impact.

The second innovation is melodic. The blues scale appears to be a variation on the Western minor scale, but with some wrinkles. The most significant is that the intervals of the third and the seventh are sometimes flattened to varying degrees and sometimes not, often within the same song or phrase. With these so-called blue notes added, blues melodies, especially when played or sung over a series of flattened seventh chords, introduce an interesting, unstable harmonic ambiguity into the performances.

The third, and perhaps the most important, innovation concerns song structure and phrasing. The lyrics are usually rhyming couplets, with the first line being repeated twice, sometimes with slight variation. Classic twelve-bar blues is structured this way: the first two bars contain the vocal phrase, the next two are left open for an instrumental variation; then the first vocal phrase is repeated again over a new chord, followed once again by a two-bar space for instrumental response; the second line in the rhyming couplet is then sung for two bars, followed by a two-bar instrumental "turnaround," and the cycle begins again.

All of these innovations have the effect of creating a fertile context for almost unlimited individual and collective improvisation. If solo performers are playing an instrument—typically a guitar—and singing, the lyric structure, with repeated lines and simple rhyming couplets, allows them to make up the verses as they go along, according to their mood, their listeners, and the occasion. They punctuate their singing with improvised instrumental passages after each phrase. Where the two-bar call, two-bar response structure of the blues becomes even more useful is when a number of people are playing together. Here each performer can add her or his improvised flourishes and rhythmic variations—often responding directly to the previous person—while the whole group still sounds good together.

The character of blues performances—a solo performer face to face with listeners or a jam session with or without an audience—demonstrates the extent to which they are deeply embedded in vernacular tradition. For example, various levels of talent and skill can be accommodated. Because the basics of blues performance are simple to master, almost anyone can participate and contribute. But for those who are more skilled, the structure provides opportunities for virtuosic demonstration. In Louis Armstrong's recordings of blues tunes made in the late 1920s, for instance, listeners can readily hear the loose, energetic performances of his band members, who get caught up in the frenzy of the music, while recognizing that Armstrong himself had a gift for phrasing and rhythmic variation that goes far beyond the competence of his fellow musicians. Small posits that blues follows "the conventions of harmony in a simple kind of way" but removes all of the drama, making the harmony one of the "givens of the performance." The predictability of harmonic movement permits the players to have "much more direct and intimate" reactions in the moment of performance.

And they can establish a very direct response to one another which is outside the limits of what is possible within the classical tradition. And you can play it simple or complex, you can be as creative or elaborate as you're capable of becoming. There is a whole spectrum of skill which the thing will allow. And to go with that there is this common stock of material, both in terms of riffs and musical material, and also in terms of poetic material which you can draw on.

Unlike audiences for today's classical concerts, who are obliged to sit quietly, contemplating the music in stillness, blues audiences (and band members) are expected to shout, clap, dance, and otherwise respond to the music. One of the features of live blues concerts (and most rock concerts as well) is how the listeners inspire the energy and direction of the music.

While the band's playing it's perfectly okay to talk. You can do anything. You can clap, of course. The performance is creating as it goes, so what you are watching is not just one feat of reconstruction but a number of daring and exciting feats, so okay you applaud them as they come along. And the audience has the power to influence the performance. We've all been to performances where that marvelous thing happens where you feel energy coming to you from the band and you feed it back and they feed it back again and the thing grows and grows and grows, and you come out feeling absolutely marvelous.

And it's quite interesting what they've done to that essentially individualistic, Western technique. They have drained, as it were, the individualism out of it and it's become a communal art, a common property, and something which creates an altogether different social situation.

A consequence of the popularity of music in the African-American tradition, particularly rock music in all its incarnations, and now world musics, is that people around the world have learned to play guitars, hand drums, and other instruments, and can easily sing basic harmonies. Jam sessions and other forms of "kitchen music" based on African-American forms are commonplace in many parts of the world among both social majorities and social minorities. These forms of music can even be found on university campuses and among retired people in middle-class North America. They are, perhaps, less common among people with jobs and children in the West—because these people are too busy fulfilling their obligations as *homo economicus*.

POSTMODERN SQUATTERS IN THE FOURTH WORLD

■

The plane landed in Mexico City at 1:00 a.m. This is one of the world's truly gigantic megacities. Population estimates range around thirty million people. No-one knows for sure because a census would be impossible even if some government wanted to pay for it. There are almost as many people in this cramped mountain plateau as in all of Canada. It is impossible to pump enough water up the mountain to supply the most basic needs of the city. The air is terribly polluted, and the traffic is ridiculous.

I had never been to Mexico before. My Spanish was terrible. My hosts had provided me with the name of a taxi company with a stand at the airport. Under no circumstances was I to take an offer from any other company. Unscrupulous cabbies had killed too many *gringo* tourists for their wallets. Even *chilangos* (Mexico City inhabitants) live in fear of theft and violence on the streets. I found the stand and signalled to a bored young man behind a screen, showing him my destination written out on a scrap of paper. He conferred with one of his drivers and I was escorted to a rather rusty car parked outside. The driver opened the door, let me in, took my piece of paper, and went off to discuss something with the other drivers. He was gone for what seemed like a long time. When he returned he smiled at me and we took off.

Since I could not talk to him, we drove in silence, careening through the early-morning traffic at breakneck speed. We must have jumped twenty red stoplights without even slowing, barely avoiding the dozens of oncoming cars that blared their horns dispiritedly. I later found out that Mexico City has one traffic accident every fourteen minutes. I can see why. I looked around for a seat belt, but none were to be found. Then the streets turned empty and dark.

Casa Gonzalez, the guest house I had booked long-distance from Canada, was on a quiet back street. They knew I was coming. Finally we arrived at the address. I looked out the taxi window and saw a small industrial building, all closed up for the night. Not a soul in sight. I looked closely at the address on the door. It said 96. I wanted to go to 69. Okay, the cabbie was dyslexic. I used all the Spanish I had ever learned to explain to him, calmly, that he had reversed the numbers. He understood. Finally we made our way to the right place. The old woman who was supposed to be waiting for me had fallen asleep. It took her a long time to come down and open the heavy padlock on the gate. As I waited, the kind cabbie lingered patiently in his car until I was safe. "*Mucho gracias,*" I called as he drove off.

I had come to Mexico to visit with and interview Gustavo Esteva, co-author of *Grassroots Post-Modernism*. I wanted Gustavo to show me some examples of vernacular culture in the country he knew so well. Our letters and emails had been cordial, but I was not prepared for his generosity and hospitality, or for the extraordinary places and people he introduced me to in a few short days.

We met the next morning at the modest offices of the non-governmental organization where Gustavo works when he travels to the city from his home in a small Zapotec village in the state of Oaxaca. We sat in the coffee shop on the ground floor and talked for several hours. I described what I meant by vernacular culture and he assured me that there were many eye-opening things to see. One problem we discussed was how, without fluency in Spanish, I would visit communities and talk with the people. Gustavo knew people I could hire as interpreters for my visits. They were not professional translators but were comfortable in both English and Spanish and closely acquainted with the places we would visit. That afternoon I met Mojdeh Hojjati, an Iranian-American woman who worked as a consultant for the Levi Strauss and Kellogg foundations, advising them on how to give money to grassroots organizations throughout Latin America. She became my guide and translator in Mexico City.

■

Our first stop the next day was the old neighbourhood of Tepito in the heart of the city. Tepito has long been famous as a "bad" neighbourhood, full of poverty, crime, and violence. Yet it was also the place where middle-class Mexicans came to buy cheap consumer goods, often well-made copies of brand items like Levis, Nike, and Rolex (complete with counterfeit labels). Even though the housing in Tepito was substandard, it was rent-controlled, so it had become an affordable place in which poor Mexicans, many of them indigenous people from rural areas, could live close to the downtown core and ply their "grey-market" trade. Because the city government and police force kept out of the way, Tepitians turned to each other to form loose social and cultural organizations and to more or less govern themselves. Photographer Carlos Plascencia, a long-time observer of Tepito, told me how the Spaniards had "arrived with the cross and the sword, they arrived with Catholicism and they set up their statues, but behind every Catholic figure, there was also the physical presence of a native divinity." This process, he said, resulted in a kind of religious syncretism, and the same kind of development extended into the realm of political authority. People in Tepito, he said, would take advantage of any corruption tendencies within political authority and exploit those tendencies to establish their own forms of self-government.

> Part of the success and even the survival of this urban zone, this urban experience, is due to its fragmentary structure: there've been so many organizations of craftspeople, of sellers, neighbourhood committees. This diversity has protected Tepito from falling under the formal control of authorities.

In Tepito Hojjati and I sat down with people's muralist Daniel Manrique, who grew up in the neighbourhood. Manrique had a passion and talent for painting from a young age, but because of his social class he couldn't break into the Mexican "art scene." Sometime in the 1970s, rather than stop painting, Manrique made an original choice that would have lasting implications for his life and the life of the community. He decided to commit what he called "a social suicide." He decided, as he put it, "to *not* look for recognition, for fame, for wealth—to not play the system's game." He would do his painting in the streets of Tepito, and he would create works aimed at helping his fellow Mexicans recognize themselves, as Mexicans. Going to the street did not mean taking his canvases out to the sidewalk. Rather, his canvas became the sides of buildings and the interior walls of one *vecindad* (courtyard) after another. The challenge for him was to locate themes and figure out how he would draw and place the figures, and "not to have a swift brush."

In the end his beautiful, playful, and political murals covered and changed the neighbourhood. He was not being paid for this art, but things worked out. The community recognized what he was doing: "So I did not go hungry. I had no money but I never felt hungry either, because people invited me over to eat." But it did not end there. He was asked to become more involved in the community, and he agreed. Then, he said, "I had to contribute to groups or to the community *my* ideas, *my* observations, about how I started to re-understand my neighbourhood of Tepito, my people, our lifestyle."

Yet Manrique has an interesting idea about consultation with his modest patrons. He seldom depicted what the people asked for.

Occasionally people suggested what I should paint: I never agreed because popular taste, in terms of painting, is corny, ordinary. They wanted me to paint seaside landscapes, nature landscapes. But my work deals with human beings in the city, what we do in the city. Most often, I ended up painting the human figure walking out of the walls.

Many of Manrique's murals from the 1970s were destroyed in the 1985 earthquake when 40 per cent of Tepito's badly built housing collapsed. The only record is an extraordinary set of photographs taken by Carlos Plascencia in 1979. Manrique continues to paint brilliant and complex murals in many of the poor barrios across the city.

Next we visited Manrique's friend, Luis Arevalo, in a tiny ground-floor apartment in one of the few old courtyards still standing. It was located in a dangerous section of the neighbourhood, and some of my Mexican friends thought it was too risky for me to go there.

I decided to brave it. Hojjati's husband, Felipé, drove us in their Mexican Volkswagen. Felipé left the car in a special guarded parking garage, and I gave the attendant an extra large tip to watch over the vehicle, which was absolutely necessary in this part of town, Felipé informed me. We made our visit and returned to the car without incident. What saved us, I believe now, was that Mojdeh and Felipé had to bring their tiny baby with them: Kia was only a few months old. While it slowed down the party—everyone, including complete strangers, had to stop, admire, and converse with the infant for long periods—it undoubtedly discouraged any would-be thieves from going for my camera pack.

As we walked up to Arevalo's workshop, I noticed that the many tiny apartments around the cramped *vecindad* had outdoor cooking facilities. When we went inside, Arevalo introduced us to his young assistants and his little grandson playing on the floor next to his bench. Arevalo was a skilled shoemaker who had decided to set up a workshop for local youth. His goal was to help them become financially self-sufficient so they could get off drugs and live a more sustainable lifestyle. His idea, according to Manrique, was "not to create slaves for shoe factories, but people who can learn to work independently." It was a difficult process with many setbacks, but after a while he achieved some successes. Other barrios asked him to set up workshops in their neigbourhoods. Manrique later told me that the New Tepito Workshop project was "not simply about new shoes." They knew they also had to provide a space for creativity. At first the work of shoe design could fill a part of that need, but eventually they "realized the project could be a lot bigger." The kids he trained could copy and improve on the design of U.S. name brands, build their own designs, or repair shoes found in the street or relegated to the garbage by the urban middle class. They could make their own work. "The main goal here is self-employment," Manrique said. "If the company owner doesn't hire you because he says there's no work, why the hell do I want a stupid boss, if I can employ myself?"

■

A key event in the history of Mexico City occurred one night in 1971. A presidential decree announced that anyone who built a house on unoccupied land around the outskirts of the city could keep the land as their own. Overnight some twenty-five thousand homes made of cardboard, scrap wood, mattresses, and plastic sheets appeared on several hectares of unusable wasteland near the university. The squatters were called *paracaidistas* (parachutists), and over the next few weeks thousands more of them arrived to build on the uneven volcanic rock—a terrain hospitable mainly to scorpions, spiders, and snakes. Today the community of Santo Domingo de los Reyes has a population of five hundred thousand. The houses there are made of mud brick, and many boast tiny front gardens overflowing with flowers and vegetables.

In the beginning the city administration was unable to provide the squatter community with even basic services. As Esteva writes: "Everything has been done, literally, 'of, and for the people': the building of the houses, the streets, the shops, the common spaces, including their own system for disposing of their garbage. And most of it has been done by women." The community also set up its own school. All this was done without formal leaders or financial support from outside.

When we arrived in Santo Domingo on a hot July day, we went straight to the beautiful community centre designed and built by volunteers. As Hojjati and I waited to see Fernando Díaz Enciso, one of the community's founders, we admired an enormous mural several stories high. It told the story of Mexico's turbulent past from the viewpoint of the indigenous people, and it was, of course, painted by Daniel Manrique.

Enciso was a survivor of the famous Tlatelolco massacre, when hundreds of peacefully protesting students were gunned down by police in the Plaza de las Tres Culturas ten days before the 1968 Olympic Games. Some three years later he threw his lot in with the homeless squatters and their land invasion, and he is still there. He told me about the evolution of the community of Santo Domingo de los Reyes: "What started happening was some kind of primitive communism. Because wherever you looked, you saw men, women, children and elderly, opening the streets, digging up rocks, filling up the paths with earth, preparing their plots for housing. It was all about having a little plot to live on."

We also met Maria Castañón, one of the community's important female leaders. She added to Enciso's description:

> If a woman had to go to the market without her kids, she could leave them because there'd always be someone to look after them so they wouldn't wander off. Neighbours would keep them. There was always a lot of trust among neighbours. That's what it was like, as organized people: we'd look after one another, we'd protect ourselves from the *comuneros* and the police.... It's like being in a village where we all know each other and we all take care of each other.

In 1997 the community proudly opened its "ecological park" on the site of what was once a foul garbage dump. Hundreds of volunteers cleared the mountains of rubbish and did the landscaping. I strolled through lush gardens and trees, gazing at dozens of imaginative sculptures made by community members. People played in one of the basketball courts; others enjoyed the cool breeze coming from the new artificial lake that had been stocked with its own fish. Bird life was abundant. What was most striking to me, coming as I did from a prefabricated urban environment designed by developers and planners, was how the local people had inscribed their own local history and geography into their park's design. Black rock outcroppings and craters still dominate, and many of the park's buildings suggest their wood and cardboard heritage. Teresa Rodriguez, another long-time resident and activist, told us how the park came about.

> When we arrived here in 1976, this place was a garbage dump. This zone was fought over quite a lot. First of all, the unionized teachers wanted it for housing. As a community, we got organized for this not to happen, because what we wanted was a park since there were no spaces for the community. Also a bus company wanted to turn this into bus garages. Other people came here, saying they were the owners, and they took over for almost a year. But the community organized to fight for this space to become a park, as we had planned.
>
> We said: let's protect this area. There were four or five projects in a contest and everybody discussed them. One was chosen. Then we started defining each zone: this section for ecology, this for culture, this for sports. It was elaborated with people's input. Also, political parties and social organizations got involved. So we talked it over until we reached a consensus, and this became what it is.
>
> After twenty-two years of efforts and inviting people to join in the preservation of this park, here it is, preserved.

■

The next day Esteva and I caught a bus to take the six-hour journey south down the single, two-lane highway to Oaxaca. In the bus, as most of the travellers enjoyed two movies, one Mexican and the other from Hollywood, Esteva and I talked. I would occasionally look out the window. At various checkpoints along the road, military personnel with rifles and machine guns were stationed prominently—yet another reminder of the deep rifts that cut through this country and of the standing war between the extremely poor, exemplified by the Zapatistas, and the newly globalized professional classes. I stayed the first night at Esteva's beautiful adobe home high up on the hillside overlooking Oaxaca City.

The next morning I drove off in a weathered Mazda driven by Oliver Froehling, a language teacher with strong ties to local activists and the indigenous community. Also in the car were two U.S. students interested in alternatives to development. I was sure the old Japanese compact couldn't survive the elephant-sized potholes and hairpin turns we encountered as we climbed into the Northern mountains of rural Oaxaca. Our destination: San Andrés de Chicahuaxtla, population eight hundred; number of telephones, one. The inhabitants speak Triqui, an ancient tongue. Many never get around to learning Spanish. Their village is literally in the clouds, but on a clear day you can see the Gulf of Mexico hundreds of kilometres to the east.

Esteva had suggested the remote community as a place to explore how unconventional local cultures were evolving in response to the radical technological and economic changes associated with globalization. At first I thought Esteva was wrong. Chicahuaxtla seemed pretty traditional, reminding me of indigenous communities I had visited in Northern Ontario. Apart from the health centre and the school, most of the buildings were fashioned from wood and adobe. Many had mud floors and no running water. The women wore brightly coloured robes called *huipiles*, the product of hand-loom weaving skills that women there begin learning at an early age. The people work little pockets of rocky soil by hand or with donkeys.

This first impression, however, was dispelled within a few hours of my arrival. "You're the Canadian filmmaker?" asked Fausto Sandoval, the local schoolteacher who had grown up in Chicahuaxtla. "We've been expecting you. We want to show you our videos."

It turned out that Sandoval had left the village to study and work in the city. But like many Mexicans who travel this path, he could not resist the lure of his roots. Fausto ushered me into a small video-editing suite at the community centre. I watched imaginatively made, technically sophisticated, short videos dealing with local festivals and garbage disposal. They were all in Triqui with Spanish subtitles. One exposed the dangers and myths of AIDS and gave detailed instructions on how to use a condom.

"Of all the important subjects to make videos about, why did you choose AIDS?" I asked. "You seem quite isolated here. Is AIDS really a big problem?"

"We may appear isolated," he explained, "but most of the men in the village spend time in the United States. They bring back all kinds of diseases. We hope this video will make people here more aware of the problem."

Despite its homemade furnishings, Sandoval's tiny dwelling, just off the village square, appeared more modern than did the houses of his neighbours. His family enjoyed running water, a gas stove, and a TV. But I was not prepared for what I saw next. Under a hand-woven cloth on a corner table was a shiny new Pentium computer. "For desktop publishing," he said, matter-of-factly.

When he began teaching, Sandoval wanted elementary school textbooks in Triqui. With the help of linguists from the city, he created a written version of Triqui using syllabics, similar to the system that European missionaries used in North American when they translated the Bible into indigenous languages. He then proceeded to write and publish textbooks in small quantities for both his own school as well as others in the area. "This way we preserve and strengthen our local oral tradition," he told me.

Not all modern conveniences are treated so positively. Sandoval's mother had turned down his offer of a modern gas range. She insisted on continuing to cook meals squatting beside a fire pit in the centre of her kitchen. "If I cooked on the gas stove," she explained when I went to visit her, "I would have my back to the activities of the room. Now I am at the centre of everything." For her, the social empowerment that her tools provided trumped convenience.

Back at Gustavo's house I prepared my video camera and microphone to conduct an extended interview. When the camera was rolling, I asked him what he thought of the villagers in San Andrés de Chicahuaxtla and their selective embrace of modernity. When these people are working with video cameras and computers to help communicate, he mused, "I can see very well that they are no longer traditional people and they are not modern people. They have their tradition fully alive—there is no rupture with the past—but they are accommodating their traditions to create opportunities for personal initiative—and personal creation—without becoming isolated 'individuals.'" Local cultures that mix electronic media with traditional ways, he reasoned, could provide models for a more sustainable world that rejects untenable Western assumptions.

A few days later, back in Canada, facing a barrage of dreary responsibilities at work or rushing through the supermarket for the week's groceries, I thought about how much wisdom there was wrapped up in this simple rejection. A refusal, not of everything that the new, globalized world has to offer—but certainly a rejection of the breakneck speed and crazed competition that is so much part of everyday life in the "developed" world.

LITERACY AND ITS DISCONTENTS

■

Old men forget; yet all shall be forgot,
But he'll remember with advantages
What feats he did that day. Then shall our names,
Familiar in his mouth as household words. . .
Be in their flowing cups freshly rememb'red.

— SHAKESPEARE, HENRY THE FIFTH,

ACT 4, SCENE 3

When William Shakespeare died in 1616, only a few of his plays had been published. Most of those were unreliable editions made without his approval. It was not until seven years after his death that two actors, John Hemings and Henry Condell, published a folio edition of thirty-six plays that they claimed were "cured and perfect of their limbs . . . as he conceived them." The technology they used to reproduce this book, the moveable-type printing press, was less than two hundred years old. Without the efforts of these two friends, William Shakespeare would have been a footnote in the history of English literature rather than its most central figure. The manuscripts from which these plays were typeset have long since disappeared. Countless scholars, from the seventeenth century onwards, have been amending and correcting what they consider to be faulty transcriptions of Shakespeare's words. In addition there has been considerable speculation, going back over two hundred years, about the authorship of these texts; many notable readers, including Mark Twain and Sigmund Freud, have doubted that Shakespeare of Stratford wrote them at all.

This story is well known to every English major. What I want to point out is how odd it appears when viewed by the uncontroversial assumptions of our own time and place. We know that the plays Shakespeare composed for his company were popular among Londoners of the time. We know that he made a respectable income from their performance. He ended up being a well-off landowner. Yet as far as historians can tell, the Bard went to his death at the age of fifty-two caring little for publication or posterity. In our text-centred culture, in which ideas about individual authorship and intellectual property rights have been assimilated into everyday life, the notion that an artist would be unconcerned with the preservation of his or her work seems inconceivable.

To comprehend Shakespeare's attitude to preservation we need to understand that he stood on the shore of what Ivan Illich and Barry Sanders have called the "island of writing," with one foot firmly planted in the vast ocean of orality. Shakespeare merely shared the attitude of his many predecessors who had spun yarns for their suppers: there would always be others to tell the stories again, or make up new ones. In fact, the assumption that creators have intellectual property rights is a modern notion, closely linked to the rise of capitalism over the last two centuries. Before that time, the relationship between individual authors and their imaginative works was of a very different order.

■

What are the characteristics of human communication in the realm of what Walter Ong calls "primary orality"—that is, among groups of people who do not know, and have never known, writing and reading? First, the utterance of words is, by definition, ephemeral. The moment a sound is spoken, it is gone. Words are on the wing, always in flight. There is no trace, no residue that can be reviewed or recalled. There are no pages or hard drives on which memories and ideas can be stored. What is remembered in a primarily oral community is what is spoken of regularly and repeatedly. Everything else fades from consciousness. What is recalled is shaped into narratives, usually spoken with standard mnemonic devices such as rhythmic emphasis and rhyme. There are also "nuggets of speech"—bits of wisdom that are recalled as necessary to remind, challenge, and teach. These nuggets are sometimes called proverbs. There are no authors as we understand that word. Without the possibility of imagining or putting words on paper, systematic thought—the conscious working through of contradictory ideas and strategies—can only be done in a conversation. Truth is arrived at by consensus. In this way, the invention of the alphabet, the recording and recalling of verbal utterances, changed not only how people communicated, but thought itself.

Human cultures have always used signs, images, and objects to represent things that are absent. Hunters are good at "reading" the tracks and stools of their prey. Lovers carry objects representing their beloved. The beads on a necklace can record the amounts involved in a transaction. Most religions have objects, like the Christian Cross, that represent powerful ideas. Most, but not all, of the great civilizations of the world between 3000 and 1000 BC developed some form of writing based on images—Egyptian hieroglyphics and Chinese logograms, for example—to express their ideas, keep records, and tell stories. Because these scripts often contained thousands of different letters, reading and writing were highly specialized activities requiring years of training. The alphabet is something else. With the alphabet, signs indicate sounds rather than things.

The alphabet was only invented once, by the Semitic peoples who lived around 1700 BC in the area between modern Syria and the Sinai Peninsula. These people, possibly descended from slaves in Egypt, and the ancestors of modern-day Jews and Arabs, took from Egyptian hieroglyphics a subset of twenty-two signs representing the consonant sounds, and threw away all the rest. From these "letters" they were able to record the sounds of their language on papyrus. This original alphabet had nothing to represent vowel sounds. These had to be guessed at from the words and the context. (This is still true today with modern Hebrew. Learners are provided with special signs above or below the letters to indicate vowels.)

The Phoenicians, one of the Semite groups using a version of this alphabet, were trading with the Greeks, and around 800 BC the Greeks took the Phoenician alphabet and began to use it. Some of the letters represented sounds that they decided were "un-Greek," and they took these letters and used them to represent vowel sounds. The revolution was now complete. For the first time in the history of the world, someone had come up with a complete "technology" for recording, not thoughts, not ideas, but sounds—sounds made by the human mouth and throat while engaged in interpersonal conversation. As a result, speech fragments could be frozen and later "played back" in another time and place. Because there were only twenty-four letters and a limited number of sounds represented, almost anyone, even a child, could learn the rudiments of reading and writing. The alphabet could even record and play back a language that the writer and the reader could not understand. It is precisely the mechanical accuracy of this technology that allows us to "hear" Homer's voice, in the form of a verbatim transcription, intoning *The Iliad*, while we are looking silently at a page. It is only because of the alphabet that Milman Parry could propose that *The Iliad* is a recording of an oral performance.

When compared with oral communication, alphabetic writing offered its users radically new possibilities. First, through standard grammatical rules and subordination, writing can convey complex ideas more precisely and coherently than speech can. Second, writing transfers sounds into a permanent visual medium, thus allowing "backward scanning" and review, a prerequisite for scientific thinking. When internalized, reading and writing encourage analytical, abstract thought—what many people call left-brain dominance—compared with the more intuitive, experiential modes of thinking associated with the right brain and sound-based oral communication. As Marshall McLuhan pointed out, reading and writing also privilege the eye over all the other senses. Because writing is permanent and portable, it allows communication (of a particular type) to happen over time and space. We can read the exact words of authors who have long since died or who live halfway around the world—people we will never meet. In addition, as writing became more dominant in modern cultures, the text became the key metaphor for individual human consciousness: "My life is an open book," and "Marriage represents a new chapter in everyone's life."

■

For those of us living in the high literacy of modern urban life, it is almost impossible to imagine a world without reading and writing, or to think that some forms of experience might be lost when writing dominates orality. For that perspective we have to rely again on literate witnesses at the threshold. One of the most thoughtful, subtle, and articulate of those witnesses was Plato. Living less than four centuries after the introduction of alphabetic literacy to Greece, and deeply influenced by his teacher, Socrates, who refused to write anything down, Plato was very aware of the limitations of the written word. In one letter attributed to him, Plato made the statement that he would never use the written word to express things that were really important to a general public. This seemingly contradictory statement has been analyzed by other philosophers in many ways, but some have suggested that Plato meant that he would never express his opinions without putting them in the form of a dialogue to recognize their dialogical character. What is clear is that Plato, one of the world's first great writers, harboured a deep ambivalence about the recently invented medium.

He articulates this ambivalence in a dialogue known as the *Phaedrus*. Here Plato has Socrates, his favourite discussant, debate meaningful communication with his friend Phaedrus. First Socrates points out that human communication has two purposes—for persuasion or to encourage understanding in the soul. He thinks the latter is the more noble cause, but also more difficult. In order to bring understanding to the soul, Socrates argues, there are four requirements: the speaker must have knowledge of the nature of the soul and the varieties of souls; he must understand how each listener's soul responds to various ideas and circumstances; he must be able to use different rhetorical skills in various situations; and, finally, he must have enough understanding to be able to use the first three appropriately, even when meeting a person for the first time. In short, Socrates argues that good, meaningful communication is *context-dependent*.

He goes on to outline the deficiencies of writing and reading for these purposes, and he does so by using the typical oral device of attributing ideas to ancestors: "What I've heard the ancients said."

First of all, Socrates tells Phaedrus, rather than improving memory, writing will actually make people's memories worse. "They will not practice using their memory because they will put their trust in writing, which is external and depends on signs that belong to others, instead of trying to remember on the inside, completely on their own." Furthermore, he argues, writing fosters only the illusion of wisdom, not its reality. As a result, people will be "difficult to get along with, since they will merely appear to be wise instead of really being so." In addition, writing cannot choose its readers and it is entirely possible for writing to fall into the hands of people for whom it will be inappropriate: "It doesn't know to whom it should speak and to whom it should not." Another problem with writing, according to Plato's Socrates, is that writing is unresponsive. If you ask a piece of writing a question, it simply responds with the same inadequate words that it uttered in the first instance. Connected with that—and this is perhaps the most important in Plato's and Socrates' dialogical world—writing cannot defend itself against unfair objections. For all these reasons, Socrates believes, writing may be useful as an amusement and as "a reminder" for certain mundane details, but it is not suitable as a means of nurturing wisdom in the soul and of communicating important ideas.

■

Socrates' complaints against written communication compared with context-dependent oral dialogue—written almost 2,500 years ago—are similar to observations made more recently about human communication and the commodification of culture. Of course, alphabetic literacy itself can also be divided into both vernacular and commercial practices. For example, literate people communicate with friends and family using written notes, letters, emails, and other personal texts: mostly one writer, one intended reader, at one moment in time. Writing each morning in a journal—in a sense, a letter to oneself, a tool for thinking and remembering—is yet another kind of vernacular literacy. Manuscript culture from the classical age to the Renaissance, which included the composing and copying of single, often priceless manuscripts, and the reading of these manuscripts aloud in social groups, maintained a tangible connection to the vernacular roots from which it arose.

The invention of the moveable-type printing press around 1440 is rightly regarded as being a major influence on the rise of individualism, scientific thinking, and democratic ideals in Europe after the Renaissance. It preserved and enabled great works of literature—Shakespeare's plays being a prime example. But the benefits of the typographic era, as shaped by the individuals and social forces of the time, did not come without a price.

Reading, writing, and publishing, by allowing for silent reflection, analysis, and discussion of one's place in the community, provided a hitherto unknown critical distance from the tribe. While consciousness of one's individual identity as separate from one's community identity is absolutely central to modern dissent and activism, its side effects can include alienation, loneliness, and also, increasingly in high-technology societies, a lack of social graces.

While speaking comes naturally and is grasped by most children before their third birthdays, literacy is seen as something that must be taught, more often than not, as part of a compulsory education. As a result, reading and writing in school—who can do it and who cannot, and how well—introduced a special kind of inequality into everyday social relations. This inequality is reinforced by most forms of schooling because of the institution's hierarchical and classificatory functions in society—which may explain why many parents who normally read very little or not at all, and who don't see the importance of literacy in their own lives, nonetheless demand hyper-literacy for their children. It is precisely this tendency of Western-style education to introduce new levels of inequality into traditional communities that makes some social majorities ambivalent about the benefits of this kind of schooling.

The printing press, by turning an utterance, a social act, into a thing, transforms what was once ephemeral into a reproducible object that can be sold like potatoes. Copyright laws—unknown and unimagined in oral and manuscript cultures—are central to the functioning of a society based on printing and other forms of mechanical replication. The history of copyright is another example of the ways in which mechanical reproduction disembeds cultural practices from their social context and transforms them into commodities. While copyright was initially invented as a way in which writers and publishers could see some financial gain for their work for a limited period of time, while still allowing the texts to become part of the public stock of cultural materials, it has increasingly, over the last two hundred years, been used as a way in which elites control cultural expressions. In 1800 the author's copyright on a book lasted fifteen years. The time period has steadily increased with each revision of copyright acts in the Western world. In the United States in 2004, copyright was extended for the author and his or her descendants to eighty years. And no longer is it just tangible objects like books and recordings that seek protection. Claims to the ownership of cultural ideas—labelled with the oxymoron "intellectual property"—have become rampant. Fame and celebrity, someone's *name*, can thus become a thing that needs protection from poachers. We have, for example, the extraordinary story of civil rights activist Rosa Parks's heirs successfully suing the musical group OutKast for mentioning her in the title of a song without getting their permission (and presumably an associated payment).

It is a paradox that, while print is widely credited as an agent of democracy in the West, the material and economic structures that underpin its use are theoretically more autocratic and centralized than either face-to-face interactions or the exchange of manuscripts. The mechanical reproduction of words and sentences enabled new and unprecedented forms of one-way communication, across time and space, from the few to the many: few writers, many readers. This made book publishing financially profitable, but it also foreshadowed and enabled modern forms of censorship and political control. Yet this, too, is complicated. For publishing to become a tool to extend and consolidate power, something else was needed: codified national languages.

■

On August 3, 1492, three small ships set sail from the port of Palos in Southern Spain. They were commanded by a charismatic Italian self-promoter named Christopher Columbus. He intended to sail these recently invented caravels to Cipangu, another name for China, which he had computed was a few weeks' sail to the west. To pay for his voyage, Columbus had lobbied for close to seven years just to get an interview with the famous rulers of Spain. Isabella of Castile's marriage to Ferdinand of Aragon united the two largest kingdoms on the Iberian peninsula. Together these innovative rulers were engaged in the construction of Europe's first Christian nation-state. They finally agreed to meet Columbus just after they had conquered Granada, the last Muslim stronghold in the region, and had driven the infidels out. When Columbus first put his case for a trip to Asia before the monarchs, Isabella, after consulting her advisors, turned him down, saying that the journey would take too long and the ships would never return. This was sound advice; China was a lot further from Spain than Columbus could possibly have sailed. Since the time of Eratosthenes of Cyrene in 255 AD, most intelligent scholars had known that the Earth was round and had estimated its size correctly to within 5 per cent. Later, swayed by her husband and some zealous Franciscan friars who wanted to see the Cross planted on distant lands, she changed her mind. In all, Columbus made four voyages to the "New World." He went to his death in 1506, a rich and celebrated hero, still convinced that he had discovered not a new continent, but the eastern shores of Asia.

In the same month and year that Columbus set sail on his historic first voyage, another event happened in Spain that was possibly even more important to the history of Europe, but which is seldom recognized in popular accounts. On August 18, the first edition of Elio Antonio de Nebrija's *Gramática de la Lengua Castellana* came off the printing press in Salamanca. Nebrija, a renowned Latin scholar, had synthesized parts from the dozen or so distinct vernacular, unwritten dialects spoken by the Queen's subjects into an *artificio*, a created language "similar to the three great languages given to us by God—Greek, Latin and Hebrew." Ivan Illich, in an article written in 1980, argued that this publication of a Spanish grammar was the beginning of a tectonic shift in relations between rulers and the ruled that would dominate the next five hundred years. What was at stake was nothing less than the control of language, written and spoken, and thus the everyday life of the people.

Nebrija *manufactured* the Spanish language. It was a radical achievement. No-one before him had ever imagined doing such a thing. To this day, his grammar and dictionary are still the best reference works available for scholars of Old Spanish. However, similar to that of Columbus, Nebrija's project was originally rejected by the same Queen. Early in 1492, around the same time as the Columbus meetings, Nebrija brought a draft of his grammar to the well-read Isabella to get her support and approval. Illich described the thinking behind the Queen's initial response:

> But while Isabella is able to grasp the achievement of his *letro*—the description of a living tongue as rules of grammar—she was unable to see any practical purpose for such an undertaking. For her, grammar was an instrument designed solely for use by teachers. She believed, however, that the vernacular simply could not be taught. In her royal view of linguistics, every subject of her many kingdoms was so made by nature that during his lifetime he would reach perfect dominion over his tongue *on his own*. In this version of "majestic linguistics" the vernacular is the subjects' domain. By the very nature of things, the vernacular is beyond the reach of the Spanish Monarch's authority. But the ruler foraging the nation state was unable to see the logic inherent in the project. Isabella's initial reaction underscores the originality of Nebrija's proposal.

In the first edition of *Gramática de la Lengua Castellana* that came off the press in August, Nebrija penned an introduction addressed directly to the Queen. In it he outlines the reasons why this project is so important for her reign. In Illich's view, "He offers Isabella a tool to colonize the language spoken by her own subjects; he wants to replace the people's speech by the imposition of the queen's *lengua—her* language, *her* tongue." Nebrija's introduction begins with this paragraph:

> My Illustrious Queen. Whenever I ponder over the tokens of the past that have been preserved in writing, I am forced to the

very same conclusion. Language has always been the consort of empire, and forever shall remain its mate. Together they came into being, together they grow and flower, and together they decline.

What Nebrija was doing here was evoking a concept that is still powerful in Spanish—*armas and letras*—the sword and the book. He was proposing to the architect of the modern, bureaucratic, imperialist state that she needed both to conquer and *civilize* her own subjects and the rest of the world. This, the "first modern language expert," advocates that the state needs to take control over the development of the language. He calls the language that people use every day "*la lengua suelta y fuera de regla*," unbound and ungoverned speech, and declares that it is a problem in need of a solution.

So far, this our language has been left loose and unruly and, therefore, in just a few centuries this language has changed beyond recognition. If we were to compare what we speak today with the language spoken five hundred years ago, we would notice a difference and a diversity that could not be any greater if these were two alien tongues.

But, with the help of teachers—a new kind of soldier—he will instruct the Queen's subjects to use a state-sanctioned version of their own tongue: "By means of my grammar, they shall learn artificial Castilian, not difficult to do, since it is built up on the base of a language they know; and then, Latin will come easily."

One reason he thinks it is necessary to do this is because, in the two and a half decades since Gutenberg first introduced the moveable type printing press, there had been an epidemic of untutored and uncontrolled *reading*.

Your Majesty, it has been my constant desire to see our nation become great, and to provide the men of my tongue with books worthy of their leisure. Presently, they waste their time on novels and fancy stories full of lies. . . . I have decided, therefore, that my most urgent task is to transform Castilian speech into an artifact so that whatever henceforth shall be written in this language may be of one standard tenor, one coinage that can outlast the times.

Historians estimate that by the time of Nebrija's grammar there were more than seventeen hundred printing presses in three hundred European towns and cities. Some forty thousand books had been published, about a third of these in the vernacular, created without the benefit of conventionalized grammar or spelling. Many were, as Nebrija says, "novels and fancy stories full of lies" as well as do-it-yourself books meant for unschooled readers. One interesting example of the latter was William Caxton's best-seller *The Arte and Crafte to Knowe Well to Dye*. This book gave suggestions to readers about how to die with dignity without the help of physicians and clergy. The effect of these books went beyond people who had taught themselves how to read. During this time reading was not a silent, solitary activity as it is today, but was usually practised aloud and with others in a social context. It is precisely this kind of unmonitored vernacular reading and writing that Nebrija wanted to suppress.

Lastly, Nebrija offered, in Illich's words, to forge "a language of propaganda—universal and fixed like Latin, yet capable of penetrating every village and town, to reduce subjects to modern citizens." Here is how Nebrija himself put it:

Greek and Latin have been governed by art [by this he means literacy], and thus have kept their uniformity throughout the ages. Unless the like of this is done for our language, in vain Your Majesty's chroniclers . . . shall praise your deeds. Your labour will not last more than a few years, and we shall continue to feed on Castilian translations of foreign tales about our own kings. Either your feats will fade with the language or they will roam among aliens abroad, homeless, without a dwelling in which they can settle.

In the end, in classical rhetorical style, he returned to and directly addressed her initial question.

You asked me what end such grammar could possibly serve. Upon this, the Bishop of Avila interrupted to answer in my stead. What he said was this: "Soon Your Majesty will have placed her yoke upon many barbarians who speak outlandish tongues. By this, your victory, these people shall stand in a new need; the need for the laws the victor owes to the vanquished, and the need for the language we shall bring with us." My grammar shall serve to impart to them the Castilian tongue, as we have used grammar to teach Latin to the young.

According to Illich, this radical innovation in the art of empire-building chillingly foreshadowed the next five centuries of brutal political and cultural colonization, not just by Spain but by the entire continent of Europe. For him what was new was how the autonomy and self-determination of human groups, as expressed in their constantly changing vernacular dialects, were eroded by the centralized control of professionals:

The new state takes from the people the words on which they subsist, and transforms them into the standardized language which henceforth they are compelled to use, each one at the level of education that has been institutionally imputed to him. Henceforth, people will have to rely on the language they receive from above, rather than to develop a tongue in common with one another. The switch from the vernacular to an officially taught mother tongue is perhaps the most significant—and, therefore, least researched—event in the coming of a commodity intensive society. The radical change from the vernacular to taught language foreshadows the switch from breast to bottle, from subsistence to welfare, from production for use to production for market, from expectations divided between state and church to a world where the Church is marginal, religion is privatized, and the state assumes the maternal functions heretofore claimed only by the Church. Formerly, there had been no salvation outside the Church; now, there would be no reading, no writing—if possible no speaking—outside the educational sphere. People would have to be reborn out of the monarch's womb and be nourished at her breast. Both the citizen of the modern state and his state-provided language came into being for the first time—and both are without precedent anywhere in history.

Nebrija's dictionary, written at the same time as his grammar and published only a year later, already contained evidence of this new future. From Columbus's account of his voyage a new word had entered into the taught national language of Spanish: *canoa* (canoe). The stage was set for Europe's enslavement of the New World through arms and letters.

■

It is tempting to extend this story into the present and to imagine the modern nation-state as a conservative, self-interested force imposing its will through official languages and compulsory schooling. This would be a dangerous oversimplification. Much has changed in five hundred years. In the globalized world of today, nation-states, public education, and print culture are all in defensive retreat. The empire has taken on new forms. The Nebrijas and Isabellas of the twenty-first century live in Los Angeles and New York. Their tools are television networks, the World Wide Web, and the shopping mall.

151

THE INVENTION
OF THE SPECTATOR

■

*When personality entered the public realm, the identity
of the public man split in two. A few people continued to
express themselves actively in public, continued the imagery
of man-as-actor which oriented the ancien régime. These
active few had by the mid-19th Century become professionals at it, though; they were skilled performers. Another
identity grew up alongside this one; it was that of the
spectator. And this spectator did not participate in public
life so much as he steeled himself to observe it. Unsure of
his feelings and convinced that, whatever they were,
they were expressed wholly beyond his will, this man did
not desert public society. He clung to the belief that
outside the home, in the cosmopolitan crowd, there were
important experiences for a person to have; unlike his
predecessor in the ancien régime, for him this fulfillment
in public was to be not of his social being, but of his
personality. If he could only prepare himself, above all if
he could discipline himself to silence in public, things
would happen to his feelings which as an individual
he could not make happen for himself.*

— RICHARD SENNETT

It is deeply puzzling that, at the same time that democracy—the idea that groups of people can talk through, negotiate, and make decisions collectively without monarchs or wars, along with its attendant ideals of freedom, equality, personal responsibility, and a more nuanced notion of individuality—became widely espoused in Europe and North America during the eighteenth and nineteenth centuries, most people experienced a profound reduction in their individual autonomy, even when compared to agricultural life.

At the dawn of industrialization, plantation workers, miners, factory labourers, and even the newly affluent bourgeoisie were subjected to physical and psychological discipline as wide and harsh as that imposed on the slaves of antiquity. The character of this discipline changed over the course of the twentieth century, but it nonetheless remains a powerful force in the twenty-first. While many workers in North America and Europe have achieved important concessions from employers, sweatshop discipline is still common in most of the world. This core contradiction remains at the heart of our current discontents.

By example and design, the economic and social changes of the last two centuries profoundly transformed artistic practices as well. Culture, including both the high culture of the privileged and the vernacular cultures of the people, was refashioned in the image of the factory and the store. An essential ingredient in the transition from the carnivalesque public displays of the eighteenth century to the private pleasures of the iPod in the twenty-first was the evolution of a new category of participant in the artistic event—a category that, except in certain special circumstances, was hitherto unknown in human society: the spectator.

■

In the cultural histories of Asia, Africa, pre-contact America, and Europe before modern times, there is little evidence of the spectator. Unless you were a monarch or an aristocrat, the idea of paying money to stand or sit in a prescribed location as a means of simply observing a performance of professional musicians, actors, or dancers was a radical one. There have always, of course, been observers and bystanders whose participation in cultural events has been more peripheral than that of the main performers, but in these cases the line between performer and bystander remained blurred. A bystander one day could be a major performer the next. Even in the case of a procession during a medieval carnival, it would have been hard to find anyone who was just watching. As Peter Burke points out: "There is no sharp distinction between the actors and the spectators, since the ladies on their balconies might throw eggs at the crowd below, and the maskers were often licensed to burst into private houses."

The few exceptions are revealing. In certain very large cities in the ancient world—Athens, Rome, Mexico City—the authorities organized large theatrical, sporting, or religious events that citizens attended but could not participate in. These examples reveal a close relationship between urbanization, centralized power, and spectatorship. According to Richard Sennett, who has written a history of the transition from public participation to privatized spectatorship in modern Europe, the evolution of the modern spectator really began in the seventeenth century in Europe's biggest cities.

Between 1600, when Shakespeare's plays were being performed regularly, and 1750, the population of London grew from 200,000 to 750,000. The population statistics for Paris over the same period show a similar increase. Cities of this size were unprecedented in medieval Europe. Most, if not all, of this increase was due to immigration from the surrounding countryside. The new inhabitants of these Renaissance cities were almost all young, single men and women intent on improving their lot. Shakespeare himself is an early example of this. He arrived in London from Stratford, a town about two days on foot from the city. Even though he was married, he lived and worked in London for three decades without his family.

By today's standards, these cities were chaotic, dangerous, and unhealthy. They had no running water, garbage collection, or police. What is amazing is how well they actually worked considering their lack of any municipal infrastructure.

These new city dwellers had to solve a novel problem. In the small, largely rural communities of early modern Europe, people watched each other grow up. The people with whom they came in contact each day were known to them. In the large cities, most if not all of the citizens were strangers to each other. Except for the so-called "Irish horde," London had none of the identifiable ethnic groups or neighbourhoods that are part of the twenty-first-century multicultural city. Because most people were strangers to each other, clues to identify social class and status were unreliable and could lead to embarrassing misunderstandings.

The solutions to this problem, fully developed by the end of the eighteenth century, were as effective as they are bizarre to our eyes today. In the *ancien régime*, before the French Revolution, the main way in which people in the rapidly growing urban centres dealt with constant and potentially stressful interactions with strangers was to develop elaborate codes of behaviour based on roles. Dress, speech, and manners were determined not by individual personality but by a person's station in life. It was a period, then, in which the actor was supreme. Skill at performing one's role was admired. The private, intimate domain was clearly bracketed from this public sphere. It was in private that a person could express individuality and intimacy. In public people did two things to play their parts. First, both men and women began to treat their bodies as mannequins—covering them with elaborate clothing, wigs, perfumes, and face makeup that communicated social class and profession. Appropriate clothing and appearance in public were actually legislated in city bylaws. In addition, a new, more impersonal use of language between strangers was developed, something that Sennett calls "using words as signs." The residue of this practice still exists today in the convention of discussing the weather and other neutral subjects with strangers as a way of "making conversation" and forming social bonds. By using this impersonal language, the new urban dwellers could negotiate numerous potentially embarrassing situations between social betters and inferiors with grace and élan. In 1747 Philip Stanhope, Fourth Earl of Chesterfield, better known as Lord Chesterfield, wrote a series of letters to his son. These letters contained advice on how to survive the "snares" of living in Paris and London.

> Of all things, banish the egoism out of your conversation, and never think of entertaining people with your own personal concerns or private affairs; although they may be interesting to you, they are tedious and impertinent to everybody else; besides that, one cannot keep one's private affairs too secret.

People became skilled at keeping their personal affairs private and becoming an actor in the *theatrum mundi* (theatre of life). They performed their parts in the cities' many public sites. The old city squares were gathering places filled with food stalls, entertainers, coffeehouses, and taverns. People of all social classes, by necessity, had to interact with each other. A cosmopolitan, market language developed.

THE INVENTION OF THE SPECTATOR

As a result of these new rules of dress, verbal language, and manners, the city dwellers of eighteenth-century Europe were able to establish, despite great differences in status and values, a remarkably fertile and passionate public sphere, both in politics and the arts. The public and the private, at least for a time, seemed to be in a fragile, delicate balance for many of the aristocrats, commoners, intellectuals, and artists of the time. The situation appeared to be similar, despite bitter class differences, among the servants and tradespeople. According to Sennett, this balance was maintained in the public arena by "action at a distance from the self" and "the experience of diversity."

> The modes of public and private expression were not so much contradictions as alternatives. In public the problem of social order was met by the creation of signs; in private the problem of nurturance was faced, if not solved, by the adherence to transcendental principles. The impulses governing the public were those of will and artifice; the impulses governing the private were those of restraint and the effacement of artifice.
>
> This balance was structured by what we now call impersonality; neither in public nor in private were "the accidents of individual character" a social principle.

In private, families of all classes continued to practise homemade music-making, storytelling, amateur theatrics, and games of all sorts. In his book *Centuries of Childhood: A Social History of Family Life*, French historian Philippe Ariès found considerable evidence that in pre-revolutionary Europe these participatory games and pastimes were much enjoyed features of everyday life. But it was the principle of performative impersonality among strangers that informed the actions of audiences at the theatre, the opera, and the ballet in the new cities. The performing arts were extensions of the public geography. As another historian put it, they became "rehearsals for collective political action."

■

In 1794, at the height of *la Terreur* following the French Revolution, when thousands of men and women were guillotined for allegedly harbouring monarchist sympathies, an actor named Arouch was put to death in Bordeaux.

Arouch was performing at the Grand Théâtre in a play called *Life Is a Dream*, written in 1636 by the Spaniard Pedro Calderón. In the third act, supporters of the fictional King Basilio attempt to stop his son from overthrowing him. In the script, one of the supporters, played by the poor Arouch, shouts, "Long live our noble King!" At that moment in the Bordeaux performance, the audience became so angry that they called for the police. All eighty-six members of the cast were arrested and imprisoned. Hearings lasted several weeks, after which everyone was released except Arouch because it was determined he had spoken the offending line. According to contemporary reports, he went to the guillotine repeatedly calling out to anyone who would listen, "But it was in my part!" As far as we know, he is the only actor in history to be put to death for the sins of his on-stage character.

Outrageous as it is, this story provides important insights about the assumptions of urban audiences in the late eighteenth century. The border between the stage and the street, between fiction and fact, art and life, was a lot more porous than it was even a century later. Not only did audiences of that time witness all the mechanics of scene changes and theatrical artifice, but they also understood the plots and characters in the dramas as part of an ongoing public dialogue. James H. Johnson, in his remarkable study of audiences, *Listening in Paris: A Cultural History*, makes the following observation about the post-revolutionary opera in France:

> In reducing the distance between art and life these works did not so much represent—understood in both senses as performance before passive observers and as actors expressing the will of the people in their stead—as encourage a radically democratic participation in the drama. By dressing in ordinary clothes, and singing the songs of the people, performers became citizens. . . . The persona was the person . . . the spectators became the spectacle.

When they arrested the cast members of *Life Is a Dream*, the authorities of the day were honouring a widely accepted tradition of audience sovereignty at public performances that had deep roots in the agricultural traditions of carnival.

For centuries, outside the large cities of Renaissance Europe, professional theatre companies travelled the countryside performing in town squares or inside tavern houses, passing a hat at the end of a performance. They relied on securing rich patrons to make their payrolls. Performances usually revolved around the patron, who would sit in a place clearly visible to everyone else at the event. Audiences were as concerned with the patron's responses as they were with the performance itself. The shows were meant to be enjoyed by all social stations and, much as it was for carnival, people conversed and mingled throughout performances and were not afraid to loudly express their displeasure or excitement with the offerings. Audiences of the time "asserted their rights to judge and direct performances," and the performers presumably acquiesced.

The first commercial theatre in London—the Red Lion in Stepney—opened in 1567. We do not know how many people it held, but we do know that by the time Shakespeare arrived thirteen years later, London had half a dozen such theatres, each holding about two thousand paying customers for every performance. To make a profit, these theatres had to have a changing repertoire of five or six plays per week. They commissioned as many as twenty new plays per year. As the seventeenth century progressed, permanent, licensed theatres and operas were built, like the Comédie Française, founded in 1680 in Paris, which charged admission at the "box office" before each performance. While all classes enjoyed the performances, the position from which people watched the show was a function of their place in the social hierarchy. The aristocrats and rich merchants and their wives could afford the boxes close to or on the stage; journeymen, apprentices, and servants stood in what the English called the pit and the French dubbed the *parterre* (the modern orchestra, but without seats); the prostitutes and others who wished anonymity could still catch the show from the benches in the balcony (sometimes called "the gods" in England). According to historian Richard Butsch:

> The separation between audience and performance is of modern origin. In the past the distinction between performer and audience was less clear and more open. Just as the line between work and leisure was less clear, so too the line between entertainment and other, more participative leisure. Plebeian entertainments, with the exception of a few theaters in the major cities of London and Paris, in early modern Europe were street events, part of fairs and markets. Street theater, such as *commedia dell'arte* and forms of carnival, and amateur theater blurred the lines between performer and audience. Community celebrations and parades, games and parlor theatrics were more common and participative than theatergoing.

The behaviour of mid-eighteenth-century audiences at the theatre and the opera revealed just how closely the events were still influenced by the social, participatory carnival traditions that they came from. It was common practice for wealthy audience members, sometimes called "fops," to sit right on the stage, next to the actors. They would walk around, interrupt the performance, and occasionally grab at the actresses. While sometimes attending to the performance, they treated the theatre "as a place to chat, play cards, argue, and even occasionally duel." During operas it was common for prominent families to bring their servants with them so that they could dine and receive messages during the show.

The plebeians in the pit ate, drank, socialized, moved around freely, engaged in repartee with the food vendors, shouted insults at the fops, sang along to popular operas, and otherwise make a lot of noise while enjoying the show. (It is interesting how closely this account might also describe people's behaviour at rock concerts today.) They expressed their collective opinions of the show by shouting, whistling, stamping their feet, or throwing flowers or rotten fruit onto the stage. Since the house lights were as bright as the stage lights, people at the theatre spent as much time watching each other as they did the performance, and they were usually rewarded. The most prominent audience members were expected to make a racket and display their reactions. Women swooned and wept in the tragic parts, while everyone hissed, booed, or shouted their compliments throughout the other big moments. Steady waves of applause greeted successful performers all through the show, not just at the end. The most successful playwrights and performers knew how to take advantage of rowdy audiences. The popular British actor Richard Tarlton was famous for taking the audience into his confidence with out-of-character asides during the show. Plays were intentionally written to provoke loud displays from the audience and to compensate for the intermittent attention of the crowd.

Rather than the extended dramatic unfolding of narratives over time that we are familiar with in modern theatre, opera, and symphonic music, performance in the eighteenth century was more about "moments." Operas, for example, were structured as a series of arias, with interlinking passages called "recitatives," or story bits, filled with sung dialogue advancing the plot. Since most people already knew the plot, it was commonplace for audience members to talk among themselves until the arias came up. Both actors and singers engaged in a practice called "pointing." When a good part came up—a point—the performer would leave the other characters and come downstage to deliver the monologue or song directly to the house. If the audience members approved they would applaud and shout "encore." The performer was then required to repeat the point again. It was not uncommon for songs and monologues to be repeated as many as six or seven times. (This is the origin of the term "show-stopper.") If audience members disliked what they saw or heard, they would hiss and boo the performer off the stage before the point was even finished. "Settling" was another common practice. If actors forgot a line they would quietly ask the prompter for a cue. When audiences heard this, they would humiliate the poor thespian by making so much noise he or she would be unable to hear the prompter.

Unlike today's audiences, which tend to revere great performers as almost superhuman, the people who went to the theatre in the eighteenth century viewed actors, singers, and musicians as merely high-class servants—which did not detract from their enjoyment of what those servants created. For most, audience participation lent performances a playful, convivial atmosphere, as long as everyone recognized that these audiences were as concerned about spending time with each other as they were with attending the show. The performances were, according to Butsch, "embedded in the activities of a community of peers." As time went on, an increasing number found this kind of audience behaviour unacceptable because it often seemed on the verge of getting out of control. Audience riots occurred from time to time, and the more rowdy, working-class, variety-show venues in Britain had to be rebuilt regularly due to damage caused by audiences expressing their collective views.

Within a hundred years, this dialogic conviviality had all but vanished. In its place was the silent spectator, politely waiting until the end of the performance to applaud. James Johnson begins *Listening in Paris* by asking: "Why, over the hundred years between 1750 and 1850, did audiences stop talking and start listening?" The answer only becomes visible through the wider lens of social history.

■

The end of the eighteenth and beginning of the nineteenth centuries in Europe were a time of catastrophic change, not only for work and consumption, but also for human consciousness. It was the time when what William Blake called the "satanic mills" transformed the physical and social landscape forever. The building of factories for the mass production of goods required two things in abundance: raw materials and labour. These requirements were met, to some extent, in the conversion of the countryside. It had been a place in which thousands of peasants—yeoman and share croppers—subsisted on traditionally determined common land. Now it became filled with vast empty fields in which valuable wool-providing sheep could graze at will. These "enclosures" of the commons in the United Kingdom, in particular, led to unprecedented migration by those country folk left without homes or land. Many emigrated to places like Canada and Australia, but many also moved to the new industrial cities to feed industry's appetite for factory workers. As the European cities enlarged with these new workers, the fears and fantasies of the more established inhabitants increased. The impoverished and uncouth bumpkins were of course necessary to provide the labour for the new factories, but they were also seen as dangerous and unpredictable by the emerging mercantile middle class.

The first generation of urban planners in England and France started redesigning the old medieval cities to deal with these fears. Their primary tool was the building of squares to establish suburban neighbourhoods. In London, starting shortly after the great fire of 1688, a grid of streets and squares was laid out according to rational principles. Unlike the squares of the past, however, these new public spaces were not filled with local vendors and gathering places. Instead the new parks in London were filled with trees and gardens. They were "museums of nature." In Paris the new planners built to a monumental scale. Cityscapes like Jules Hardouin-Mansard's place Vendôme (1701) or Jacques Ange Gabriel's place de la Concorde (1763) were meant to be *observed* by travellers going from home to work. As Sennett describes them, "These squares were not designed with a lingering, congregating crowd in mind." In his case, Hardouin-Mansard turned his attention to the elimination of "stalls, bands of acrobats, and other forms of street trade from the squares." His plan was to keep cafés out of sight, behind doors. In the process the historic life of the square was weakened. The previous "multiplicity of functions," with an overlay of urban activities, became "fragmented and dispersed." Crowds became limited to three areas: the café, the pedestrian park, and the theatre. Over time the old local markets disappeared. Instead of walking to the end of the street to buy food and clothing, city dwellers increasingly found it necessary to travel to large, centralized open-air markets like the foires des Halles in Paris and Covent Garden in London.

The idea of segmenting the city into residential neighbourhoods and commercial centres reached its pinnacle with the remaking of Paris by Baron Haussmann in the 1850s and 1860s. Here social classes were isolated from each other to an even greater extent than before. Work was increasingly separated from home, and the very idea of home as a respite from the world of work began to take shape. It was also a time when the "men's club" first became popular. Instead of frequenting coffeehouses or taverns, bourgeois men could go out to clubs and thus avoid interacting with people outside their social class. By the middle of the nineteenth century, shopping was one of the only cosmopolitan activities left in which social classes mixed.

Changes in how goods were manufactured also precipitated changes in how they got sold. Economic historian Karl Polanyi described these changes as a "disembedding" of economic relations—"the market"—from their traditional social contexts.

> Obscure as the beginnings of local markets are, this much can
> be asserted: that from the start, this institution was surrounded
> by a number of safeguards designed to protect the prevailing
> economic organization of society from interference on the part
> of market practices. The peace of the market was secured by rituals and ceremonies which restricted its scope while ensuring
> its ability to function within given narrow limits. . . . The gearing of markets into a self-regulating system . . . means no less
> than the running of society as an adjunct to the market. Instead
> of economy being embedded in social relations, social relations
> are embedded in the economic system. The vital importance of

the economic factor to the existence of society precludes any other result, for once the economic system is organized in separate institutions, society must be shaped in such a manner as to allow that system to function according to its own laws.

The changes in retail merchandizing caused by industrialization altered not just *what* people purchased but *how* they interacted with each other. Before the nineteenth century most food and clothing had variable pricing, and the vendor's right to operate in a particular location was protected. Buyers and sellers in the local markets had to haggle over the price for each sale. (This is still the case in many traditional markets in the world today.) Shopping necessitated dialogue, with significant consequences for both parties. Being a good actor in public was a necessity. People of different social classes were obligated to have daily interaction.

In 1852 an ambitious entrepreneur named Aristide Boucicaut took over a *magasin de nouveautés* (fancy goods store) called Le Bon Marché on Paris's Left Bank. The store sold gloves, hosiery, lingerie, shawls, woollens, silks, and something new: ready-to-wear clothes. Before this time most clothing was made-to-measure. Within twenty years Boucicaut expanded the business into the world's first department store and made retail history. His success was based on several radical innovations that he had developed while working as a clerk at another store. First, he had a large number of mass-produced items, purchased in bulk, that were sold for only a small markup. Frequently, these items would go "on sale." Second, all the goods had "fixed prices" clearly marked—no haggling necessary. If people changed their minds, they could return the goods for an exchange. Lastly, people were encouraged to "browse" without feeling any obligation to buy. While all of these seem like wonderfully sensible innovations, they had unintended consequences for human sociability in the public sphere. In Bouci-caut's store the shopper was transformed from a performing actor into a silent observer.

The idea of shopping as silent observation was also encouraged by the rise of marketing. As the production capacity of the factories vastly outstripped consumer needs, manufacturers realized that they had to create demand for their products. Through a process of trial and error, retailers learned how to encourage buyers to invest machine-made goods with personal meaning far beyond their use value. Marketers increased demand by putting visually stunning advertisements for their products in the new daily newspapers, and by making department stores themselves into spectacles: large plate-glass windows overflowing with goods, and elaborate store displays. These in-store displays, according to one commentator, were meant to both mystify and disorient the shopper. This new trend of emotional investment in consumer objects combined with silent observation by the shopper inspired Karl Marx, writing at the same time, to come up with the term "commodity fetishism."

Alterations in marketing and consumer behaviour interacted with new forms of religious belief to fashion a novel paradigm in human consciousness: the personality. Today the idea that each human being is special and has a unique destiny is commonplace. Before the nineteenth century this was a novel concept, even within the privacy of the family. Up to that point the majority of people in Europe had lived like most people in other parts of the world: their everyday culture was oral, communal, and filled with a belief in the supernatural. People placed their fates in God's hands or believed in the great order of nature. Starting in the fifteenth century, some people, mostly those who had learned how to read the new books coming off the recently invented printing press and who were part of the emerging mercantile class, rejected these ideas. Humanism, a belief that concrete human matters were more important than divine or supernatural conditions, emerged along with the "disenchantment of nature" and the rise of the scientific world view: the conviction that objective knowledge of the world was possible through observation and rational thought. Industrial time was measured by a clock, and the notion of progress, the idea that time keeps moving forward at a regular pace, was widely accepted. Concomitant with these developments was the "invention" of the private individual who was free and responsible for his (and much less often her) own actions—an idea with roots in the early history of the Christian church but that now took on a decidedly secular flavour. Philosopher Charles Taylor explains it this way:

> In order to see what is new in this, we have to see the analogy to earlier moral views, where being in touch with some source— God, say, or the Idea of the Good—was considered essential to full being. Only now the source we have to connect with is deep in us. This is part of the massive subjective turn of modern culture, a new form of inwardness, in which we come to think of ourselves as beings with inner depths.

As Sennett puts it, "As the gods are demystified, man mystifies his own condition; his own life is fraught with meaning, yet it remains to be played out." An individual's personality was something that needed to be discovered and developed through acts of will. People began to ask "who am I?" Playing a role in public was slowly replaced by being a personality. The "domain of appearances" was no longer ruled by the old standards. Clothing and behaviour in public, instead of providing raw materials for the role-playing actor, became the carefully controlled code that subtly revealed a person's authentic personality; but because of the immanence of feeling and perception associated with authenticity, there was always the risk that one's inner life could be involuntarily revealed to others in unacceptable ways.

The scientific world view compelled people, if they wanted to understand the world, to observe events dispassionately, at a distance, and in silence. The privileging of the eye over the other senses, which began long before the printing press, reached a new level. "To know one must impose no coloration of one's own, of one's own commitments; this meant silence in public in order to understand it, objectivity in scientific investigation, a gastronomy of the eye. Voyeurism was the logical complement of 19th century secularity."

The introduction of personality into the public life of industrial, commercialized Europe and "silent observation as a principle of public order" had curious effects. People became extremely self-conscious about the involuntary expression of feeling. Spontaneity was viewed as deviant. Clothing was designed to cover and hide the body and to make everyone look the same. To decode the truth behind the appearances, one had to become a detective, looking for tiny clues—the tying of a cravat or a significant eye movement— that revealed important social information. It is no accident that Sherlock Holmes became one of the most popular literary characters of the late nineteenth century, or that Freud's psychology provided a brilliant explanation for the discontents of his age. As Sennett argues, these developments make sense when we look at their larger context: "Today, a person trying not to feel seems headed toward disaster. A century ago, perhaps a whole class of people did experience a psychic disaster because of their attempts to ignore or suppress their impulses. But the reason they attempted to do this was logical. This was their way of coping with the confusion of public and private life." In other words, people became wary of involuntarily

revealing their deeply felt emotions to family and friends and especially strangers. The clothes they wore served to deform their
bodies and thus contributed to this effect: "If one has effaced all
traces of nature, one has reduced one's vulnerability in the eyes of
others . . . a protection thought necessary, given the new psychological sense of public life."

These new attitudes to the self had profound effects on the attitudes and behaviour of people in public spaces. The seats of theatres
and opera houses of the nineteenth century were filled, for the first
time, with the modern "spectator": one who watches, listens, and
feels—who participates with the art work inwardly—but never acts.

■

The middle-class bourgeois audiences of the nineteenth century
learned to be silent and attentive in ways that we would recognize
today as conventional. Individual audience members, in public but
isolated from each other, could feel privately and safely the most
shocking and abnormal emotions. It was essential, however, as it
still is today in serious theatres, for audience members to show few
outward signs of emotion. Indeed, by the 1850s it was considered
very bad manners to cry openly at a play. People were ridiculed if
they lost control. Pointing and settling were both considered bar-
baric procedures. For the first time, booing, hissing, or other verbal
displays were considered to be signs of poor breeding and lower
social status. This attitude increased the social pressure to conform.
A "proper" member of the audience at a play or concert would
sneer at anyone who showed emotions. The order of the day was
restraint, and it was used to draw a line between the middle-class
audience and the working class. The "respectable" audience, according to Sennett, "could control its feelings through silence; the old

spontaneity was called 'primitive.' The Beau Brummell ideal of restraint in bodily appearance was being matched by a new idea of respectable noiselessness in public."

The only residue of audience sovereignty to persist in this new environment was applause, but this too was disciplined. By the end of the nineteenth century it was unacceptable to applaud in the middle of a scene or even after a movement in a concerto. Audiences were expected to wait until the end of the play or the piece to show their appreciation. Change, however, was slow in coming: nineteenth-century audiences applauded for longer and with greater enthusiasm than do their counterparts today. Modern audiences at live events, accustomed to movies, television, and audio recordings that request no response whatsoever, often find applause an unnecessary burden, and provide only the most perfunctory ovation, even after very good performances. A history of applause has yet to be written.

Gone too were the seats on stage. The house lights were dimmed. Indeed, everything was done to create a sharper boundary between theatrical illusion and the spectator. The emphasis turned to a celebration of spectacle and material objects, "an advertisement for consumption." The design of Richard Wagner's Bayreuth Opera House, completed in 1876, is a perfect example. Every seat had a perfect view of the stage, but it was difficult to see other audience members. Wagner was also the first to hide the orchestra from the audience. He believed that the machinery behind the illusion should be invisible. The hidden orchestra and the second proscenium over the orchestra pit all added to what he called the *mystische Abgrund*—the mystic gulf.

One of the things masked by this silent isolation in public was a deep insecurity on the part of audiences. In a world in which shock and spontaneity were idealized on stage but forbidden in daily life, audiences could no longer trust their own reactions. It was only in this period that entertainment critics achieved commercial influence. Their job was to advise consumers on what was worth seeing and how they should spend their money, but they also explained what audiences *should* be feeling and thinking while watching a particular performance. Of course, audiences often disagreed with critics' judgements. It was probably at this moment that the stereotype of the misunderstood artist at odds with his public, but recognized by the insightful critic, was first constructed.

No example better illustrates the evolution in listening than the reaction of Paris audiences to Beethoven's music over two decades. When Beethoven's music premiered in Paris in 1807, audience reaction was almost uniformly negative. Listeners said it "grated on the ears while freezing the soul" and was full of "German barbarisms." His ideas were said to be "frenzied" and his themes "grotesque paths." One witness commented, "He seems to harbor doves and crocodiles at the same time." Just twenty years later, when the *Fifth Symphony* was first presented in Paris, audience response was the opposite. Instead of using the music as a backdrop to casual conversation, people actually began to listen and to respond with rapt attention. The waves of applause and cheers continued through all the movements, much like the behaviour of audiences in more recent times to performers like Elvis Presley and the Beatles. In subsequent performances, the orchestra was obliged to repeat the third and fourth movements before the listeners would go home. At the time, novelist Honoré de Balzac described the *Fifth* as "fairies who flutter with womanly beauty and the diaphanous wings of angels." It was not so much that the music had changed; it was how people listened to it. Beethoven, more than his contemporaries, anticipated—and partly precipitated—a shift in the horizon of possible aesthetic experience for urban concertgoers.

Building on the operatic tradition, Beethoven, and those influenced by him, composed instrumental music that told stories without words: stories about the individual in conflict with the group, fate, and nature, but who usually finds reconciliation in the final movement. The central point of these musical stories was to stimulate indescribable emotions in the hearts of individual listeners. To succeed, subtler forms of harmonic complexity became necessary, and aesthetically the results required the full attention—and thus the silence—of the listener. As Johnson argues, it was "the acceptance of harmony, more than anything else, [that] defined romantic musical experience."

> Socially, it made the hall a metaphor for the street. And its political applications spanned the ideological spectrum. Harmony momentarily suspended the mistrust. It permitted spectators to tell themselves that all men really were brothers, just as the chorus sang out in Beethoven's Ninth at the Conservatoire. It sanctified individuality without sacrificing the community.

To develop these harmonically complex narratives, composers had to experience the intense emotions in private and record and revise their musical imaginings on paper. Beethoven is an interesting example of this; he composed many of his well-known works while suffering from almost complete hearing loss. Only later were the representations of these intense emotions translated into sound in the concert hall. European musical performance, well into the eighteenth century, had been a more collective, improvisational affair. With the great symphonies of the nineteenth century, the orchestras became much more disciplined, requiring for the first time an individual whose only job was to provide decisive leadership: the conductor. Unlike the past, members of the orchestra were required to play precisely the notes written in advance by the composer and to follow the instructions of the conductor.

The primary solo instrument of this period was the piano. While clavichords, harpsichords, and organs existed before the piano was invented, it was the piano keyboard that defined European art music of the nineteenth century. Unlike their predecessors, pianos could be played softly or loudly according to how heavily the keys were pressed, thus making possible a more emotionally nuanced performance. (Pianoforte, the instrument's full name, means "soft-loud.") Most importantly, the piano made it possible for one single individual to have simultaneous mastery over all the tones in the orchestra. It was the private laboratory for the composer of symphonies and chamber music, but also the supreme medium for the *individual* expression of the complex harmonic architecture of romantic music. The piano helped to transform music from a primarily collective public event into the expression of certain gifted individuals.

Dramatic performances also went through far-reaching innovations. Unlike the theatre of the eighteenth century and before, in which the street and the stage were almost continuous, the audiences of the new century demanded a stage that provided the opposite. It was in art that they sought the display of authenticity and transparency missing from everyday life. Realism and precise historical accuracy were required of the theatre. The actors no longer delivered their important lines to the audience. Instead an imaginary "fourth wall" was erected between the action on stage and the spectators. The action could then be observed voyeuristically from the darkened theatre. Actors were expected to transmit their emotions and motivations unambiguously. The most successful performers were those who, contrary to their audience, could display strong feelings spontaneously in public. Everything about the system encouraged people to think of these public performers as a special kind of human being, set apart from the rest of humanity. Consequently, it was the time of the great virtuosos.

■

The natural twin of spectatorship is the idea of creative genius. Originally the word meant a guardian spirit, but around the end of the eighteenth century the word "genius" became transformed into its modern meaning, denoting a person with exceptional natural ability, creativity, and intelligence. The original prototype for this special person was the violinist Niccolò Paganini, who achieved great fame between 1810 and 1840. Paganini had extraordinary technique, but rather than put it in the service of the musical text, as the rest of the orchestra was required to do, he sought to make the audience forget about the music. Paradoxically, he attempted to transcend the composition with his own personal, spontaneous feeling—with his personality. He constantly added exaggerated pauses and tempo changes. He engaged in antics such as forcing the orchestra to stop playing in the middle of concerto, sometimes for up to two minutes, while he waited for inspiration; or he would arrange for three of his strings to break, one by one, during a performance so that he would have to finish a particularly difficult passage on the low G string alone. The great pianists Liszt and Chopin learned from Paganini how to engage in extreme shock theatrics while playing impossibly difficult pieces. Audiences loved it.

In a similar way, the two greatest actors of the century, Frédérick Lemaître and Sarah Bernhardt, both worked to transcend the text with their own personalities and spontaneity. The new importance of personality reveals itself most in the obsessions of their audiences with finding out the smallest details of their private and romantic lives—much like today's Hollywood star system—while often paying little attention to the plays in which these actors performed.

The veneration of the extraordinary performer, at the expense of the "merely competent," changed the terms under which the performing arts were produced and experienced. The results can be seen in the statistics for the size of audiences for music recitals in Vienna in the nineteenth century. From 1830 to 1870 the audience size for the average piano recital increased by 35 per cent. At the same time the number of piano recitals fell sharply. Some reports suggest that the number of people working full-time as musicians dropped to half of what it had been at the beginning of the period, despite a significant increase in population. Audiences were apparently more interested in listening to the few international celebrities who came through town than they were in going out to hear music performed by less-well-known local performers.

The seating capacity of new theatres and concert halls in the second half of the century increased accordingly. From a purely financial point of view, larger audiences and fewer performances made for higher profits—which is no doubt one of the main reasons why the star system was first implemented and is still sustained today. But this same system deeply discourages a large number of extremely talented and skilled performers who want to practise their art, but are not fortunate enough to make the big time.

The evolving spectator-artist relationship introduced a novel form of inequality into the public sphere. Whereas in the eighteenth century actors and musicians (including Bach and Mozart) were viewed by their patrons as hired help, by the end of the nineteenth century the reverse was true. The great virtuosos and actors, through their manipulation of the emotions of the silent, insecure audience, using their charismatic personalities, had become the masters. This, in and of itself, is not necessarily bad when it is confined to the stage. But if it becomes a model for other forms of public action—such as politics—it can have dangerous, unintended results. With the shift in audience behaviour, in the age of silence as "the agent of dependence in art, of isolation-as-independence in the society," as Sennett puts it: "The whole rationale of public culture had cracked apart. The relation between stage and street was now an inverted one. The sources of creativity and imagination which existed in the arts were no longer available to nourish everyday life."

This phenomenon suggests an interesting question. Is it possible that the disempowerment of the spectator and the displacement of his and her creative energies is perhaps partly responsible for new, particularly twentieth-century, forms of political domination?

The final consequence is perhaps historically the most important. By redefining the work of art as an object prepared in private and then presented unaltered to an individualized audience, by widening the gulf between the act of creation and the moment of reception, the architects of nineteenth-century performance practices unintentionally prepared the way for the next stage in the evolution of culture: the absolute separation in time and space between the artist and the audience wrought by the new media of cinema and radio.

PETE'S
PROPOSAL

∎

*Us folksingin' types are asked to donate our caterwauling
skills at a hell-of-a lotta benefit concerts: and so we do. The
last one I did with Pete was (as well-meaning occasions
often are) very poorly organized and swiftly proved to be a
festival of tension and frustration backstage. So there I was,
hiding in my dressing room, head hung low, wondering,
"Why, why, why does it always have to be like this?"—
when suddenly the sound of laughter made me lift my head.
I ventured into the green room to find Pete leading everyone in an ad-hoc rehearsal for the closing number of the
show. The backstage was slowly transformed into a magical
circle of song. Pete, in his inimitable style, had transcended
it all once again, and brought everyone with him. Amidst
the snarling and flailing about, he cleared a place for us to
sit down, relax, and sing together. I've seen Pete change the
world around him. I've seen him set about fixing things big
and small, in an everyday kinda-way. And I think if I've
ever known peace in this world, it's been in his voice.*

— ANI DIFRANCO

My first encounter with Pete Seeger came in the fall of 1969. I was working as an assistant film editor at the Canadian Broadcasting Corporation in what was called the "rushes room." Our job was to synchronize the recorded sound to the visuals when the film first arrived from the lab. There was usually some fairly simple method of establishing sync, like a clapper board, but occasionally things would go wrong and someone was given the rather tedious job of lip-reading and lip-synching each shot.

One day the word came down from management that an entire two-hour concert had been filmed without any synchronization marks. I was assigned the job of sorting it out. Reluctantly I bade goodbye to my fellow workers. I was to work in an entirely windowless room where the one "two-headed" Steenbeck editing table was stored. For the next two days I would sit alone lip-reading a bunch of songs.

As I began to sort out and view the material, I entered a musical world unlike anything I had ever experienced. The project in hand was a Pete Seeger concert at Massey Hall in Toronto. On stage was a rail-thin man who looked more like a lumberjack than a pop singer. The first thing that struck me was how he took up acoustic space: the complete absence of other musicians; no drums, no bass, no keyboard, no horns, no harmony singers. Just one human being on the large stage alone singing, playing a banjo and occasionally a guitar. The second thing that struck me as unusual was the complete lack of pretension: a direct sincerity without "vocal stylings" or sentimentality. Then there were the songs: a remarkable variety of genres and styles. Instead of schmaltzy love ballads or macho rock posturing I heard songs that were truthful, political, challenging—songs that provided insight into daily life or provided refreshingly comic commentary on current issues. Then, as the concert progressed, Seeger actually asked the audience to join in. First, it was just on the choruses. Then he got them to carry one part while he sang another. Astonishingly, the audience complied. Finally, as a kind of grand finale, he divided the 2,750 people in the hall into four sections and proceeded to teach them a simple song in four-part harmony.

This spontaneous, dangerous, fragile experiment in unrehearsed group singing brought tears to my eyes. It sent a courageous, powerful message about solidarity and collective action. I was hooked. I remember leaving the room at one moment and searching out a colleague who played guitar.

"Do you know who Pete Seeger is?" I asked.

"Oh, yeah, he's someone who influenced Bob Dylan," my friend responded.

Later on I learned that, despite the novel circumstances surrounding my first exposure, I was far from alone in my response to Pete. He opened the ears and eyes of thousands of North Americans of a certain generation and political persuasion—not only to new musics but, more importantly, to new ways of thinking about and doing music. As legend has it, one 1954 Seeger concert in Palo Alto, California, inspired both Joan Baez and Dave Guard (of the Kingston Trio) to commit their lives to folk music. He sent the message loud and clear that music was something anyone could do, should do. It was not the exclusive domain of the "talented." Within a year of my editing-room introduction, I had purchased a Gibson long-neck banjo and Seeger's self-published little book on how to play it. As Studs Terkel mused years later, "His influence among the young was so pervasive that it brought forth this thought: When you see a kid with Adam's apple bobbing and banjo held chest-high, you know that Pete Seeger, like Kilroy, was there."

Today Pete Seeger's status has gone through a curious transformation. Pete once said about the song "L'Internationale": "They made a big mistake, they made it official. I've decided there is one thing worse than banning a song. That's making it official. . . . When they make things official they slow 'em down. You only hear the first verse anyway." He might have been talking about himself. Once famous for being banned from TV's *Smothers Brothers* for expressing his pacifist views in the era of the Vietnam War, Seeger was, in 1994, named a Kennedy Center for the Performing Arts Honoree. In the publicity associated with the event, he was called "arguably the most influential folk artist in the United States." Some two years later he was inducted into the Rock and Roll Hall of Fame. That same year he was awarded the Harvard Arts Medal, even though he quit attending that university before the end of his second year to become a left-wing journalist. In 1997 he won a Grammy for Best Traditional Folk Album, and in April 1999 in Havana, Cuba, Pete accepted the Felix Varela Medal, that nation's highest honour, for "his humanistic and artistic work in defense of the environment and against racism." In 2006 the Boss himself, Bruce Springsteen, released an album devoted to Pete and the songs he made famous. Called *We Shall Overcome: The Seeger Sessions*, most of it was recorded live in Springsteen's farm house in New Jersey with all the musicians jamming "kitchen style." Seeger's ninetieth birthday party was held at Madison Square Garden in 2009 with Springsteen as the master of ceremonies.

Seeger deserves all the honours he has received—he has worked tirelessly and courageously his entire adult life for social justice and people's music. But because he is so closely associated with the ferment of the 1960s and 1970s, he is often thought of as a man whose relevance was exhausted by it. At the same time that Seeger has become an object of nostalgic adoration for aging boomers, he has lost any real currency among younger generations of activists. If his name comes up at all, he is usually associated with a discredited bygone moment in America's pop music history. When seen through the cynical lens of post 9/11 consciousness, Pete and his folk music buddies seem unbearably naive.

This is a mistake. Contrary to that view, I would argue that, of all the great pop artists of the twentieth century, including the Beatles, Dylan, and (insert the name of your favourite singer-songwriter here), Seeger ultimately has the most to teach us about appropriate forms of music-making in a globalized world. I am making this claim *not* on the basis of his songwriting—others penned more and better songs—or on the evidence of his vocal or instrumental abilities—many members of his generation were better singers, guitarists, even banjo players. I'm not even making the claim for Seeger's relevance based on his influence on others. Instead I want to focus my attention on how Seeger structured and performed his concerts during his solo period, from 1957 until the 1990s. Indeed, the *form* of these concerts is more important, more applicable, to twenty-first-century preoccupations than is their content.

■

Pete Seeger was born in 1919, just one year after his famous musicologist father was fired from the University of California, Berkeley, for his left-wing, antiwar views. The events leading up to the firing caused Charles Seeger to have a nervous breakdown and precipitated a rift in his marriage to Pete's mother. Both parents came from wealthy, well-established New England families. The Seeger estate on Staten Island spanned twelve acres. Charles conducted at the Cologne Opera before becoming the youngest faculty member at Berkeley ever to be given a full professorship. Pete's mother studied classical violin at the school that would become Juilliard, and later she taught there. Pete was sent to boarding school at the age of four and saw his family only on holidays and during summers. His parents divorced when he was eight. It was his father who was the first major influence on the socially reticent young boy. As Pete once said, "My father was the one person I really related to."

Charles Seeger was a skilled performer, composer, and musicologist. While teaching at Berkeley during the First World War he transformed himself from conservative to socialist to radical. He stubbornly rejected all compromise, refused the draft, and spoke publicly against the war. Finally, it was "mutually agreed" that he should leave the university. For years after that he could not find permanent employment, but he became a key member, along with Aaron Copland, of the communist-influenced Composers Collective in New York City. Later he got a permanent job at the New School of Social Research and, along with his second wife, Ruth Crawford Seeger, became one of the key researchers in the academic discovery of American folk music during the 1930s. His associates included John and Alan Lomax, whose recordings made in the U.S. South became the basis of the Smithsonian Folklife Archive in Washington. It was through his father that young Pete was able to circulate in the philosophically explosive communist circles of New York during the Depression of the 1930s and also attend "hillbilly" music and dance festivals. When Pete became interested in learning to play the five-string banjo, his father drove him down to North Carolina to meet Bascom Lunsford, one of the great authentic performers on the instrument. It was through his father that Pete met Huddie Ledbetter, better known as Leadbelly, a black ex-convict musician who became a *cause célèbre* for the radical left in New York. His association with this world also led Pete to the one man who would have the most profound influence on his life: Woody Guthrie.

Woody was about as rural and poor as Pete was urban and privileged. Yet they became close friends. Just seven years Pete's senior,

Guthrie had survived a hard Oklahoma childhood before making the dust-bowl migration to California, earning his living picking grapes and hauling wood. He was staggeringly prolific: singing and performing songs from an early age. He would sometimes write several new songs a day and was famous for making up new lyrics mid-performance. Guthrie was also a lifelong trade unionist and activist, contributing a regular column, "Woody Sez," to the *Daily Worker* and *People's World* newspapers. His was political country music, sung in a dry matter of fact voice, describing all the injustices suffered by the poor and working class he was part of. Woody lived and loved passionately. He once confided to a friend, "That guy Seeger, I can't make him out. He doesn't look at girls, he doesn't drink, he doesn't smoke, the fellow's weird." Despite their differences, Woody and Pete both believed that people's music could influence others when connected with political activism, and they set out to do just that by forming the Almanac Singers in 1941.

Seeger's one brush with commercial success came in the late 1940s when he helped found a folk quartet called the Weavers. Their rendition of Leadbelly's "Goodnight Irene" was number one on the hit parade charts for ten weeks in the fall of 1950. The Weavers were later blacklisted during the McCarthy era, and Seeger himself was charged with contempt for refusing to co-operate with the House Un-American Activities Committee. After the Weavers disbanded in 1957, Seeger began to pursue a solo career as a blacklisted former "pop star."

Today, when I listen to Weavers records, I find the slick harmonies, orchestral strings, and jazzy horns incongruous. This is folk music tamed for mainstream fifties America. Gone is the raw sincerity of Leadbelly or the simple directness of Woody Guthrie. The Weavers' recordings are a good example of how form can transform content into its opposite. There is evidence that Seeger himself was well aware of this transformation. From the mid-1950s on, Seeger's solo performances and recordings returned to the minimalist roots that had first inspired him.

Banned from night clubs and television, Seeger more or less invented the college circuit as a way of earning a living as a musician. Friend and fellow musician Don McLean put it this way:

> Pete went underground. He started doing fifty-dollar bookings, then twenty-five dollar dates at schoolhouses, auditoriums, and eventually college campuses. He definitely pioneered what we know of today as the college circuit. . . . He persevered and went out like Kilroy, sowing seeds at a grass-roots level for many, many years. The blacklist was the best thing that ever happened to him: it forced him into a situation of struggle, which he thrived on.

Seeger used what he called "cultural guerrilla tactics" to publicize his gigs.

> I'd call up the local TV or radio station, and say "is there a TV show I can come on?"
> "Who are you?" they'd ask.
> "Pete Seeger."
> "Well, what do you do?"
> "I sing folk songs"
> "Oh, you were with the Weavers. Sure, I remember, 'Goodnight Irene.' Come on up, we'll chat a moment. I'll play your record—singing at the local college tonight? Good."
> I'd go up there and we'd talk for five or ten minutes. Then he'd play some songs, and I'd be away before the American Legion could mobilize itself to protest this Communist fellow on the air.

It was in the crucible of these small-scale performances that the subversive Seeger promoted his message of self-reliance in the face of consumer culture by developing the "gimmick" of getting his audiences to sing along. For the uninitiated it was disquieting. In 1953 a writer with the *Providence Journal* remarked: "The concert was like none I've ever seen. He let us sing the ballads with him."

Slowly, using trial and error—and motivated by a deep commitment to democratic culture—Seeger amassed a range of techniques to get audiences to participate in concerts. As his popularity grew, he brought these techniques into larger halls. By 1969, when I first experienced his work in the film editing room, he was directing impromptu choruses of thousands.

■   **187**

In 1980 Folkways Records made a remarkable recording called *Singalong* that provides a useful starting point for grasping Seeger's approach. In the liner notes, Seeger explained the thinking behind the project:

> Before my voice, memory, and sense of rhythm and pitch are too far gone I decided, at age sixty, to ask Folkways Records to document one of my 2-hour "concerts" such as I have given for over twenty-five years, usually at colleges. They are not concerts so much as singalongs. My main purpose on this record is to show people how good it is to sing together and to show future songleaders some of the techniques they can use in teaching songs without everyone's nose being buried in a sheet of paper. And if they listen critically, as they should, they can perceive some things worth not emulating.

Unlike most live concert recordings, this one includes "most of the talking, tuning, the mistakes, fluffs and goofs." Sound engineer John Nagy set up dozens of microphones in the audience and recorded everything to a twenty-four-track master tape.

Everything about the concert was geared to encourage audience participation, including the physical setup of the room and the stage. Seeger picked the old Sanders Theatre at Harvard University because it had good natural acoustics and the seating was arranged in curved rows around the stage, making it possible for audience members to see and hear each other better. As usual he performed without a backup band. It was one person with a few readily accessible acoustic instruments—banjo, guitar, recorder—alone on stage, and Seeger also tended towards restraint in the use of these instruments. Instead of banging away on full chords for every beat, as most pop-folk artists do to keep up the energy, Seeger, in "Twelve Gates to the City," for example, plucked only two notes on the banjo a fifth apart leaving room for the sung melody in the middle. During his long-metre-style rendering of "Amazing Grace" near the beginning of the concert, he played syncopated banjo chords. Standard arrangements of folk songs use loud pounding drums and full guitar chords, and bass lines fill in all the spaces. They *complete* the songs, leaving nothing for the audience to add. The audience members are superfluous except as listeners. But when faced with only the barest outlines of the song, audiences feel more compelled to join in and complete the music, especially when they are encouraged to do so.

Another key element in Seeger's approach was the complete absence of "paper." Often at Christmas singalongs, and in most community choirs, those in attendance receive printed lyrics and music to read as they sing. Seeger strongly opposed "everyone's nose being buried in a sheet of paper." In addition to its obvious disadvantage—

if people are looking at paper they are not looking at (or listening to) each other—reading is a visual, right-brain, linear activity, whereas music is an auditory, left-brain, holistic experience. The reading inhibits the music-making.

All of this is predicated on the assumption that a majority of the people in the audience have acquired a basic competency in the rudiments of vocal music performance. A short-term musical memory is helpful. Audience members should also be able to find and hold accurate pitches and be able to keep to their harmony line while the melody is being sung. A basic sense of rhythm comes in handy. While these skills are easy for 99 per cent of the people in the world to acquire, there was no guarantee that white middle-class North Americans sitting in that hall had acquired them. Here Seeger cheated a little. Part of it was expectation. People who went to Pete Seeger concerts could and wanted to sing along. It was a simple case of self-selection. But Pete did not stop there. On the evening before the concert he met with eighty members of the Boston Folk Music Society and the Lowell House Singing Club. He taught them the choruses to a couple of unfamiliar songs and emphasized the importance of a good bass line. He said to them, "You are my leaven in a loaf of bread. If you sing well, the rest of the crowd will rise to the occasion."

The choice of material was also important. While he was famous for his left-wing views, on *Singalong* Seeger did only a few overtly political songs. Mostly we hear sad love songs, satirical ballads, working songs, and religious hymns. Politics appeared more often in the song's introductions, in the implicit meanings, but most importantly in their form. When this concert was recorded over a quarter-century ago, much of the material was already "out of date" by the extremely fashion-conscious standards of pop music. Yet this feature had certain advantages for Seeger's purposes. Many, perhaps most, of the songs were already familiar to the audience. Familiarity encourages group singing. The lineup also had considerable variety: songs from many traditions and styles, often in different languages. Seeger sang in the original language first (with a bad accent) and then provided a spoken translation. He expected the audience to try as well. "Not only Canada needs to be bilingual," he told his Boston audience before teaching a song from El Salvador in Spanish. Seeger never did accept the appropriation argument—that white North Americans have no right singing the music of workers, blacks, aboriginals, or others. For him, through experiencing other traditions viscerally, not just intellectually, greater understanding and tolerance became possible. He once wrote:

Some critics sneer to hear a Kentucky miner's song sung by a middle-class college student; but is it not just as strange to have a Carnegie Hall audience composed of Catholic, Jew, Protestant and atheist applauding Lutheran Bach chorales? Or city dwellers decorating their apartments with sculpture carved by distant tribesmen?

It would *all* be laughable, if we in the 1960s did not use these works of art of the faraway and long gone to help us in our own lives to create anew, to be more than mere spectators.

The other interesting characteristic of the songs on this recording is their harmonic and rhythmic simplicity. This also encourages audience participation. Many of the songs have repeated choruses and refrains, but other structures also appear—call and response, rounds—all developed in grassroots cultures in which group singing is the norm. That is why Seeger, who admits he's an atheist, loves the songs in the African-American sacred tradition.

I do not *love* all the songs on this recording. Seeger himself was critical of a few. After singing the "Homestead Strike Song," he acknowledged that it was sexist, and proceeded to do a feminist parody of the famous "I Know an Old Lady Who Swallowed a Fly." His version was called "I Know a Young Woman Who Swallowed a Lie." Certainly someone trying to do the same thing today would have to choose material more appropriate for today's audiences. What matters more, in my view, is how well the content and form of the songs worked to elicit participation. The singing audience was the deepest political statement of this performance, and it was grasped by the bodies and souls of those present.

The very first song set a tone of informality and experimentation that lasted throughout the concert. Seeger frequently readjusted the tuning on his instruments. At one point he changed the key of a song when he realized it was too low for the basses. He often interrupted songs after the first or second verse for long spoken asides or translations. Seeger's direct, unaffected voice matched perfectly with the voices in the audience. He also offered considerable flexibility when it came to pitch and rhythm. Songs slowed down and speeded up as they went along. Seeger knew how to bend the sevenths and thirds in African-American pieces. Beats were often skipped or bars extended (as is common in most folk traditions, but uncommon in Western pop). A perfect example of this is the way in which he handled "The Water Is Wide," an old British ballad. Seeger sang the song very slowly, again to encourage the audience to join in—but there was no chorus. The song was more or less in four-four time, but Seeger played an eight-twelve guitar backup and occasionally shortened bars strategically to keep the song flowing and interesting. The result was loose and uninhibited.

He also frequently used humour to reduce audience inhibitions. Other singers who have tried Seeger's approach say that getting the audience to laugh is the first step towards getting them to sing. Satirical songs with choruses were placed in the program at regular intervals, and the introductions, even to very serious songs, were peppered with jokes. At one point Seeger said, "It's a nice song to harmonize on—literally any note works, I've found (laughter). I think they call it 'tone clusters' (louder laughter)." The humour was a little naughty, but both you and your grandmother could laugh at it. It was not the kind of humour that excludes.

Communication with the audience took many forms, both verbal and non-verbal, providing constant encouragement and feedback. At one point teetotaller Seeger yelled out, "We need more tenors. Imagine you're in a bar." And because the audience was miked we can immediately hear the difference. He taught the lyrics and melodies to unfamiliar songs in three ways. In the pre-song intro-

duction, as is common with choir leaders, Seeger sang each line of the chorus and asked the audience to repeat it back. In addition, during the performance, he practised his trademark habit of speaking the lyrics to the audience just before they sang them. Finally, for the Latin American song with Spanish lyrics, Seeger held up enormous cardboard cue cards. He sang most of the songs very slowly so that the multitude of voices had a chance to lock in. He added a lot of repetition, sometimes repeating the whole song twice (as he does with "The Water Is Wide') or reprising the chorus multiple times. "Just make sure everyone agrees," he warned would-be song leaders about repetition.

Getting the audience to sing harmony was more complicated. It's not something that comes easily to most North Americans. Some critics were infuriated by Seeger's habit of singing bits of the harmony instead of the melody at strategic points in songs as a way of encouraging timid harmonizers to sing out. On more familiar songs, Seeger let the audience hold the melody while he sang only harmony parts, sometimes sliding effortlessly between alto, tenor, and bass. (Some have suggested that Seeger's loss of singing voice in his old age came from singing outside his range for too long.) Towards the middle of the concert at the Sanders Theatre, he actually took time to teach the harmony parts, one by one, for a series of songs. He started with "We Shall Not Be Moved," quipping, "Musicians can show the politicians—not everyone has to sing the melody." After teaching three different harmony lines, he instructed: "If you hear too many people singing high, you sing low. If you hear too many people singing low, you sing high. And a few slither in the middle." Next he tried the African "Somagwaza," which has two different repeated patterns superimposed. Once the audience singers were secure in their two parts, Seeger sang a descant that soared above the others. Finally, he tried a little chant, composed by a friend, which was similar to the African song. Here again he quickly taught the primed audience all the parts, and the recorded results were remarkable. But he didn't stop there. His final tour de force came five songs later with "Jacob's Ladder." Building on the African-American sacred singing tradition, Seeger encouraged the audience not only to harmonize freely, but also to syncopate and improvise outside of the melody line. Astonishingly, they tried it with great success.

As the concert wound down, the audience was offered two non-singing opportunities to participate. The first occurs in "Twelve Gates to the City," another African-American sacred song. ("Us born-again atheists sing a lot of Christian hymns," Seeger observed in the liner notes.) The audience began clapping on the offbeat: on two and four in each bar. This clapping has become overdone at rock and folk concerts these days, but this time it worked well. Lastly, as an encore, Seeger played the tune for "Greensleeves" on his recorder. Pretty soon the audience started humming along.

After they had locked in, he began an extended free-flowing solo on the recorder as the audience kept humming the melody. He occasionally returned to a bit of the melody if he sensed the audience was losing the thread. He kept going, and the effect was beautiful and calming. That was it. The concert was over.

■

Some five years after *Singalong* was recorded, I had a chance to meet Pete Seeger in person. I was producing a radio documentary on vernacular culture and Pete agreed to do an interview. He was performing in Toronto with Arlo Guthrie, once again at Massey Hall. When I went to his hotel room the next morning, we had a good talk. He was intense and serious. Very little of the on-stage humour was apparent. He was in activist mode. But he was extremely articulate about his views on the dangers of a narrowly scientific world view. At one point, to explain why resistance to consumer culture was so important, he told me a story, which, he said, he had made up and "hardly ever tell—but sometimes I tell people."

There was once a tribe living in a beautiful valley. They hunted animals. They dug for roots and gathered berries. And life was difficult but loving. They lived in family groups. They gathered round the fire to tell stories and sing songs.

Then one family discovered some delicious berries on the side of a neighbouring mountain. It was a steep cliff but there were ledges between the cliffs, and on these ledges were these delicious berries, and small rodents also lived there, also to eat the berries. And the families started gathering these berries and even living up on the side of the mountain. Pretty soon the entire rest of the tribe decided to follow their example. And they congratulated themselves on the beautiful views that they got from this mountain, and the tasty berries and the generally higher standard of living. They swung from ledge to ledge on long vines that reached down the cliffs.

Nine months after the tribe had started living on the ledges children were born with no hands. Now the wise men discussed "what have we done to offend the gods?" They couldn't figure out what was wrong. Then a baby was born with perfectly normal hands. The woman who gave birth to the child with normal hands, she herself had no arms. Her husband had always had to carry her when they travelled from ledge to ledge. Her arms had been normal. They were destroyed in a terrible accident.

Now the wise men were really stumped. They tried cutting off the arms of other women. Now they found that babies started to be born with normal hands, but the women said, "You are not going to cut off all our arms so that babies will be born with arms! You mean to say that all those women are going to have their hands cut off and all the men carry them?" This led to great confusion.

They did some more experiments. One woman said: "I'm not going to touch these vines; my husband is going to carry me." And they found that when that was done, as long as the women did not touch the vines, the children were being born with normal hands. But then the men said, "This is not fair, we can't do all this. We can't be carrying half the population around."

They determined that there was some kind of poison in the vines that caused the children to be born with no hands. And the entire tribe decided to go back and live in the valley. But the only way they could get back to the valley was by swinging on these vines.

Similarly, today, I believe the only way we'll get back to living more sensibly is to realize that our goal is to use less technology, less power, less information.

So it is with Pete: he has shown us how to ride the poison vines of commercial, technological culture—a culture that both disempowers and enables—back to the vernacular valley.

13

THE
RETRIBALIZATION
OF THE WORLD?

■

Even when you find utopia, you bring the snake with you.

— RICHARD HOLLOWAY

Marshall McLuhan, a Canadian originally from Winnipeg,
attended Cambridge University in England during the mid-1930s.
There he converted to Catholicism and developed a particular
interest in the poetry and prose of the English Renaissance. He
eventually got a job teaching at the University of Toronto in 1946.
McLuhan never much liked television. His house was the last on
the block to have one, and he relegated it to the basement so that
it would not interfere with his enjoyment of the fireplace. But he
began to notice significant changes in the behaviour of not only
the undergraduate students he taught but also his own six children, and he suspected that these changes had something to do
with this increasingly ubiquitous piece of furniture. He told his
colleagues that children should not be exposed to the toxic medium
of television for more than one hour a week.

Consumer culture, especially as served up on TV, both appalled
and fascinated him. His first book, *The Mechanical Bride: The Folklore of Industrial Man*, was nothing less than a witty and far-ranging

attack on the whole of modern Western civilization, including adventure movies and comic books, paying particular attention to whisky, automobile, and perfume advertisements.

The book was a complete failure. Despite getting mostly positive reviews, it sold only a few hundred copies. According to his biographers, McLuhan was devastated. He began to rethink his whole approach. He decided that he would never again play the angry moralist, raging against capitalism, consumerism, and industrialism. Henceforth he would adopt the stance of the cool observer reporting on the facts of the evolving cultural world as he saw them. He coined the term "global village" to describe what he saw happening as the result of electronic media. It was meant to be descriptive, but many people who worked in the emerging medium of television took the term as an intellectual affirmation of their own importance. According to Glen Willmott, after that moment the public McLuhan became a carefully constructed masquerade, much like the carnivals of earlier times in which "men acted as women, women as men, kings as beggars, servants as masters, acolytes as Bishops." McLuhan's critique of modern life took the form of guerrilla theatre. Willmott states: "McLuhan always avowed that the Global Village was antithetical to him personally. If he nevertheless paraded his Global Village identity (and to the hilt), it is because he wished to play the normal social life of modernity in reverse, raising its unconscious technological modes of life to conscious satire."

Two books later McLuhan had become one of the most important public intellectuals of the twentieth century. His picture appeared on the cover of *Newsweek* magazine, *Playboy* interviewed him, and he appeared countless times on television. Madison Avenue advertising executives sought him out. He played himself in Woody Allen's movie *Annie Hall*. Most people believed, with his clever aphorisms like "the medium is the message" and "medium hot and cool," that he was a kind of high priest for the transformation of the world by technology. Years later, *Wired* magazine, a popular voice for techno-utopianism, made him their "patron saint."

Not long before his death in 1980 at the age of sixty-nine, McLuhan attempted to come clean in a *Washington Post* article, "What Television Is Doing to Us—and Why." He urged readers to "pull the plug" on television. "Electronic man is in desperate need of roots," he wrote. "He's lost his body, his physical body and his private identity. He has an image, but no body." By that point his many disciples could dismiss old McLuhan as simply being nostalgic for the obsolete, literate human of his generation and social class—nostalgic for a figure whose influence began to wane when the first televisions entered the living rooms of the nation. **199**

■

McLuhan was the most famous in a long line of intellectuals and social commentators in the twentieth century—Harold Innis, Walter Ong, and Joshua Meyrowitz are three others—who focused their observations on the specific effects of different technologies on human consciousness. These thinkers have been so influential that it is now commonplace to casually remark that television causes violence or that the Internet brings people together. While it has some merits, this particular way of thinking—that machines are agents in the evolution of culture—obscures the extent to which all the mechanical communication technologies of the last century—the phonograph, the still camera, motion pictures, radio and television, the networked personal computer—are first and foremost *social* arrangements.

People go to the movies, watch television, or set up a Facebook profile for many often inchoate, perhaps irrational reasons: contingency, convenience, novelty, curiosity, diversion, pleasure, loneliness, boredom. But surely a big part of the reason that people do these things is social. Human beings want to feel part of their community; they want to share and discuss common experiences with their families and friends. This is true even of seemingly anti-social technologies such as books and iPods, because solitary reading and listening have ways of feeding back into social relationships. In this regard the cultural tools of the last hundred years and their contents are part of today's vernacular life. In other important ways they are something new: vernacular's opposite.

The media environment we live inside today is the fruit of choices made by millions of people over many decades. If we see this media environment as the inevitable result of disembodied machines making us do things in a certain way, then human beings have little motivation to do things differently; if we see ourselves as choosing and shaping the *machines*, we can then understand how things in the past might have been formulated differently—and imagine that perhaps they still could be.

■

In June 1889, a month after the Eiffel Tower opened in Paris, the famous U. S. inventor Thomas Alva Edison assigned a young employee named William Dickson to develop a motion picture apparatus. Edison imagined a "coin operated entertainment machine" to accompany his highly successful phonograph. After looking at the work of Eadweard Muybridge, Étienne Jules Marey, and other inventors, Dickson began experimenting with the recording of a rapid sequence of still photographs on perforated celluloid. By

1892 he had designed the Kinetograph, a battery-powered camera weighing several hundred pounds. The machine could record black and white moving images at sixteen frames per second. Dickson could not solve the problem of how to synchronize sound; that would take another thirty-five years.

Edison then decided that the future of motion pictures was in small viewing machines that could be used by one customer at a time. The first Kinetoscope parlour was set up in 1893 in a converted shoe store at 1155 Broadway, New York City. For a nickel, customers could watch short performances by vaudeville performers or mildly pornographic items like *The Gaiety Girls Dancing*. Edison's vision of the individualized viewer watching a tiny screen alone was a century too early. It would not materialize until the iPod and YouTube were developed and marketed in the twenty-first century.

The novelty of Dickson's invention was quickly overtaken by events on another continent. Shortly after Christmas in the year 1895, the brothers Auguste and Louis Lumière rented a basement room in the Grand Café on the boulevard des Capucines in Paris. They projected on the wall a program of ten "films" to a small group of spectators. On the program were *La Sortie des ouvriers de l'usine Lumière* (Workers leaving the Lumière factory), *Déjeuner de bébé* (Baby's lunch), and *L'Arroseur arrosé* (The sprinkler sprinkled), an early slapstick about a boy and a gardener. Perhaps the most famous of the one-minute films was *L'Arrivée d'un train en gare* (Arrival of a train at a station), during which it was widely reported that audiences shifted in their seats out of fear as the train approached. Like so many apocryphal stories in the history of show business, this one too has proven false. It was a rumour spread by the brothers as a publicity stunt. Admission that day was one franc, and the receipts for the first screening were only thirty-five francs. A month later the same program was bringing in seven thousand francs each day.

For his part, Edison, who originally had no interest in projection, began searching for someone to develop a projection system in North America. The success of projection over the Kinescope says more about the historical conditions—who was using cinema and what their expectations were—than about the technology itself.

Cinema began life in the vernacular ocean. Between 1880 and 1930 over twenty-seven million immigrants flooded into the United States, twenty million of those entering through Ellis Island off New York City. They came from Italy, Eastern Europe, Russia, Germany, Britain, Canada, Scandinavia, and Mexico. In a flow that was similar to changes in urban life in Europe a century earlier, as the factories and the immigrants moved into downtown areas, the middle classes headed for the rapidly growing suburbs, creating, in all major cities, new class divisions. Torn from their vernacular roots in farms and villages, the displaced, urbanized working-class people were hungry for a sense of belonging and new myths appropriate to their new lives. The grainy, jerky, black and white moving images at the corner nickel show provided them with some semblance of what they searched for. Motion pictures were successful partly because they came out of the very communities they served. For several decades those who made movies and those who watched them came from the same social class. Most of the first generation of great filmmakers and producers—Edwin S. Porter, Charlie Chaplin, Mack Sennett, William Fox, Adolph Zukor, Louis B. Mayer, the Warner brothers, Carl Laemmle—started out as penniless immigrants. As film historian Richard Sklar points out, "The urban workers, the immigrants and the poor had discovered a new medium of entertainment without the aid, and indeed beneath the notice, of the custodians and arbiters of middle-class culture."

Dozens of movie houses opened in immigrant neighbourhoods. On their way home from a twelve-hour shift at the factory, the men and women working in the sweat shops on the Lower East Side of Manhattan would pay a nickel to attend a twenty-minute compilation of short subjects. The middle class considered these establishments to be dangerous breeding grounds for social unrest and moral turpitude. The atmosphere in the theatres was loud and raucous. Children and adults crowded in each night. Unescorted women often attended. There was nothing silent about these screenings, and the passive spectator was nowhere in sight. Besides the shouts and sighs of the viewers and the general conversation, movies had, from the beginning, live musical accompaniment: usually a piano or organ, often played by women. In some theatres a live narrator filled in the storyline for people who could not read the intertitles. The musicians and narrators prided themselves on being able to respond spontaneously to the mood of the audience and the specifics of time and place. Later, when studios started sending out written scores to go with their A pictures, the keyboard players resisted these attempts at centralized control and continued to improvise for their local viewership.

In a pattern that would become commonplace in the popular media for the rest of the twentieth century, movie producers tapped into the rich trove of vernacular stories and performances that lived on in the recently urbanized working classes. They refashioned these, added new ideas about individual freedom and equality, and marketed the results back to their new audience. The stories told and the myths generated were transformed by the new medium: the romance, the farce, the Western, the murder mystery, the morality tale—filled with folk heroes, ghastly gangsters, beautiful women in need of protection, and monsters of all kinds. Movies represented the sex and violence, amorality, and tragedy that were a common part of the emerging urban life of North American and European cities.

Within a couple of decades movie watching changed. Exhibitors and theatre owners began to search out and attract middle-class patrons. Their motivation was frankly commercial. Well-heeled audiences could afford higher ticket prices. But these patrons would only come to the cinema if the audience behaved with greater civility—in other words, audiences had to be taught to keep quiet. Producers began making movies that conformed more to middle-class mores. Theatre owners attempted to enforce new rules of behaviour in their movie houses. This project was abetted by the invention of synchronous sound tracks at the end of 1920s. With sound movies, audiences had to remain silent if they wanted hear the dialogue. In practice the transformation was slow to take hold. The 1988 movie *Cinema Paradiso*, set in Sicily in the days after World War II, colourfully illustrates these tensions in audience behaviour. The largely peasant audiences depicted in the film, unsocialized in the conventions of urban cinema watching, comment loudly, shout, socialize, insult each other, engage in sexual adventures, and otherwise pay less than full attention to the screen. In the larger historical sense, however, silent spectators experiencing their emotions privately in public—an expectation first imagined in the concert halls and theatres of nineteenth-century Europe—became the ideal and later the norm in movie houses worldwide.

Since film could capture performances and reproduce them indefinitely, it began to replace live local performers. The advantages of this for the owners of entertainment venues first became obvious as early as 1900. When theatre managers in New York started deducting 10 per cent from performers' salaries as agent fees, vaudeville performers went on strike. In the absence of live shows, managers filled their programs with motion pictures, and the audiences kept coming. The strike was broken. After that, movies remained a standard part of vaudeville programs and eventually replaced them altogether. The long tradition of live entertainment as a site of working-class solidarity and collective action was dealt a fatal blow.

As with any medium, cinema has seen many producer-artists who refused to accept the conventional forms embraced by mainstream Hollywood. Over the years innovators have used the medium for non-commercial purposes: experimental film, socialist cinema (especially in the early Soviet Union), documentaries as agents of democratic debate, and artistic expression. Film artists have attempted to forge new, more critical forms of audience engagement with the images and sounds that movies can reproduce so well. While remarkable examples of this work continue to appear at the margins of the international movie business, cinema as an influential cultural force is waning and thus so too are its finest artists. Susan Sontag, in her widely reprinted 1996 article "The Decay of Cinema," declared:

Cinema's 100 years seem to have the shape of a life cycle: an inevitable birth, the steady accumulation of glories and the onset in the last decade of an ignominious, irreversible decline. It's not that you can't look forward anymore to new films that you can admire. But such films not only have to be exceptions— that's true of great achievements in any art. They have to be actual violations of the norms and practices that now govern movie making everywhere in the capitalist and would-be capitalist world—which is to say, everywhere. And ordinary films, films made purely for entertainment (that is, commercial) purposes, are astonishingly witless; the vast majority fail resoundingly to appeal to their cynically targeted audiences. While the point of a great film is now, more than ever, to be a one-of-a-kind achievement, the commercial cinema has settled for a policy of bloated, derivative film-making, a brazen combinatory or recombinatory art, in the hope of reproducing past successes. Cinema, once heralded as the art of the 20th century, seems now, as the century closes numerically, to be a decadent art.

Increasingly, audiences are turning away from the social rituals of the movie house and choosing instead to stay home in front of their electronic hearth and its portable surrogates.

■

In the beginning all radios were two-way: transmitters as well as receivers, little more than a wireless extension of the telegraph and the telephone. The first commercial radios were used for ship to ship and ship to shore telegraph messages like the ones used by the *Titanic* after it hit the iceberg in 1912. When Reginald Fessenden and Lee de Forest invented amplitude-modulated signals that allowed for sound to be sent over the air, radiotelephones became common. At this time there was little in the way of regulation, the equipment was hard to operate, and professional operators competed with passionate amateurs for available frequencies. Nonetheless, a strong community developed among radio operators, particularly the amateurs.

During World War I governments on both sides took over all radio frequencies for military use. At the end of the war these same governments were reluctant to return the airwaves to private citizens. Different solutions were found. In Britain, for example, control of all useful radio frequencies was turned over to the General Post Office. In the United States, a giant cartel of radio manufacturers, including General Electric, Western Electric, and AT&T, was formed. This new organization, called RCA, was granted the licence to control all one thousand radio patents "in the national interest."

Amateurs were left with the frequencies at the extreme end of the spectrum, the shortwave band. Then, by a strange quirk in the contingencies of corporate wrangling, a strategic decision was made that would have profound consequences on world media culture.

One radio-maker was frozen out of the U.S. cartel: Westinghouse Electric and Manufacturing Company. Faced with impending bankruptcy, the company came up with an ingenious solution to its predicament. One of the company's senior engineers, Dr. Frank Conrad, had been transmitting music recordings from an amateur radio set in his garage. He used the word "broadcasts" to describe these transmissions, borrowing the term used by farmers when they sowed seeds in their fields. When these broadcasts became popular, Westinghouse got the idea of manufacturing a radio "receiver" that could not transmit, thus bypassing government regulations and RCA's monopoly. In 1920, in order to make the receivers attractive for purchasers, Westinghouse also set up a radio station that produced regular, publicized broadcasts each night.

So began radio broadcasting in the United States. It proved so popular that RCA soon entered the broadcasting field as well with a packed schedule of recorded music, live lectures, variety, and drama programs. Stations sprang up everywhere. Many department stores operated stations "as a public service" to advertise their wares. Rich individuals, laundries, chicken farms, and at least one stockyard also operated stations.

Radio's success was coupled with major social and economic changes that transformed the North America of the 1920s: household electrification, the automobile, new ideas about gender roles, sexual mores, and child-rearing practices. Cheap radio receivers became the bearer of many of these new ideas. From 1923 to 1924 the number of radios in U.S. homes increased twenty-fivefold. In the beginning families and invited guests would listen to shows in rapt silence. Later, when radio became more commonplace, people put it on in the background and went about their household chores.

The problem of how to pay for radio programs was solved in several ways. In Britain all radio owners were charged an annual licence fee. The money generated paid for programming on the government-sponsored British Broadcasting Corporation. In the United States someone proposed that commercial messages, inserted into the middle of "free" programs, could pay for shows and also provide marketers with a new advertising medium. Amazing as it seems today, indignation about this idea was swift and articulate and came from some surprising sources. Few commentators believed that audiences would ever agree to have programs interrupted for commercials. David Sarnoff, the general manager of RCA, believed that commercial messages would destroy radio's potential for quality and public service. Secretary of State Herbert Hoover, soon to be U.S. president, declared in a 1922 speech: "The ether is a public medium and must be used for the public good. It is quite inconceivable that it should be used for advertising." Others suggested as an alternative that radio outlets, like libraries, should be publicly funded.

Alas, once a few stations started doing it, the dam burst and radio commercials became commonplace. Advertisers thrilled at the possibilities. One marketing specialist, in 1931, ruminated:

> For years the national advertiser and his agency have been dreaming of the time to come when there would be evolved some great family medium which should reach the home and the adult members of the family in their moments of relaxation, bringing to them the editorial and advertising message. Then came radio broadcasting, utilizing the air we breathe, and with electricity as its vehicle entering the homes of the nation through

doors and windows, no matter how tightly barred, and delivering its message audibly through the loudspeaker wherever placed.

In other words, radio was an advertising executive's wet dream.

Over half of all homes in the United States had a radio by the beginning of the Great Depression. For people without jobs or prospects in those lean years, radio provided an important source of free information and entertainment. The medium reduced the sense of isolation for farming families. Under these circumstances, most listeners learned to tolerate and sometimes even enjoy the commercials, as have generations since. Commercial-free radio was always a viable idea, and remains quite successful in other parts of the world, including Canada. Had things progressed differently, with different decisions made in high places, mainstream radio and television broadcasting might have become something very different from what it is today.

■

Audience silence and the privatizing of experience in public brought on by darkened theatres and sound movies formed only a prelude to what happened with radio. The story of contemporary consumer culture took a significant plot turn at this moment. When the wireless carried public performances into private living rooms, a deep well of vernacular traditions, including family conversation, storytelling, music-making, game playing, reading aloud, and other forms of homemade entertainment was replaced by commercial, massproduced culture. In the United States between 1923 and 1929 the production of musical instruments dropped by over 50 per cent. Piano and sheet music sales decreased even more dramatically in the same period. Without constant practice, people's ability to entertain themselves began to atrophy.

Television began life as little more than an extension of radio. The same networks that monopolized radio broadcasting, NBC and CBS in the United States and the BBC in Britain, for example, were the same ones that brought television to market. The same types of programs, often with the same performers, became standard fare on the new medium. In the United States, television commercials took over where their radio counterparts left off, and television was welcomed into the home in much the same way. Like all novelties, watching was intense and focused in the beginning, but later televisions became part of the furniture. They were used as an aural and visual accompaniment to the busy lives of baby boomers and their parents.

Like cinema and radio before it, television's rise in popularity corresponded to a time of significant cultural and economic change. The first televisions went on the market in the late 1940s when the Depression was still a vivid memory and World War II had just ended. It was a time of economic expansion and the optimistic celebration of childhood and the nuclear family. It was also a time of mass exodus from city centres and the creation of suburbs, commuting, and conspicuous consumption. People became more concerned about safety and risk than they ever had before. Television did not create these phenomena, but it was certainly used by taste-makers and nation-builders to promote them. As Joyce Nelson explains in her book *The Perfect Machine*, television show genres reflected and reinforced these emerging attitudes. Situation comedies portrayed domesticity as warm and humorous. Cop and doctor shows, in contrast, painted the world outside the home as treacherous: full of criminality, disease, and tragedy. Television news also reported on dangerous threats elsewhere, at the same time giving viewers the illusion of participation in public life while staying at home. All of this was interspersed with TV commercials, which provided optimistic messages about new and improved products that would make life easier and more fun. The dichotomy between the safe, product-filled domestic space and the dangerous public arena depicted in television programming hastened the demise of the already eroding public sphere and its replacement by the shopping mall.

People went out a lot less. Movie attendance, in absolute numbers, peaked in 1946 when 4.1 billion tickets were sold. After that, admissions suffered a steady decline until they levelled off at around one billion per year in the early 1960s. Despite rising population figures, that number has not changed significantly since and television is often cited as the primary cause. Critics also blame television viewing for the drop in recreational reading, reduced participation in sports and other group activities outside the home, and the "obesity epidemic." In his celebrated book *Bowling Alone: The Collapse and Revival of American Community* (2000), Robert Putnam makes a case for the decline of active civic engagement by ordinary citizens, what he calls "social capital." He uses the example of bowling leagues. While the number of people who bowl has increased, membership in leagues has gone down. He places the blame squarely on the isolating tendencies inherent in the role of electronic media in modern society.

The social arrangements of television hastened the dismantling of vernacular culture that was already set in motion by radio. In the 1950s Americans watched television for an average of four and a half hours every day. By the 1980s viewing had climbed to an astonishing seven hours daily. No one knows how many people watched television during supper, but the popularity of TV dinners suggests that the practice was common. Poet Adrienne Rich grieved eloquently over all that was lost:

The television screen has throughout the world replaced, or is fast replacing: oral poetry, old wives' tales; children's story-acting games and verbal lore; lullabies; "playing the sevens"; political argument; the reading of books too difficult for the reader, yet somehow read; tales of "when-I-was-your-age" told by parents and grandparents to children, linking them to their own past; singing in parts, memorization of poetry; the oral transmitting of skills and remedies; reading aloud, recitation; both community and solitude. People grow up who not only don't know how to read, a late-acquired skill among the world's majority; they don't know how to talk, to tell stories, to sing, to listen and remember, to argue, to pierce an opponent's argument, to use metaphor and imagery and inspired exaggeration in speech; people are growing up in the slack flicker of a pale light which lacks the concentrated burn of a candle flame or oil wick or the bulb of a gooseneck desk lamp: a pale, wavering, oblong shimmer, emitting incessant noise, which is to real knowledge or discourse what the manic or weepy protestations of a drunk are to responsible speech.

It is wrong to blame dumb machines for these developments. It is, after all, people who choose to utilize the available technologies in these ways; they could, of course, use them differently. Video technology is cheap and relatively easy to use. It is entirely possible for people to employ video or small-scale television broadcasts as artistic media and as adjuncts to local vernacular cultures. Indeed, many people, especially in the global South, already use them this way. But we seldom hear about these examples because they fail to confirm common beliefs about how electronic media work. Commercial television is based on the selling of heads—individual audience members—to advertisers. The price is determined by the number of heads delivered (which is perhaps why McLuhan once remarked that we do not watch television, television watches us). The small numbers of people who make up audiences in local markets do not have economic value and, according to the simple test of popularity, have low social status as well. But we would do well to pay more attention. It is precisely these examples that might provide us with a way out of the electronic media labyrinth.

■

In the summer of 1999 almost three hundred people gathered in an abandoned factory in Montreuil, on the eastern edge of Paris. They were there to film a dramatization of the story of the Paris Commune of 1871, when the people of Paris set up their own government against the wishes of French state. Only a handful of those gathered had any previous motion picture experience. The project was the brainchild of British filmmaker Peter Watkins, who won an Academy Award in 1966 for *The War Game* and had been making films outside the mainstream system for three decades. In the 1980s he produced *The Journey*, a fourteen-hour film about the threat of nuclear war. Funded entirely with small donations from individuals around the world, *The Journey* was presented to groups of viewers in short segments, each ending with a large question mark on the screen. The viewing groups were supposed to stop the projector at these points and discuss the issues being portrayed. I once spent a weekend involved in a marathon *Journey* screening complete with discussions. The thought-provoking intensity of that experience is something I remember vividly. In 1999 Watkins was once again experimenting with process as well as product.

Working with labour unions and leftist theatre groups, Watkins recruited over 220 people from all over France to portray the working-class population of the eleventh district of Paris in the second half of the nineteenth century. Through the conservative press he enlisted other non-professionals, with opposing political views, to portray the politicians and generals who crushed the Commune. Each performer was required to research the particular historical figure that he or she had been assigned to portray. When the filming began in July, the dialogue and much of the action on the semi-realistic set were improvised from the historical record and photographed as if they were events being captured in a documentary. From time to time the actors would step out of character and start reflecting on the relevance of the past to pressing problems in the present. At one point the women protested that Watkins was not giving them enough screen time, and he agreed to film and include a sequence in which the women talk about feminism in the past and the present. The finished program, almost six hours long, includes a dramatic climax during which hundreds of Parisians are slaughtered by the government army. In a brilliant, theatrical gesture, however, the violence is neither realistic nor graphic, which somehow makes it all the more disturbing.

La Commune was partly funded by La Sept Arte, a French television channel. It was shown only once on national TV and was invited to a few film festivals. If that was all, it would have disappeared, like so many other programs, deep into the archives. Fortunately, as part of Watkins' concept, the performers and their friends set up an organization to screen *La Commune* in meeting halls around France. At these screenings, usually attended by cast members, the historical and contemporary issues explored in the video, and the process of making it, were readdressed in face-to-face discussion.

By collaborating with a majority of non-professionals on the *Commune* project, Watkins questioned the idea that only a schooled elite can create meaningful media. By working with a minimal means and showing the lovingly constructed but only semi-realistic set, he also challenged the idea that historical renderings can only be made with big budgets and sophisticated special effects. By improvising around a loose structure he relinquished much of the control conventionally held by the producer-writer-director team in narrative filmmaking. This process honoured the individual contributions of the cast members and inscribed the collaborative process into the final work. Lastly, the collaborative process whereby history is negotiated and redramatized continued even after the "product" was complete because of the active way in which the film was watched and disseminated in public space. *La Commune* rekindled vernacular traditions of storytelling and homemade theatrics. It directly challenged how homogenized, passively consumed electronic media is created and experienced in contemporary life.

215

■

The 1980s marked the return of naked, ruthless capitalism and its global expansion. Radical changes in social and political life ensued: Asian and Latin American sweatshops, increasing division between the rich and the poor, destruction of the environment, global climate change, the crushing of labour unions, unbridled competition, the dwindling of free time, and the corrosion of character in corporate life. It is not an exaggeration to suggest that without personal computers and telecommunications networks this transformation would not have been possible. To make it work, millions of people had to learn to love the keyboard and the screen. The tools had to be domesticated and fetishized. And they were. In the Western world, networked computers have become as necessary to daily life, and almost as passionately embraced, as food and shelter.

I remember the moment in which this phenomenon seemed to take hold in my life. It was the winter of 1994. Professors at the university were invited to a demonstration of something called the World Wide Web. We sat in a lecture theatre watching a video screen. Technicians from Computing Services explained that it was possible, using free software called Mosaic, to connect to a remote computer and display text and images available there. On the screen we travelled to the Louvre in Paris and looked at reproductions of the *Mona Lisa* and other famous paintings. Making websites was easy, they told us. Anyone could do it. I was immediately aware of the implications that such a tool might have for vernacular culture. I turned to a colleague and confessed that I wanted to learn more.

A couple of months later I attended two concurrent conferences. "Multimedia '94" was a glossy, breathless trade show held at a big convention centre in Toronto. A few blocks away, in an opera house rehearsal space, the non-commercial types gathered for "Culture, Technologies, Convergence." While some attempts were made to integrate the two events, the gulf between them was immense. The keynote speaker at "Multimedia '94" told his audience that "we are inventing the goose that lays the golden egg," and huge profits will be made from the World Wide Web. The only barrier, he added, was excessive government regulation.

At the opera house cautious intellectuals and imaginative artists presented their views on the potential of the World Wide Web to empower, educate, and govern. Very little was said about its ability to earn money. I found their views about the future more to my liking. I wrote an optimistic article about the conference and began learning HTML. What these people were saying about the Web sounded very similar to things I had been saying about vernacular culture. It empowered grassroots creation by people who normally had no access to the public sphere. Because it was cheap, it flattened hierarchies: in cyberspace the powerful and powerless were both on the same level. Rather than encouraging the passive response of a television viewer, the Web was interactive by design. It demanded participation and encouraged dialogue and collaboration. One presenter described his idea of "complex, compound, electronic documents," written by groups, anticipating by a decade wikis and Wikipedia. Stories would no longer have one plot. Instead, people could navigate their own way through the material, changing the narrative as they went, much like a constantly revised bedtime story. I was interested in the subversive effects that such a celebration of amateurization would have on the cultural professions.

Not long after, software became available to include audio and even video on websites. I set about creating an interactive multimedia documentary that would be available online. Using as my model an intellectual, non-violent computer game called *Myst*, I created a virtual museum that, appropriately, explored the history and characteristics of vernacular culture. Using rough, handpainted graphics and a playful tone, Memory Palace invited audiences to wander the halls, often looking in forbidden places to find subversive gems. They could leave their comments and discuss issues using an online forum. The site was filled with hundreds of photographs and audio interviews that I had recorded with people such as Raymond Williams and Pete Seeger. The project was well received. It was nominated for awards. An article about it appeared in *Forbes* magazine. I was invited to lecture about the work on several occasions.

But my enthusiasm for the World Wide Web was short-lived. When I asked people to describe their experiences of Memory Palace, I received distressing responses. A typical comment was, "It looks really interesting, but I only stayed there for about five minutes. I plan to go back and spend more time very soon." In my naïveté I had expected the average participant to use the site for an hour or more at one sitting.

It would be easy to say that I misunderstood how the Web really works and thus produced something inappropriate for the medium. That is undoubtedly true. But as I began to grasp the ways in which most people actually used the medium in the real world and what the consequences were for the public sphere, I became less and less convinced that it was a format friendly to vernacular life.

■

Many years ago, when telephone voice mail first became popular, I saw a clever cartoon. An old gentleman has just answered the phone in his hallway. The caption quotes what he hears: "Oh, George, you're home. I was just phoning to leave a message on your machine. I'll call back later." The joke is funny because it reveals a dirty little secret about modern life. People, it seems, often prefer to leave messages or send emails rather than engage in actual dialogue, with its expectations of politeness and small talk. Electronic technologies enable geographical and temporal separations between the senders and receivers of messages. Paradoxically, while making it easier for people to communicate, these tools also create conditions that breed anti-social attitudes and behaviour.

Cyberspace privileges the distant over the local, the virtual over the real. Everyone at some point has been in a store, a classroom, a restaurant, or other public place and been struck by the extent to which people are focused on their cell phones or Blackberries instead of attending to here and now. At some points it is almost comical, as when young Parisian couples sit side by side in the cafés drinking their morning lattes, conversing with other people on their cell phones or checking their emails instead of talking to each other.

There is a dark side to this. The individual, the economic unit of the new capitalism, watching his or her own private screen, hearing the world through his or her earbuds, is an increasingly anti-social being. The structure and culture of commercialized personal computing encourage individuals to think of themselves as living in a customized bubble. Other human beings increasingly get cast as more or less useful players in one's personal cybernetic fantasy. Children are now growing up in the embrace of temporary electronic pseudo-communities that require few, if any, long-term commitments.

While the Web encourages participation and involvement, the opposite is often the norm. The term "lurking" says it all. The anonymity of the technology makes possible a passive, superficial sampling from the smorgasbord of choices available, with little involvement or commitment on the part of the user. The result is the distracted focus and pseudo-knowledge of the perpetual observer rather than the wisdom of direct experience.

It is precisely the tendency of people to use digital gadgets as a way of disengaging from age-old traditions of human hospitality and reciprocity—traditions that limit narcissistic desire and behaviour—that makes cyberculture an enemy to vernacular life.

Rather than resisting commerce, the World Wide Web is consumer culture on steroids. Like television and radio, most websites advertise an endless parade of products or personalities; but, even more, the do-it-yourself fan culture of YouTube and Facebook represents a new level of customer engagement. Instead of having professional marketers selling products to consumers, we now live in a world in which customers increasingly market products to each other. When customers produce their own YouTube videos, they try to replicate the slick, fashion-conscious popular culture that they are enchanted with. The results are for the most part embarrassing and silly. Web insider Lee Siegel calls them "cautious and derivative—

pre-certified by popular culture." These homemade media works are the opposite of playful. They are about "me as a brand" and "going viral." In Siegel's words, "The wolf of unbridled appetite slips into everyday convention in the sheep's clothing of commercial language."

People think and do things differently with digital media. There is no way we can go back on that. Some products of this paradigm shift are beneficial. I am not one of those people who criticize Wikipedia because it is written and maintained by amateurs. I have no doubt that Wikipedia provides accurate and current information to millions of people daily. It also challenges many assumptions about expertise and specialization. Skype, a free software that turns your computer into a video phone, is a good example of a new convivial tool. It allows two people to look at each other in real time while conversing over long distances. It increases reciprocity and engagement.

The cybernetic dream and its consequences are far from comprehensive. Human beings still love deeply and want to spend "face time" with each other. Family and traditional community bonds remain profoundly important, for many, perhaps the majority, of people now living in the world. We find all kinds of ways to retain our humanity in the ruins of modern life. Refuges from the tyranny of economic compulsion and the generalized speed-up include, for example, friendly conversation, slow food, slow sex, yoga, meditation, camping trips, and guitar playing. But it is unlikely that any of these vernacular subversions will have much effect on the relentless advance of the digital mindset.

In the end, cyberculture will be transformed not because of its anti-social tendencies or commercial excesses. The Achilles heel of the digital revolution has always been its refusal to acknowledge the material conditions of its existence. To build the machines that keep this new culture operating, millions of workers, most of whom will never be able to afford the gadgets they make, toil away in Asian sweatshops for a few dollars a day. The promoters of the bitsphere like to think that their mode of life is environmentally neutral, especially compared to the previous industrial era of smoky factories and truckloads of goods crisscrossing the globe. Nothing could be further from the truth.

Digital devices contain a range of heavy metals—lead, mercury, and cadmium, as well as gold, silver, copper, and zinc. The minerals are often mined in Africa and South America, where labour costs are minimal and environmental standards low. As a result, poorer countries bear a disproportionate amount of the environmental and human costs of gadgets. In the Congo, for example, the profits from coltan mining (an essential ingredient in cell phones) are used to finance both a civil war and fighting in neighbouring Uganda and Rwanda. A copper, lead, and zinc processing plant in Peru that supplies the computer industry has caused nearly all of the community's children to suffer from lead poisoning.

The manufacture of billions of silicon chips used in all digital devices requires untold gallons of water, as well as tons of toxic solvents and caustic solutions that end up in rivers, aquifers, and the air. Many of these pollutants are known carcinogens. The National Science Foundation estimates that 1,600 grams of fossil fuels and chemicals are used to produce a microchip weighing one gram. In addition, the secondary products that go into each chip equal 630 times the mass of the final product.

The electrical power needed to run these gadgets is another seldom told part of the story. Google, Yahoo, and Microsoft are all building "server farms" on the banks of the Columbia River in order to tap into the cheapest (and dirtiest) electricity in the United States. Google's operations will include over one million interconnected servers in three giant buildings. According to the industry's own estimates, this complex will draw 103 megawatts of electricity—

enough to power eighty-two thousand homes. Google and other companies are also looking to Siberia, Shanghai, and Ireland as locations to build farms, based on the availability of cheap, carbon-heavy power sources.

E-waste, generated by the extraordinarily rapid obsolescence of electronic equipment, has now reached unimaginable proportions. Some estimates put the amount at seven million tons annually in the United States alone. Some 90 per cent of that waste finds its way directly into landfill sites; and two-thirds of all heavy metals and 50 per cent of the lead found in landfills is the result of e-waste. These dangerous toxins leach into the water table and harm everyone's health. Recycling the remaining 10 per cent is extremely difficult and labour-intensive. That is why e-waste is sent by the shipload to China, India, Pakistan, and West Africa, where workers, without masks or gloves, boil circuit boards over homemade braziers to extract microchips that are then soaked in vats of acid for their gold and precious metals. In the Chinese city of Guiya, 80 per cent of the inhabitants are engaged in the primitive recycling of millions of tons of electronic waste, exposing themselves and their children to untold dangers, for pennies a day.

For all these reasons, the networked digital world should never be seen as a sustainable tool for remaking vernacular cultures. If anything survives of human civilization, once the full effects of climate change are felt in this century, the success will be partly due to some kind of disciplined reduction or elimination of electronic gadgets. Who knows, in a couple of decades we may find ourselves like the embargoed Cubans with their 1950 American cars: patching together with wire and duct tape our ancient Pentium dual-cores for just a bit more word processing or perhaps an old game or two. The rest of the time, those who have preserved and cultivated the skills of face-to-face vernacular culture will be in great demand.

14

THE POLITICS
OF PLAY

■

In late September 1981 some friends invited me to an unusual performance. I was told to meet them at 5:00 a.m. in front of the Royal Conservatory of Music in Toronto. There was a light, misty rain falling and the sky was black. We boarded a chartered bus and headed north through damp, empty streets.

About forty minutes later, still in pitch black and rain, we found ourselves deposited in the parking lot of a suburban conservation area. Volunteers with flashlights ushered us down a wooded path to the beach of a small lake. Many audience members, attired in rain gear of varying effectiveness, had already found places to stand or sit on the sand. The performance would begin at around 6:00 a.m.

We had assembled to witness an outdoor opera called *Princess of the Stars*. Musicians—four of them, playing a variety of instruments including flute, clarinet, trumpet, horn, trombone, tuba, and percussion—were hidden in strategic spots in the forest that encircled the lake. Beautifully costumed and masked singers, actors, and dancers performed in large canoes some distance out from the shore. The canoes were paddled by a group of hearty volunteers. We could make them out quite clearly in the dim, pre-dawn light. The libretto was in an invented language, and the show thus required a translator in his own canoe. The translator (played on this occasion by poet b.p. Nichol) came close to the beach and spoke to us in a magisterial voice.

This is the story of the Princess of the Stars,
Daughter of the Sun-God and herself a Goddess.
Her name is in the stars and you have seen it there.
Each night she looked down on the earth,
Blessing it with kisses and light.

At certain times a solo singer or horn player performed directly across from us on the other shore of the lake—almost a kilometre away—but, in the silence of the early hour, we could hear everything clearly. The performance was haunting. At dawn, a few minutes after 7:00, an enormous Sun Disk made its entrance by canoe and turned the plot in a new direction. I imagined how this might have looked had the morning sky been clear, but even in the mist, with the real sun absent, the moment resonates in my memory. Minutes later we were heading back to the buses, the city, and a good breakfast. The rain had subsided.

That was my first experience with the outdoor music theatre pageants of R. Murray Schafer. Less than two years later I found myself standing outside the Ontario Science Centre at dusk on a clear night in May with seventy-four other "initiates" to partake in an eleven-hour performance of Schafer's *Ra*. During the night we would dance, sing the sacred tones, identify incense and other scents, have a nap and a meal, feel our way through hazardous rooms blindfolded, and emerge at dawn to the exquisite sounds of an aria sung by two sopranos. Most theatre critics, it seemed, could not stand it, but I was hooked.

In the years following *Ra* I witnessed a number of other performances in England and the United States that, while coming from different traditions, had similar characteristics to Schafer's musical theatre.

The first was in 1985. I attended the one-hundredth anniversary of the birth of D.H. Lawrence in the little Nottinghamshire town of Eastwood, where the British novelist was born. A group called Welfare State International had created a playful and subversive funeral procession for the great man, who was known partly for the sexual themes he explored in his novels. The floats were fashioned on top of barely functioning cars borrowed from the local wreckers. At various moments along the route, an enormous D.H. Lawrence puppet, complete with the easily recognizable, well-trimmed beard, would slowly rise out of the centre of a giant coffin into an upright position that clearly suggested an erect penis. The parade ended at a carnival site set up in a field just outside of town.

A week later I had a chance to sit down with John Fox and Sue Gill, the founders of Welfare State, and talk about their approach to public performance. This influential group was founded in the late 1960s by British visual artists interested in making their art more collaborative and pertinent to communities outside the art world, and I was curious about the relationship between the collective, communal work and the artists who initiate the project and see it through. What the group attempts to do, John Fox told me, is build "structures where people can 'blow' along with the master musician." In other words, although the aim is communal, the path to the performance requires an artist, a composer, to create the structures that "give access to a lot of people for their own blowing, for their own improvisation." Fox argued that even in what are seen as

THE POLITICS OF PLAY

more simple or primitive economies—and, he said, "It may be a romantic rereading of the Middle Ages and primitive cultures in order to project a model of a potential utopia, for which I make no apologies at all, so it may very well be a false pattern"—the artist still has a personal role and significance. "There is, I think, a more collective way of working and more of a democratic structure, but I wouldn't wish to pretend that it was some kind of a perfect euphoric situation where everybody bubbled up with immense creativity and there weren't some people better at it than others."

Today this work is sometimes grouped under the umbrella term of "celebratory theatre"—a kind of theatre exemplified by the U.S. troupe Bread and Puppets Theater, founded in 1962-63 in a Delancey Street loft in New York City. Fox acknowledged that the inspiration for Welfare State came after he saw a Bread and Puppets street performance outside the Oval House in South London in 1965.

In 1989 I finally got to see Bread and Puppets for myself when I attended the annual Domestic Resurrection Circus at their large farm in Northern Vermont. There I pitched my little tent in a neighbouring field and walked through the woods to the enormous natural amphitheatre on the grassed-over remains of a stone quarry. The performance area spanned twenty acres. The troupe was expecting over ten thousand people that weekend, even though there was no publicity whatsoever for the event. Many participants had already arrived. I lined up to get my piece of coarse sourdough bread spread with aioli. Offering audiences free bread as a gesture of hospitality has been a tradition of Bread and Puppets since the beginning. The day I got there, Peter Schumann, the troupe's founder and artistic director, rose before dawn to bake the bread himself, with assistance from volunteer helpers.

The Domestic Resurrection Circus, which was held every summer from 1970 to 1998 without any admission price, had several interlinked parts. Visitors could visit the Puppet Museum in the old barn or buy "cheap art" and posters in a renovated bus. Scheduled performances happened each night over the weekend, and "sideshows," created by associated theatre groups, could be enjoyed each morning in the woods next to the quarry. The two main events, for which thousands of people gathered on the side of the hill, were the circus and the pageant. The circus, which took place in the afternoon, was accompanied by raucous music and a master of ceremonies shouting into a megaphone. In the circus ring, performers in costumes and masks, interacting with oversized puppets, performed a series of humorous and ironic skits on current political issues. Apart from the small permanent troupe, all of the hundred or more performers were unpaid volunteers.

Later on, as twilight descended on the meadow, the crowd gathered again to witness the spectacular, wordless, giant puppet pageant that combined political and religious themes. Some of the puppets made their entrances and exits half a kilometre away from the audience. Each year the story followed a similar mythological trajectory. Some major disaster had been caused by "the Man"—a thirty-foot-high puppet in a business suit. Redemption arrived in the form of an even larger Mother Earth figure. Operated by over fifty puppeteers working in unison, the Mother Puppet torched the Man with a giant match. The pageant ended with the Man being engulfed in flames while white bird puppets circled and called in the surrounding darkness.

Bread and Puppets' art is anarchic, subversive, "deprofessionalized," convivial, and prophetic. Schumann, a deeply committed visual artist, made a conscious decision early in life to reject the "enclosed and self-absorbed world" of avant-garde American art and bring his moving sculptures out into the streets, making them available to everyone. As one commentator put it:

The pictures and sculptures which are the meat of puppetry, are ordered by a strange ambition: to provide the world with an unfragmented and uncontrollably large picture of itself, a picture which only puppetry can draw, a picture which praises and attacks at the same time, a *theatrum mundi*, which includes the desire of the world to be what it can be.

The anti-consumer, homemade aesthetic and inclusive process have made it a prototype for many other vernacular performances.

■

Dozens of celebratory theatre groups around the world draw their inspiration from these early pioneers. In Canada, for example, Shadowland in Toronto and Public Dreams in Vancouver both claim direct links to Welfare State. The giant puppets in peace and anti-globalization demonstrations have their roots in Bread and Puppets' ground-breaking work in the streets of New York during the Vietnam era. More recently, the large-scale cultural event held each year in Northern Nevada called Burning Man also draws on many of the ideas and practices of the pioneers. All of these spinoff companies and events have gone in their own directions, and some have moved away from the community-ritual focus of their mentors, but the priorities of the originating companies still provide the key to understanding the significance that this work has for the new century.

Baz Kershaw, in his book *The Radical in Performance: Between Brecht and Baudrillard,* writes that the Western theatre is "past its sell-by date . . . the established estate of theatre is transformed into a playground for the newly privileged, a quick stopover site on the tourist and heritage map." Political theatre in particular is "all but dead, smothered by the promiscuity of the political in post-modern culture." He sees people in the West as living in a performative society, a state of continual crisis in which "survival depends on the ability to perform" in a globe that has been "mediaized." He maintains, "The performative quality of power is shaping the global future as it never has before." Given this condition, he argues for new kinds of performance that engage democratic freedoms. He is interested in "how radical performance can actually produce such freedoms, or at least a sense of them, for both the performers and spectators, as it is happening." Central to this project is "inserting performance into everyday life," which involves the "transformation of the spectator into participant."

While the practices of Schafer, Bread and Puppets, and Welfare State are different, and in some ways contradictory to each other, they all share one important feature: they are all carefully considered challenges to the idea of performance as a consumable product available for purchase. Each in its own way is part of the project that Kershaw envisions.

In celebratory theatre the audiences are often very large. Yet for the most part these spectators are not people who normally go to the theatre or the symphony. When I talked to him, R. Murray Schafer reminded me that "a lot of the things in the past did unite people who were living in fairly close proximity—a village, for instance, would put on a pageant or do a miracle play or something of that sort. The entire village participated." People knew each other, and they could be drawn together through the immediacy of a ritualized action. "To bring us back to some kind of re-harmonization in our lives," Schafer argues, theatre artists can strive to work for and with "the available audience"—the audience "that is right around the corner, or the audience that is on your own block, or the audience that lives in your own apartment building."

For Schafer, drawing people together in this way is "precisely what we need" in these days of dense but fragmented populations. These audiences witness dozens of people—their neighbours, friends, and family members: ordinary people—performing along with the professionals. The borders between the stage and the spectator are porous. As Schafer points out, these activities tend to encourage a sense of community: either communities that already exist, or new ones formed just for the show.

Performances take place in non-standard environments: a lakeshore at dawn, a town street, an abandoned quarry, a science museum. In many cases the performance is tied to a particular time of day—perhaps sunrise, sunset, or another meteorological event. The performances are tightly linked to these spaces and times and do not travel easily. Speaking of the show I saw in 1981, Schafer said:

> You have to go to a particular lake in order to see *Princess of the Stars*. You can't see it in London or New York or Vienna. And it therefore reintroduces the idea of pilgrimage to the work of art.
>
> By moving out to an external environment and performing at a strange time of the day, you introduce people to a relationship to that environment they perhaps haven't perceived clearly before. Maybe people have been out in the countryside of Canada. Maybe they've never actually thought of it as being somehow sacred, ritual territory, magical. The job of an artist in a way is to make those hunches that we might have, to articulate them somehow. And to draw them really to our attention so that we suddenly realize, "Yes, I see what you mean about that mountain, that lake, that is a sacred property. I never realized that before." You do that simply by creating some kind of a legend about the place, you infuse it with some kind of magic.

■

These ideas were very much on my mind one evening in March 2006 as I sat in the bleachers of an enormous circus tent near Ulverston, a market town in England's Lake District. Bundled up against the uncommonly cold winter, I was waiting for *Longline: The Carnival Opera* to begin. As the last of the three-hundred audience members—children, old hippies, townspeople, intellectuals—streamed in, I could feel the weight of the moment in the air. This series of five performances would be Welfare State International's last show. *Longline* was their "exit rite of passage," according to John Fox. Billed as an ecological fable, the opera was the culmination of a three-year community residency. Working out of a renovated architectural marvel called Lanternhouse on one of the town's main streets, Welfare State artists had been living and working in the community of Ulverston for many years: recording oral history, songs, and stories; creating rites of passage, exhibitions, installations, performances, and concerts; organizing workshops, lectures, and meetings; and producing CDs and DVDs. The purpose of *Longline* was to tie all of these strands together into a final celebration within the community. Some two weeks later, on April Fool's Day 2006, Welfare State International would cease to exist.

The circus ring stage was surrounded on three sides by audience. A five-piece band inhabited the back quarter of the stage, and above the band a collection of circular and rectangular screens projected slides and videos that ran as a kind of chorus through the show's two hours. Using wall-to-wall music and a menagerie of carnival and circus techniques, *Longline* told the story of a rock in neighbouring Morecambe Bay, starting from a million years ago and moving into the future. A number of puppet characters witnessed the changes of time and progress along with the rock:

Jack, a fisherman; Gladys, the dreamer; and the ghosts of Sam, an immigrant slave from the West Indies, and the Blue Orphan girl—so named because she was covered in blue dye from a Victorian factory, where she laboured making laundry soap.

As the story progressed the rock was swallowed up by rising levels of sea and sand caused by climate change. The other characters were subdued by the war-making institutions of contemporary life. In the end, as all celebratory pageants must, the evils were dramatically vanquished and the humble characters triumphed—in this case, the rock was transformed into a space ship. Jack, Gladys, Sam, and the Blue Orphan Girl all took off into outer space in search of a new life. The decision to make exiting the planet the only choice available for our meek victims of environmental and social collapse was just one example of the dark heart beating at the centre of this ambitious work.

How do you evaluate a performance like that? The visual images—in essence, moving sculptures—were astonishing. It was Welfare State's métier to create brilliant, heart-crushing, unsentimental images using the detritus of consumer civilization. *Longline* had moments of great theatrical power—for instance, when the Jack and Gladys puppets held hands and sang a duet of friendship, their puppeteers and singers tenderly surrounding them. The score by Tim Fleming was exceptional in the way it spanned a range of musical styles and emotional states, stepping a fine line between pop sentimentality and inaccessible avant-gardism, but never succumbing to either.

If I were to apply the shopworn standards used by critics to assess professional musical theatre, I would find a few things about this production that would not pass muster. For one thing, it was difficult to follow the plot, such as it was, especially towards the end. The characters did not have relationships beyond the most rudimentary, and the conflicts were often black and white, with obvious heroes and villains. In addition, the pace of the show was quite slow by modern standards. I noticed many examples of what French critics call *longueurs*, when the action stopped and particularly important sets of visual images were laid out for the audience to contemplate. The narrator, the one potentially integrating agent in the mishmash of performance styles and modes of address, lacked the charisma to enforce coherence.

To apply these standards to *Longline*, however, is to miss the point. Welfare State International developed a collective artistic process that Fox called "applied vernacular culture." Its goals were directly opposed to the aims of professional theatre and the international art scene. Rather than focusing on producing "great" artistic products that could be repeated, reproduced, and sold to global audiences, Welfare State was committed to encouraging non-professionals, non-artists—people from all classes and backgrounds—to not just enjoy or consume art, but to actually make it themselves alongside the professionals. The empowering of ordinary people to tell their own stories and express their own aspirations has a distinctly political dimension, as Fox explained to me in 1985: "The aims are to release creativity. This is done through working with individuals who join in community events with us. But it's also to release creativity in society at large." Fox was worried that lip service had been paid for years to the idea of creativity, but the results were not there.

> There is the same hidden curriculum both in school and in the whole society, which does not allow people to generate their own ceremonies, to create their own art, to believe that they can create for themselves. Once people start to have control over their own lives and over their own creativity, then they will

not tolerate a repressive political or any other kind of regime which stops them doing that.

These goals are at least partly achieved by giving people permission to play, because it is often in the safety of play that people can risk revealing their deepest fears and dreams. Process thus becomes as important as product. Under these circumstances it would have been counterproductive for Welfare State to attempt conventional musical theatre. Imposing those standards on non-professionals would have closed off the risk-taking, truth-telling, and spontaneity that the group was trying to tap. New goals required new standards, and any evaluation of a Welfare State event must ask how well those goals were achieved.

Children plagiarize promiscuously from their immediate material and cultural environments, creating props, characters, and story twists from what is readily at hand. Similarly, *Longline* was a strange amalgam of seemingly incompatible styles and techniques: sand painting, clowning, magic acts, trapeze artists and acrobats, puppets of all shapes and sizes, a shadow play, fireworks, dance numbers, a community choir, pantomimes, monologues, and television animations that looked like the work of an anti-social six-year-old. The materials used to make the images, puppets, and props came, for the most part, from the garbage dump. In one deeply moving scene, a crippled, deformed puppet cow made out of plastic bleach bottles hobbled in slow motion across the stage in the aftermath of environmental devastation.

Near the middle of the second act the cosmic clowns attempted to dramatize a thunderstorm using homemade noisemakers. While it was supposed to be a serious, climactic moment, they hammed it up with that slightly over-the-top, I'm-having-a-good-time-up-here posture reminiscent of adolescent role-playing. This playful approach was also apparent in many of the other performances. After a while it did not matter that the narrator, cast from the local youth theatre group, lacked the authority of a professional. It was more appropriate in this context that a recognizably ordinary person should be the story's mouthpiece.

Children at play usually have no spectators. To watch others playing is to be excluded. Welfare State International was committed to crossing and dissolving the boundary between spectator and performer. The band and lead singers were experienced performers, but the bulk of the large cast—the community choir, teenage dancers, elementary-school kids, brass band—were all local enthusiasts working as volunteers. The benefits for those on stage were obvious, but there was another benefit as well. For those in the bleachers, the meaning was in the context. Their children, relatives, and neighbours were onstage, all contributing to this community celebration. The message said, you too, you who have no "talent," can make your own art right here in your own town.

The performers transgressed the boundaries between stage and spectator in other ways. On one occasion the clowns embroiled the audience in a dispute, dividing the room in two and getting each side to compete by making louder and louder bird sounds. On another occasion, Tyndale Thomas, a gospel singer from Manchester, taught the audience two different backup parts to a song and then, Pete Seeger–style, sang the melody over top.

Children engrossed in dramatic play shape the narrative spontaneously based on their responses to each other and the flow of their imaginations. So too was *Longline* a constantly evolving process with no fixed text. In the same way that improvising musicians use a simple repeating pattern of chords to play their riffs against, Welfare State used an elementary fall and redemption narrative as the skeleton to support the rich procession of images, songs, and performances that evolved within the various communities. The cosmic clowns and other performers were encouraged to improvise their parts based on audience response. The day after each show the company would meet and hash out yet more changes. Some of these changes were significant. For example, after opening night the performers decided to take their bows before the dramatic coda (when the audience was to gather outside the circus tent for the final send-off scene) rather than at the end of the show. "We have to separate the theatre from the ritual," Fox told me. This unconventional approach, discovered during the experience of performing in front of others, was much more effective.

■

Welfare State's experiments in process, form, and context provided an empowering, embodied, and democratic model for one kind of vernacular performance in the new century. No-one can say for sure what effect *Longline* had on those who made it or who shared in the experience from the bleachers, but one thing is certain: a lot of people in Ulverston that week did not sit watching slickly made television shows produced in the United States or spend an evening playing violent hyper-real video games or shopping at the mall. Instead they joined together in a collective storytelling ritual that connected their pasts with the rivers of the future.

During the coda on the third night, I happened to turn around at one point. We were all standing outside in a petrified forest, the moon almost completely hidden by unsettled clouds. An enormous papier-mâché vessel had just taken off into the heavens in a fiery blast of fireworks. In the quiet that followed, a delicate cradle of stars, which had been conjured up seemingly through magic at the beginning of the show, slowly descended to muddy earth. People around me were openly weeping. Several couples were holding each other in their arms. I realized I too had tears in my eyes. What were we crying about? Maybe it was because Tyndale Thomas was singing a beautiful lullaby: "The world's not upside down./Follow the plough/to the pole star held forever still." Or maybe it was because Welfare State International was coming to an end. Or were we crying because of the great distance all of us there that night had travelled from our playful, empowered, hope-filled childhood passions?

15

A VERNACULAR
MANIFESTO

■

We will never see this world again. It is gone, gone, totally
gone. We are moving into an intermediate state in which
the new world is secretly growing a body. We are in fact
pregnant. And the thing that is making us feel so strange is
morning sickness. But we must take care of the child
within, no matter how we feel. That child is tomorrow,
and we must embody it with our trust and love.

— SPIRAL GARDEN CO-FOUNDER PAUL HOGAN

When I remember back to the little boy I once was, half a
century ago—playing spaceship behind the farmhouse, barely conscious of the ominous oil refinery on the horizon, sensing the outside world through the snowy images on a television screen—I am
struck by one thing more than any other. In the following decades,
the convenient, globalized consumer society, with all its admonish-
ments, labours, and joys, has become so pervasive that, for many of
us, it is impossible to imagine anything else. There have been clear
benefits, to be sure, at least for those who can afford them, but the
consequences are severe: pollution and climate change, burgeoning
economic inequality, terrorism and religious fundamentalism, a generalized speed-up in life's pace leading to an epidemic of exhaustion,

a bunker mentality leading to an obsession with security, the fracturing of face-to-face communities.

Even when faced with the catastrophic failure of the economic system in the autumn of 2008, and the widely discussed dangers of unrestrained economic activities for the world's climate, human beings will not slow the treadmill. Indeed, we are encouraged to see economic expansion as uncontrovertibly good, and spending money as a kind of civic duty. It becomes a kind of hunger that cannot be satiated, as Thomas Homer-Dixon points out in *The Upside of Down:* "Our economic role in this culture of consumption is to be little more than walking appetites that serve the function of maintaining our economy's throughput. Our psychological state is comparable to that of drug addicts needing a fix: buying things doesn't really make us happy, except perhaps for the moment after the purchase. But we do it over and over anyway."

Homer-Dixon speculates that an often overlooked reason for this tendency is the immense power of consumerism, which "helps anesthetize us against the dread produced by empty lives—lives that modern capitalism and consumerism have themselves helped empty of meaning." People today lead lives of constant stress created by rapid technology change (and the career uncertainty that brings), economic insecurity, and the resulting fragmentation of society. "The social fabric of caring, trust, and reciprocity essential to our happiness" becomes shredded. "In place of vital connections between people that come with strong communities, families, and friendships," Homer-Dixon argues, "we substitute the transitory pleasures provided by newly bought things. We also substitute the hyper-stimulation afforded by frenetic movement in cars and planes and by a torrent of incoming information from TV, video games, and the Internet." In the process our lives and social relations become even more broken down into often-unrelated bits and pieces; we lack "the period of uninterrupted time we need for the pleasure of focused activities—for pastimes like writing, reading, dancing, gardening, playing a sport or musical instrument, or playing with our children—that bring real happiness." The chronic, basic dissatisfaction leads to us buying more and more stuff in an ever-continuing effort to distract ourselves.

But every social force generates its opposite. Chronically dissatisfied and aware of their addictions, some people actively resist and challenge the status quo. Our age is a time when notions of social and environmental justice, gender equality, aboriginal rights, direct democracy, and localism are becoming more widely accepted. As always, alternative ways of living continue to be imagined and enacted. Times of crisis, when coupled with imaginative aspirations, can often produce unanticipated outcomes. If history teaches anything it is that the present is always a surprise to the past.

Cultural activities form the necessary bridges between aspirations and lasting renewal. Any change must be imagined first. Art stimulates and exercises individual and collective inventiveness, thus promoting the experimentation and adaptation necessary for people to adjust to constantly changing conditions. For example, Harold Bloom uses the term "wisdom writing" to describe the great works of the Western canon. In addition, art acts as a powerful counter-force to the centrifugal tendencies of human groups to quarrel and splinter. It unites people by constantly representing and re-enacting community. Christopher Small shows that the organization of musical performances, for example, can act as models for how human groups work together: a jazz combo or a string quartet represents one kind of human collaboration, while a symphony orchestra with its star conductor represents another.

Yet the ways in which mainstream art and culture are organized and practised in the Western world today—as beautiful and brilliant as those efforts have been—fail to do the work necessary for our times. Modern culture—the culture of professionals and spectators, of products and consumers, of experts and ignorance, of power and powerlessness, of mass reproduction and repetition—provides little nourishment for the hunger that we all share for new wisdom in this "time of punishment and ruin." Newer and better movies, books, and operas will not help. It is the form and context of artistic works that must change, even more than their content. Radical times require radical forms and radical contexts. This is precisely where ideas about vernacular culture begin to take purchase.

What might more appropriate forms of cultural activity look like in a time of deep uncertainty? What can we do differently? Well, we might begin by turning off the television. We could stop surfing the net. We could sing while we work, dance to live music, learn how to harmonize voices, play guitar instead of listening to our iPods. We could perform our own plays instead of going to the movies. We could invent new rituals, tell each other stories from memory or imagination, mythologize our neighbourhoods and make up puppet plays about them. We could build campfires and sing songs there or tell ghost stories. We could cook meals entirely from local materials and enjoy them slowly amidst honest conversation. We could work in our gardens and then work on the gardens in the park. We could tell our children stories before bedtime every night, tell stories or recite poems to our spouses, organize a lantern procession and have each person make their own lantern. The possibilities are endless and unpredictable.

These are not naive suggestions. Vernacular culture means making your own culture instead of buying it. Homemade culture—simple, flexible, improvised—has a low impact on the environment and is a powerful antidote to consumer addictions. When people are not buying objects produced in factories and shipped thousands of kilometres by truck, or travelling great distances to attend the performance of a great virtuoso, they are reducing their carbon footprint.

Consumer culture cannot operate without social inequality. Mimetic desire and envy drive acquisitiveness and competition. The poor are needed to fill the sweatshops that manufacture the objects that the rich covet. When people stop buying their culture and start making vernacular art together, they will be resisting the tidal flow of social inequality, and other, more convivial, currents will emerge. Vernacular culture encourages and supports relationships and communities that are not based on economic interests. This quiet community-building and negotiation at the local level is of crucial importance. When people spend pleasurable, public time outside their family or immediate social group, the doors of the bunker stay open, and people are more motivated to maintain good relations with neighbours. This phenomenon has particular relevance in situations in which racism and intolerance run high. When people experience those who are different not as threatening representations on the screen or as sources of labour or income but rather in face-to-face, non-instrumental cultural encounters, they find it much more difficult to harbour stereotypical views of the Other.

If it is possible to think of artistic practices as metaphors for other kinds of human collaborations, the metaphors of the Hollywood celebrity or the televised soccer game provide different models than do nighttime storytelling or neighbourhood pageants. Celebrities and commercial sport discourage participation other than spectatorship. It is no wonder that powerful elites prefer politics to be a spectator sport and look upon the mass media as tools to mollify the electorate. In their view, low voter turnout is all for the best. In contrast, stories and pageants encourage, even demand, wide participation in decision-making.

Not all instances of vernacular culture are equally good. Some standards exist and others need to be developed to critically evaluate the aesthetic practices of non-specialists. Honesty, originality, formal coherence, craftsmanship—many are the same as those used in the evaluation of any cultural act. You still need to sing in tune. But others are less conventional. Critical responses to vernacular culture must take seriously its social context. Relationships are more important than objects. Tradition and improvisation play equally central roles. Meanings and metaphors may be opaque to those outside the community of origin but deeply resonant to those within. We can recognize a vernacular culture that works by the extent to which it is participatory and resistant to commerce.

Yes, truly miraculous things are possible when professionals dedicate their lives to, for example, composing great music or producing brilliant, wise films. And what about the joy and critical distance afforded by mindful spectatorship? The professional and the spectator remain important and necessary parts of our cultural future. They will never disappear, nor should they. Vernacular culture to the exclusion of all else is neither possible nor desirable. It is the balance between commercial culture and vernacular culture, and how gifted professionals and leaders are included, that we need to reimagine.

■

At the end of *The Wizard of Oz* (1939), Dorothy discovers that she had always possessed the ability to return home—by using the ruby slippers she was wearing on her own feet. The same might be said about remaking vernacular culture in a globalized world. The tools may be hard to see, but they are already in our hands. We can begin today. Every small decision to participate in the homemade and the local instead of buying the mass-produced and the distant is another step in the journey to restore, reinvigorate, and create anew vernacular cultures for our own times.

Cultural institutions will have to change as well. Museums, arts councils, broadcasters, and universities must respond and evolve in response to an increase in vernacular practices. Social resources will need to be committed to nourish the growth of grassroots culture. The recent emphasis on community arts within these institutions in Canada is one example of how this may already be happening.

Perhaps the most significant obstacle to a renewed vernacular culture is lack of time. Here, in the West, we are suffering a pandemic of time poverty that continues to get worse. The cure is to slow down. Why is it that so few people have the courage to do it? Much of the impetus for longer work hours comes from workers as well as employers. People maximize their incomes to pay for things that they have been told are necessary. When the deep human drive to belong and be part of something bigger is satisfied by community and the simple pleasures of sharing local culture together, people will have less need for the overtime pay that those extra working hours generate. If vernacular culture is going to flourish in the uncertain future, we will need to regain some of the time that our ancestors once enjoyed. I believe this is possible if people are willing to change their priorities. Surely, just turning off the television would free up several extra hours each day that could be spent participating in vernacular culture.

Near the very end of his life, Ivan Illich began talking about a practice that was widespread in the early Christian church at another historical moment of punishment and ruin: "*conspiratio*" ("breathing together" or "mingling spirits" in Latin). When the first followers of Christ gathered, usually clandestinely because of persecution, to share a meal as an expression of their voluntary association—woman and man, slave and citizen, farmer and prostitute—they would greet each other with a "kiss of peace." This was not a sexual touching of lips, but rather a bringing together of one face to another so that each person breathed the other's breath. It is the Latin root of the English word "conspiracy." As the official church became more institutionalized and shed its sensual and ecstatic past, this kind of intimacy was frowned upon. The practice went through several variations before the present pax, where parishioners shake hands and greet each other before communion (itself a shrunken remnant of the celebratory meal that was originally at the heart of Christian practice).

When he was asked how people could possibly live in a world full of apocalyptic despair, Illich proposed a modern *conspiratio*: a practice to be performed between people today, when they come together, as an antidote to the planned, disconnected, rushed, atomized, monetized world we cannot escape—a simple gesture of embodied hope and faith. Taking his lead, I advocate here for a "conspiracy of the vernacular," a breathing together such that the crushing addictions and profitable bowdlerizing of commercial culture and its objects are pushed aside in favour of conviviality, hospitality, and imagination: not because it serves some purpose, but simply because our hearts tell us that it is beautiful and good.

ACKNOWLEDGEMENTS

The seeds for this book were first sown in a second-year social anthropology class taught by Richard Lee at the University of Toronto. They were watered by my friendship with Peter Harcourt, who taught me, among other things, that original ideas are worth having. I owe a special debt of gratitude to Peter for all those long, intense talks about art and culture that continue to this day.

When I began working as a preschool teacher I was extremely fortunate to meet Pasia Schonberg. She introduced me to Hélène Comay and Dorothy Medhurst, two of the most generous and tolerant mentors I have ever met. Pasia, Hélène, and Dorothy taught me how to foster the creativity of young children and introduced me to the writings of Herbert Read, John Holt, and Ivan Illich. Around the same time I discovered the joys of collective music-making at the Woods Music and Dance Camp and learned the politics and pleasures of contra dancing from Lanie Melamed.

An Explorations Grant from the Canada Council for the Arts in 1985 gave me the encouragement I needed to start researching the idea of vernacular culture. I bought a professional tape recorder and travelled to Britain and the United States to interview artists and thinkers. These interviews became the basis of much of the work I would undertake in the years to follow. I am deeply grateful to all of the original interviewees for their openness to the as-yet-unformed ideas of a young questioner. In Britain I spoke with Raymond Williams, Christopher Small, Ken Worpole, John Fox, Sue Gill, and Frankie Armstrong. In New York I interviewed Joel Kovel, Dee Dee Halleck, and Stanley Diamond. When I got back to Canada I recorded conversations with Susan Crean, Ron Grimes, Paul Hogan, Jan Mackie, and R. Murray Schafer. I visited Pete Seeger in his hotel room on the morning following one of his concerts in Toronto.

In the early 1990s I gathered together a group of brave souls to produce an experimental, collaborative film about vernacular culture called *Dance on the Edge* (1995). Greg Artzner, Cat Cayuga, Terry Leonino, Chris Miner, Peter Oliver, Itah Sadu, Lib Spry, and Wayne Westfall took on the project with imagination and unfailing good humour. I will be forever thankful for the friendships forged and for what I learned from that experience.

Through the continuing financial support of the Canada Council and Queen's University, I was able to produce the website *Memory Palace: Vernacular Culture in the Digital Age* (1997) and travel to Mexico to make the documentary *Disrobing the Emperor* (2000). Neither of these projects would have been possible without the quiet dedication and hard work of webmaster and video editor Peter Cassidy. It was in Mexico that I befriended Gustavo Esteva, who helped me to see the cultures of the poor and the marginalized with new eyes. Thanks also go to the extraordinary people Gustavo introduced me to: Maria Castanon, Fernando Enciso Diaz, Oliver Froehling, Mojdeh Hojjati, Daniel Manrique, Carlos Plascencia,

Teresa Rodrigues, and two generations of the Sandoval family.

Radio producer David Cayley and his partner Jutta Mason share with me a common interest in vernacular culture. I am indebted to them for their encouragement and friendship—and the many, many hours of conversations we've had over the years. It was in the Cayley-Mason living room that I spoke with Ivan Illich in person. Jutta's role in reimagining her local park is one of the stories this book tells.

The ideas in these chapters were debated and refined in the Culture and Technology class I taught at Queen's University from 1999 to 2006. The contribution of those undergraduate students to this book cannot be underestimated.

Portions of chapter 9 were published in a different form in *Pic Press*, June 2000; portions of chaper 14 were published in a different form in alt.theatre, February 2007.

I am fortunate to work at a university and in a department that strongly support original thinking and creative work. I have received grants from Queen's University Fund for the Support of Artistic Production on several occasions. Without the sabbaticals that a university position affords I could not have found the time to do the writing. Thank you to all my colleagues at Queen's Film and Media: Blaine Allan, Peter Baxter, Frank Burke, Gary Kibbins, Reena Kukreja, Frances Leeming, Susan Lord, Sidney Eve Matrix, Dorit Naaman, and Derek Redmond. Special thanks to Linda Graham, whose steadfastness and good humour make our work possible. I also want to acknowledge the wisdom and friendship of many others at the university, including Julie Salverson and Ted Rettig, with whom I have also discussed these ideas. Creative courage is an outstanding feature of the interdisciplinary course called Contemporary Cultural Performance, which I co-teach with Kathleen Sellars, Kim Renders, and Matt Rogalsky.

Early versions of this manuscript were read by Kelley Aiken, David Cayley, John Fox, Peter Harcourt, Ruth Howard, and Jamie Swift. Their honest, thoughtful suggestions, along with those from two anonymous readers at Between the Lines, made this book much better.

Many thanks too for the wisdom and hard work of the editorial board and staff at Between the Lines press, including Amanda Crocker, Paula Brill, and Jennifer Tiberio. Robert Clarke deserves special mention. He edited the manuscript once near the beginning and again at the end. Always precise, critical, and diplomatic, he is the best editor any writer can dream of.

Long-time friends who helped shape this book in more ways than they understand include Shelly and Coleman Romalis, Ricardo and Chris Sternberg, Babs Church, and Becky Schechter. My family, the extended Mackey clan, modelled the curiosity and confidence to non-conform that have sustained me over the years. Elaine, Daniel, and Annie, my immediate family, have taught me more about vernacular culture than anyone else. Without them, none of this would make sense.

Clarke Mackey,
Kingston, Ontario, April 2010

NOTES

1   **"As a twelve-year old":** Quotation on the wall of the Picasso Museum in Barcelona; allegedly said by Picasso in 1956 in a school classroom. See http://www.arthistoryarchive.com/arthistory/cubism/Pablo-Picasso. html.

1   **Studies show:** Gene D. Cohen, "Research on Creativity and Aging: The Positive Impact of the Arts on Health and Illness," *Generations*, 30,1 (2006), pp.7–15, copyright American Society on Aging.

9–10   **etymology of words for art and culture:** All of these references come from Raymond Williams, *Keywords*, rev. ed. (Oxford: Oxford University Press, 1983). The view that there are no words for art in non-Western languages is widely held. For an interesting discussion of the idea, see Mineke Schipper, "Beauty in Context: Towards an Anthropological Approach to Aesthetics by Wilfried van Damme (review)," *Research in African Literatures*, 31,4 (2000), pp.168–72.

11   **definition of "vernacular":** Ivan Illich, *Shadow Work* (London: Boyars, 1981), p.24.

12   **We have entered a period:** John Howard Kunstler, *The Long Emergency* (New York: Grove Press, 2006); and Nicholas Stern, *The Economics of Climate Change* (Cambridge: Cambridge University Press, 2007).

13 **"It is not a question of going back"**: R. Murray Schafer, interview with the author, 1985.

CHAPTER 2 – BEDTIME STORIES

19 **Gould revising Mozart:** Peter F. Ostwald, *Glenn Gould: The Ecstasy and Tragedy of Genius* (New York: Norton, 1998), pp.166, 249, and "Of Mozart and Related Matters: Glenn Gould in Conversation with Bruno Monsaingeon," *Piano Quarterly*, Fall 1976; reprinted in *Page* (1990), p.33. For a brief summary, see http://www.classicalnotes.net/columns/gould.html.

19–20 **oral storytelling:** Albert Lord, *Singer of Tales* (Boston: Harvard University Press, 1981), pp.27–28.

CHAPTER 3 – SNAPSHOTS FROM THE EDGE

25 **"It's insane to imagine"**: Jutta Mason, interview with the author, 1998.

25 **cradled in the buying and selling:** This idea is discussed by Nicholas Bourriaud, *Relational Aesthetics* (1998). His comments are quoted in Darren O'Donnell, *Social Acupuncture: A Guide to Suicide, Performance and Utopia* (Toronto: Coach House Books, 2006), pp.28–29.

26–27 **hopscotch in Ottawa:** Tony Lofaro, "Anti-Graffiti Squad Erases Children's Fun," *Ottawa Citizen*, May 5, 2007.

28 **"A day of sunshine"**: Quoted in Richard Lloyd, "Happiness Is Just a Riverside Shack for Designer Homeless," *The Times*, June 11, 2005, http://www.timesonline.co.uk/tol/news/world/article532080.ece. See also Kyohei Sakaguchi, *Zero Yen House* (Japan: Little More, 2004), architecture, http://www.oyenhouse.com/en/Zero_Yen_House/.

28–29 **"I don't want to idealize"** and **"These homes embody simplicity"**: Quoted in Lloyd Alter, "Housing Built by Japanese Homeless as Art Form," March 18, 2006, http://www.treehugger.com/files/2006/03/post_25.php#recent.

29 **"It sometimes gets cold"**: Quoted in Hiroko Tabuchi, "Structure with a Zen View," *Globe and Mail*, March 18, 2006.

30 **"collaborative process"**: Jan MacKie et al., "Foreword," *Spiral Garden Resource Book* (Toronto: Bloorview MacMillan Children's Centre, 2002).

30–31 **mythopoetics of one summer's epic:** Ibid., pp.98–99.

31 **"a reaction to consumerism"**: Jan MacKie, interview with the author, 1997.

32–34 **inventing new rites:** Ron Grimes, interview with the author, 1985.

35–38 **stories of Dufferin Grove Park:** Jutta Mason, *Cooking with Fire in Public*, 2001, http://www.dufferinpark.ca/research/pdf/CookingFireinPublicSpace.pdf, pp.2, 26–27. By late spring 2010, municipal government bureaucrats had limited or banned many of the volunteer activities in Dufferin Grove Park, saying they violate city policies.

38–40 **graffiti politics:** This story is a summary of a radio documentary produced by Elizabeth Grey, "Finding Alpha," CBC, Radio One, May 22, 2005. All quotations are from this program, http://www.cbc.ca/thesundayedition/features/alpha.html.

40 **Yves Laroche Gallery:** Joshua Knelman, "Graffiti Goes Six-Figure Legit," *Globe and Mail*, Aug. 4, 2007.

CHAPTER 4 – THE VERNACULAR OCEAN

43 **"The historian's home":** Ivan Illich and Barry Sanders, *ABC: The Alphabetization of the Popular Mind* (New York: Vintage Books, 1988), p.3.

43–44 **Shanidar Cave discoveries:** Richard E. Leakey and Roger Lewin, *Origins* (New York: E.P. Dutton, 1977), p.125.

44 **At least one novel:** Jean M. Auel, *Clan of the Cave Bear* (New York: Bantam, 1984).

43–44 **Persian jird explanation:** Jeffrey D. Sommer, "The Shanidar IV 'Flower Burial': A Re-evaluation of Neanderthal Burial Ritual," *Cambridge Archaeological Journal*, 9,1 (1999), pp.127–29.

46 **"Where every man is enemy":** Thomas Hobbes, *Leviathan*, (1973 [1651]).

46 **"noble savage":** Quoted in Peter Gay, *The Basic Political Writings of Jean Jacques Rousseau* (Indianapolis, Ind.: Hackett Press, 1987), p.25.

46–47 **Wright provides archeological evidence:** Ronald Wright, *A Short History of Progress* (Toronto: House of Anansi, 2004), pp.25, 37, 39.

47–48 **Rousseau's arguments get fresh treatment:** Hugh Brody, *The Other Side of Eden: Hunters, Farmers and the Shaping of the World* (Vancouver: Douglas and McIntyre, 2000), pp.117, 118, 155.

49 **an exchange of newborns:** A different version of this idea is in Wright, *Short History of Progress*, p.21.

CHAPTER 5 – FORAGING FUNDAMENTALS

51 **"Beyond the story of the lineages":** Brody, *Other Side of Eden*, p.115.

51–53 **Social anthropologist Richard Lee:** All quotations are from Richard

NOTES

Borshay Lee, "Eating Christmas in the Kalahari," reprinted in James P. Spradley and David W. McCurty, *Conformity and Conflict: Readings in Cultural Anthropology* (Boston: Little Brown and Co., 1971), pp.7–14.

53 **"Aggressively egalitarian":** Quoted in John M. Gowdy, *Coevolutionary Economics: The Economy, Society and the Environment* (New York: Springer, 1994), p.40, referring to a famous article by James Woodburn: "Egalitarian Societies," in *Man*, 17 (1982), p.434.

53–54 **hunter-gatherer studies:** Most of the examples cited come from research done on the !Kung over several decades. Because I studied anthropology with Richard Lee in the 1970s at the University of Toronto, these are the examples I am most familiar with. But research confirms that similar patterns exist in many other forager groups. A good relatively recent survey of the literature is *The Cambridge Encyclopedia of Hunters and Gatherers* (London: Cambridge University Press, 1999).

54 **"the original affluent society":** Marshall Sahlins, "The Original Affluent Society" (1968), in *Stone Age Economics* (London: Tavistock Publications, 1972).

54 **hunter-gatherers refuse agriculture:** Jared Diamond, *Guns, Germs, and Steel: The Fates of Human Societies* (New York: W.W. Norton, 1997), p.105.

55 **"Separation and loneliness":** Lorna Marshall, "Sharing, Talking, and Giving: Relief from Social Tensions among the !Kung," originally published 1976, in John Gowdy, ed., *Limited Wants, Unlimited Means: A Reader on Hunter-Gatherer Economics and the Environment* (Washington, D.C.: Island Press,1998), pp.65–66.

55–56 **"The term 'egalitarian'":** Diamond, *Guns, Germs, and Steel*, p.269.

56 **"In group discussions":** Lee is quoted in James Woodburn, "Egalitarian Societies," reprinted in Gowdy, ed., *Limited Wants, Unlimited Means*, p.103.

57 **Father Paul Le Jeune's report:** Quoted in Eleanor Leacock, "Woman's Status in Egalitarian Society: Implications for Social Evolution," in Gowdy, ed., *Limited Wants, Unlimited Means*, p.145. For a good survey of the literature on gender relations, see Karen L. Endicott, "Gender Relations in Hunter-Gatherer Societies," in *Cambridge Encyclopedia of Hunters and Gatherers*.

57 **"An Indian gift":** Quoted in Lewis Hyde, *The Gift: Imagination and the Erotic Life of Property* (New York: Vintage Books, 1983), p.3.

58–59 **sharing and gifts:** Marshall, "Sharing, Talking, and Giving," p.80.

59 **Police, armies, and wars:** For a contrary view of this position, see Wright, *Short History of Progress*, chs. 1, 2.

RANDOM ACTS OF CULTURE

59 **"a radically alternative mode"**: Quoted in Gowdy, *Limited Wants, Unlimited Means*, p.181.

60–61 **Marshall describes the art**: The three quotations are from Marshall, "Sharing, Talking, and Giving," pp.65–84.

61 **"In oral culture"**: Brody, *Other Side of Eden*, p.207.

61 **"The !Kung say that a song composed"**: Marshall, "Sharing, Talking, and Giving," p.66.

62 **"Though there is a keen enthusiasm"**: Megan Biesele, "Aspects of !Kung Folklore," in Richard B. Lee and Irven DeVore, *Kalahari Hunter-Gatherers: Studies of the !Kung San and Their Neighbors* (Cambridge, Mass.: Harvard University Press, 1976), p.308.

62 **"Nature is pervasively animated"**: Mathias Guenther, "From Totemism and Shamanism: Hunter-Gatherer Contributions to World Mythology and Spirituality," in *Cambridge Encyclopedia of Hunters and Gatherers*, p.426.

63 **"The entire village comes"**: Richard Katz, "Education for Transcendence: !Kia Healing with the Kalahari !Kung," in Lee and DeVore, *Kalahari Hunter-Gatherers*, p.286.

63 **"Shamanism prepares the brain"**: Brody, *Other Side of Eden*, p.247.

64 **"thick description"**: Clifford Geertz, "Thick Description: Toward an Interpretive Theory of Culture," in *The Interpretation of Cultures: Selected Essays* (New York: Basic Books, 1973), pp.3–30.

64 **sympathetic biographer**: Roy Richard Grinker, *In the Arms of Africa: The Life of Colin Turnbull* (Chicago: University Of Chicago Press, 2001).

64–69 **description of the molimo**: Colin Turnbull, *The Forest People: A Study of the Pygmies of the Congo* (New York: Simon and Schuster, 1961), pp.87–88, 150–54.

CHAPTER 6 – THE FOLK AND THEIR OBSERVERS

71 **"Popular culture is one of history's losers"**: Robert Muchembled, *Popular Culture and Elite Culture in France 1400–1750*, trans. Lydia Cochrane (Baton Rouge: Louisiana State University Press, 1978–1985), p.1.

73 **that is what a small army of historians**: The new historians of everyday life include Peter Burke, Natalie Zemon Davis, Robert Muchembled, Philippe Ariès, and several others.

74–77 **Huron feasts and rituals**: All quotations are from Allan Greer, ed., *The Jesuit Relations: Natives and Missionaries in Seventeenth-Century North America* (Boston: Bedford/St. Martin's, 2000), pp.49, 30 (emphasis added), 63, 66–68.

77 **"The neolithic saw no particular improvement"**: Sahlins, *Affluent Society*, p.35.

78–79 **"When the world was half a thousand years younger"**: Johan Huizinga, *The Autumn of the Middle Ages*, trans. Rodney J. Payton and Ulrich Mammitzsch (Chicago: University of Chicago Press, 1996 [1919]), p.1.

79 **"You really *are* San Andrés de Chichauxtla"**: Quoted in Clarke Mackey, *Disrobing the Emperor: The New Commons in Mexico*, video, 2000.

80 **"the raw into the cooked"**: *The Raw and the Cooked* is the title of a volume from *Mythologiques I-IV* written by French anthropologist Claude Lévi-Strauss; *Le Cru et le cuit* in French. "Cuit" can also denote "done," which is not necessarily obtained by cooking. Strauss's use of *cuit* implies what culture and society do to nature to make it "done" or "cooked."

80 **a myth about "witches"**: There has been considerable controversy among historians about the facts of European witchcraft and "wise women." Useful books on this subject include Barbara Ehrenreich and Deirdre English, *For Her Own Good: 150 years of the Experts' Advice to Women* (New York: Anchor Books, 1979), ch.2; and Leonard Shlain, *The Alphabet Versus the Goddess: The Conflict between Word and Image* (New York: Penguin, 1999), pp.364–77; and Muchembled, *Popular Culture and Elite Culture*.

80 **medieval European festivals:** Described in Muchembled, *Popular Culture and Elite Culture*, pp.92–93.

80–81 **carnival:** Academic interest in carnival rituals probably begins with Mikhail Bakhtin, *Rabelais and His World* (Boston: MIT Press, 1968). See also Peter Burke, *Popular Culture in Early Modern Europe* (New York: New York University Press, 1978).

81 **"misrule"**: Burke, *Popular Culture*, p.183.

81 **"these dense time cycles"**: Muchembled, *Popular Culture and Elite Culture*, pp.58–59.

81 **"where they spend the night in pastimes"**: Philip Stubbs, "Anatomy of Abuses," a Puritan tract from the seventeenth century, quoted in Christopher Rawlence, ed., *About Time* (London: Jonathan Cape, 1985), p.68.

81 **potential for societal change:** Muchembled, *Popular Culture and Elite Culture*, p.60.

81–82 **"Their more or less regular occurrence"**: Ibid., pp.58–59.

82–83 **Brothers Grimm and middle-class women:** Jack Ziples, *When Dreams Came True: Classical Fairy Tales and Their Tradition* (London: Routledge, 1998), pp.69–70.

83–84 **"I was able to obtain"**: Quoted in "An Introduction to the Collection," *The Milman Parry Collection*, Harvard University, http://chs119.harvard.edu/mpc/about/intro.html.

84 **"Was Zogic lying to us?"**: Lord, *Singer of Tales*, p.28, emphasis added.

85 **"Without telling Avdo"**: Ibid., p.78.

86 **"The individual may invent"**: Burke, *Popular Culture*, p.115.

87–88 **John Berger, in his collection of stories**: John Berger, *Pig Earth* (New York: Pantheon Books, 1979), pp.8–9, emphases in the original.

CHAPTER 7 – THE POSTMAN AND THE TILE SETTER

89 **"To the peasant"**: John Berger, "The Ideal Palace," in *Keeping a Rendezvous* (New York: Pantheon Books, 1991), pp.83–91.

90 **"What can a man do"**: Cheval's autobiography is translated and quoted in Berger, "Ideal Palace," pp.83–85.

91 **"1906, I am the faithful companion"**: Quoted in an Ideal Palace tourist pamphlet.

92 **"Here I wanted to sleep"**: Berger, "Ideal Palace."

92 **"architect of the useless"**: Ibid.

92 **"I would be the first to agree"**: Quoted in Jeremy Josephs, "The Postman's Palace," http://www.jeremyjosephs.com/postmanspalace.htm.

92 **"uncontested master"**: Ibid.

93–95 **Simon Rodia**: Much of the information about Rodia's life comes from Donald O'Donovan "Simon Rodia, Architect of Dreams," Feb. 11, 2007, http://www.associatedcontent.com/article/139761/simon_rodia_archi tect_of_dreams.html?cat=38; and from "History of the Towers," (no longer available).

95–97 **"The category of the professional artist"**: John Berger, "The Primitive and the Professional" (1976), in *About Looking* (New York: Pantheon, 1980), pp.64–65.

98 **"not as a depository"**: Ibid., p.68.

98 **"The Palace is about the experience"**: Berger, "Ideal Palace," p.86.

99 **"The elongated, arched buttresses"**: Kenneth Scambray, "The Watts Towers," *Accenti Online Magazine*, July 2008, http://www.accenti.ca/news_ item.asp?news_id=11_7. (For complete documentation of sources used in this essay, see "Creative Responses to the Italian Immigrant Experience in California: Baldassare Forestiere's Underground Gardens and Simon Rodia's Watts Towers," *The Italian American Review*, Autumn/Winter 2001, pp.113–40. A shorter version of this article appeared in *The Land Beyond: Italian Migrants in the Westward Movement*, ed. Gloria Ricci Lothrop (San Marino, Ca.: Patrons of Italian Culture, 2007).

99 **"a correct or ideal relationship":** *Canadian Oxford Dictionary* (Toronto: Oxford University Press, 1998).

100 **"the edge of history":** William Irwin Thompson, *At the Edge of History: Speculations in the Transformation of Culture* (New York: Harper, 1971).

101 **Rodia was vocal in his criticism:** "History of the Towers," KCET, Life and Times Tonight.

CHAPTER 8 – SOCIAL MAJORITIES AND SOCIAL MINORITIES

103 **"The computer has become the storehouse":** Berger, "Ideal Palace," p.90.

104 **"the true, the good, and the inevitable":** Arjun Appadurai, *Modernity at Large: Cultural Dimensions of Globalization* (Minneapolis: University of Minnesota Press, 1996), p.11.

104 **population figures:** My statistics for population and inequality come from a number of sources, but mostly from the United Nations Population Division, World Population Prospects: The 2002 Revision Population Database, http://esa.un.org/unpp, accessed in 2005; and UNESCO Institute for Statistics (UIS), Literacy and Non-Formal Education Section, July 2004, http://stats.uis.unesco.org/unesco/.

105 **what, if anything, they have gained from the modern experiment:** This comment comes out of discussions over several years with Gustavo Esteva.

105 **For these "marginals":** My understanding of the roots of the Rwandan genocide comes from the documentary film based on General Romeo Dallaire's book: Peter Raymont, director, *Shake Hands with the Devil* (90 min., 2005).

106–7 **"new resources and disciplines for the construction":** Appadurai, *Modernity at Large*, pp.3–4.

108–10 **Estava tried to explain this choice:** Gustavo Esteva, interview in Oaxaca with the author, 1998.

110 **"non-subjects":** Yvonne Dion-Buffalo and John Mohawk, quoted in Gustavo Esteva and Madhu Suri Prakash, *Grassroots Post-Modernism: Remaking the Soil of Cultures* (London: Zed Books, 1998), p.45.

110 **"disrobing the emperor":** the title of the video I made based on Esteva and Prakash, *Grassroots Post-Modernism*.

110 **Salt Satyagraha: A** good summary of Gandhi's salt march can be found at *Wikipedia*, http://en.wikipedia.org/wiki/Salt_Satyagraha.

111 **"The individual self is cut out"**: Esteva and Prakash, *Grassroots Post-Modernism*, pp.68–69.

111–12 **"There are two irreconcilably different ways"**: Ibid., p.71.

113 **"The books were all very acceptable"**: Quoted in Christopher Small, *Music of the Common Tongue: Survival and Celebration in African American Music* (Hanover, N.H.: Wesleyan University Press, 1998), p.83.

114 **"deep melodious organ-like music"**: Quoted in Small, *Music of the Common Tongue*, p.89.

114–15 **"Here ought to be considered, too"**: Quoted in ibid., p.89.

115 **"centres of resistance"**: Ibid., p.100.

116 **"The slaves' problem"**: Ibid., pp.85–86.

116 **"depended neither on written sources"**: Ibid., p.81.

117 **"improvised hymnody"**: Ibid., p.90.

117–18 **"There is no singing in *parts*"**: Quoted in ibid., p.91.

118 **"work songs, songs of praise"**: Ibid., p.97.

121–22 **Small posits that this kind of music**: Christopher Small, interview with the author, 1985.

CHAPTER 9 – POSTMODERN SQUATTERS IN THE FOURTH WORLD

123 **Fourth World:** refers to marginal, stateless societies living outside the modern industrial norm. The term has been used extensively by Manuel Castells, especially in *End of Millennium: The Information Age: Economy, Society and Culture*, vol. 3 (Oxford: Blackwell, 1998).

126 **the Spaniards had "arrived with the cross":** Unless otherwise indicated, the quotations in this chapter are from Mackey, *Disrobing the Emperor*, which was shot in 1998.

129 **"Everything has been done, literally":** Esteva and Prakash, *Grassroots Post-Modernism*, p.83.

CHAPTER 10 – LITERACY AND ITS DISCONTENTS

135 **"cured and perfect of their limbs":** "To the Great Variety of Readers," Introduction to the First Folio (1623).

136 **doubts about authorship:** see The Shakespeare Authorship Coalition website: http://www.doubtaboutwill.org/declaration (2009); and H. Trosman, "Freud and the Controversy over Shakespearean Authorship," *Journal*

of the American Psychoanalytic Association, 13 (1965), pp.475–98.

136 **"island of writing":** Illich and Sanders, *ABC*, p.3.

137 **"primary orality":** Walter J. Ong, *Orality and Literacy: The Technologizing of the Word* (New York: Methuen, 1982), p.11.

137 **systematic thought:** Illich and Sanders, *ABC*, p.84. "Only when I have gotten used to thinking as the silent tracing of words on the parchment of my memory, can I detach thought from speech and contra-dict it. A full blown lie presupposes a self that thinks before it says what it has thought."

138 **The alphabet was only invented once:** Diamond, *Guns, Germs, and Steel*, p.226. "Alphabets apparently arose only once in human history among speakers of Semitic languages in the area from modern Syria to the Sinai, around 1700 B.C. All of the hundreds of historical and now existing alphabets were ultimately derived from that ancestral Semitic alphabet."

138 **Some of the letters represented sounds:** Ibid., p.227.

140 **Plato made the statement that he would never use the written word:** Plato, *The Seventh Letter*, http://classics.mit.edu/Plato/seventh_letter.html.

140–41 **Socrates and literacy:** Plato, *Phaedrus*, http://classics.mit.edu/Plato/phaedrus.html. Well analyzed by Ong, *Orality and Literacy*, pp.78–79.

142 **a lack of social graces:** For example, see Lynne Truss, *Talk to the Hand: The Utter Bloody Rudeness of the World Today, or Six Good Reasons to Stay Home and Bolt the Door* (New York: Gotham Books, 2005).

143 **ambivalent about the benefits of this kind of schooling:** See, for example, Ivan Illich, *Deschooling Society* (New York: Harper and Row, 1971); and Madhu Suri Prakash and Gustavo Esteva, *Escaping Education: Living as Learning within Grassroots Cultures* (New York: Peter Lang Publishing, 2005).

143 **The history of copyright:** For a good introduction, see Lawrence Lessig, *The Future of Ideas: The Fate of the Commons in a Connected World* (New York: Random House, 2001).

143 **Rosa Parks and OutKast:** "Rosa Parks Settles Suit over Outkast CD," CNN.com, April 15, 2005, http://www.cnn.com/2005/SHOWBIZ/Music/04/15/parks.settlement/index.html.

145–50 **Elio Antonio de Nebrija:** All quotations are from Ivan Illich, "Vernacular Values," in *Shadow Work*, pp.29–51.

148 **Historians estimate:** The numbers come from Illich, "Vernacular Values," p.41. Elizabeth Eisenstein is more equivocal, but agrees with the basic description of the spread of early vernacular works presented here. Elizabeth Eisenstein, *The Printing Press as an Agent of Change* (Cambridge: Cambridge University Press, 1983).

153 **"When personality entered the public realm":** Richard Sennett, *The Fall of Public Man: On the Social Psychology of Capitalism* (New York: Vintage Books, 1976), p.195.

154 **discipline as wide and harsh:** Ancient slavery and early industrial servitude are different from each other in significant ways; nonetheless, there are profound limitations on personal freedom in both instances. Some household slaves in Greek and Roman times may have had considerably more freedom than a British factory worker in the nineteenth century.

154 **sweatshop discipline is still common:** Naomi Klein, *No Logo: Taking Aim at the Brand Bullies* (Toronto: Alfred A. Knopf, 2000).

154 **refashioned in the image of the factory:** R. Murray Schafer, in *The Tuning of the World* (Toronto: McClelland and Stewart, 1976), pp.108–9, quotes Lewis Mumford, who makes parallels between the symphony orchestra and the factory: they both originated at around the same time, they both require obedient workers (musicians) and a foreman (the conductor), and they are both deafeningly loud.

155 **"There is no sharp distinction":** Burke, *Popular Culture*, p.182.   **261**

156 **He arrived in London:** Samuel Johnson, in the eighteenth century, is another example.

157 **"Of all things, banish the egoism":** from Lord Chesterfield, *Letters* (London: Dent-Dutton, 1969 [1774]), quoted in Sennett, *Fall of Public Man*, p.63.

158 **fertile and passionate public sphere:** see Sennett, *Fall of Public Man*, p.87.

158 **fragile, delicate balance:** Neil Postman makes a similar argument in *Building a Bridge to the 18th Century: How the Past Can Improve Our Future* (New York: Alfred A. Knopf, 2000).

158 **"action at a distance from the self":** Sennett, *Fall of Public Man*, p.87.

158 **"The modes of public and private expression":** Ibid., p.98.

158 **participatory games and pastimes:** Philippe Ariès, *Centuries of Childhood: A Social History of Family Life* (New York: Vintage Books, 1962), pp.62–99.

159 **"rehearsals for collective political action":** Richard Butsch, *The Making of American Audiences: From Stage to Television, 1750–1990* (Cambridge: Cambridge University Press, 2000), p.12.

159 **Arouch was performing:** The story comes from historian Paul d'Estree in 1913 and is repeated in James H. Johnson, *Listening in Paris: A Cultural*

History (Berkeley: University of California Press, 1995), p.116.

160 **"In reducing the distance"**: Johnson, *Listening in Paris*, p.121.

160 **professional theatre companies travelled**: See Stephen Greenblatt, *Will in the World: How Shakespeare Became Shakespeare* (New York: W.W. Norton & Company, 2004).

160 **"asserted their rights to judge"**: Butsch, *Making of American Audiences*, p.4.

161 **"The separation between audience and performance"**: Ibid., p.8.

162 **"as a place to chat"**: Ibid., p.4.

162 **The plebeians in the pit**: Ibid., pp.3–4 and whole chapter.

162 **Steady waves of applause**: This comes mostly from Sennett, *Fall of Public Man*, and Johnson, *Listening in Paris*, and their interpretation of primary sources.

162–63 **Plays were intentionally written**: Butsch, *Making of American Audiences*, p.8.

163 **"pointing"** and **"settling"**: described in Sennett, *Fall of Public Man*, p.75.

164 **"a community of peers"**: Butsch, *Making of American Audiences*, p.10.

164 **Audience riots**: Ibid., p.6.

165 **"museums of nature"**: Sennett, *Fall of Public Man*, p.55.

165 **"These squares were not designed"**: Ibid., p.54.

166–67 **"Obscure as the beginnings of local markets are"**: Karl Polanyi, *The Great Transformation: The Political and Economic Origins of Our Times* (Boston: Beacon Press, 1944), pp.57–63.

167 **haggle over the price**: Sennett, *Fall of Public Man*, p.142.

168 **In Boucicaut's store the shopper was transformed**: This is Sennett's analysis. For a different view, see Andrew Lees and Lynn Hollen Lees, *Cities and the Making of Modern Europe 1750–1914* (Cambridge: Cambridge University Press, 2007), pp.225–26. The authors argue that the "retail revolution" promoted cultural democratization, feminized the public sphere, provided jobs for women, and thus contributed to women's emancipation from the home.

168 **Marketers increased demand**: Stuart Ewan, *Captains of Consciousness: Advertising and the Social Roots of the Consumer Culture* (New York: Basic Books, 1976).

168 **These in-store displays**: Sennett, *Fall of Public Man*, p.144.

168 **"commodity fetishism"**: Karl Marx, *Capital* (1887), chapter 1, section 4.

169 **"In order to see what is new"**: Charles Taylor, *The Malaise of Modernity* (Toronto: House of Anansi Press, 1991), p.26.

169 **"As the gods are demystified"**: Sennett, *Fall of Public Man*, p.151.

169 **"domain of appearances"**: Ibid., p.59.

170 **"To know one must impose"**: Ibid., p.153.

170 **"silent observation"**: Ibid., p.123.

170 **"Today, a person trying not to feel"**: Ibid., pp.173–74.

171 **People were ridiculed**: Butsch, *Making of American Audiences*, p.9.

171–72 **"could control its feelings through silence"**: Sennett, *Fall of Public Man*, p.206.

172 **nineteenth-century audiences applauded for longer**: Ibid., p.208. "In the 1750s, when an actor turned to the audience to make a point, a sentence or even a word could bring immediate boos or applause. Similarly, in the 18th Century opera, a particular phrase or high note beautifully performed could rouse the audience to demand that the little phrase be immediately sung again; the text was interrupted and the high note hit once, twice, or more. By 1870, the applause had acquired a new form. One did not interrupt actors in the middle of a scene but held back until the end to applaud. One did not applaud the singer until the end of the aria, not at the concert between movements of a symphony. Thus, even as the Romantic performer transcended his text, the behavior of audiences was moving in the opposite direction."

172 **A history of applause**: See Alex Ross, "Applause: The Rest Is Noise," for a good summary, http://www.therestisnoise.com/2005/02/applause_a_rest.html.

172 **"an advertisment for consumption"**: Johnson, *Listening in Paris*, p.236.

173 **entertainment critics achieved commercial influence**: This is partly my own conjecture, but Johnson, *Listening in Paris* (p.248), hints at the rise of critics and Sennett, *Fall of Public Man* (p.209), comments on audience insecurity: "The public was losing faith in its own capacity to judge."

173 **the reaction of Paris audiences to Beethoven's music**: Johnson, *Listening in Paris*, pp.257–58.

173 **"fairies who flutter"**: Quoted in Ibid., p.275.

174 **The central point of these musical stories**: Ibid., pp.273–75.

174 **"the acceptance of harmony"** and **"Socially, it made the hall**: Ibid., p.208.

174–75 **members of the orchestra were required to play precisely**: See my earlier note (p.144) about the symphony orchestra and the factory.

176 **the word "genius"**: Williams, *Keywords*, p.142.

176 **the violinist Niccolò Paganini**: Johnson, *Listening in Paris*, p.266; and Sennett, *Fall of Public Man*, pp.200–2.

177 **statistics for the size of audiences . . . in Vienna:** Sennett, *Fall of Public Man*, p.206.

178 **the agent of dependence in art:** Ibid., p.218.

CHAPTER 12 – PETE'S PROPOSAL

179 **"Us folksingin' types":** Quoted in liner notes, *Where Have All the Flowers Gone: The Songs of Pete Seeger*, Appleseed Recordings, 1998.

181 **"His influence among the young":** Studs Turkel, "Pete Seeger: Ain't No One Like Him," *The Nation*, May 16, 2005, http://www.thenation.com/doc/20050516/terkel.

181–82 **"They made a big mistake":** Quoted in liner notes, *Pete Seeger Singalong*, Smithsonian Folkways, 1991 (recorded 1980).

182 **"arguably the most influential folk artist":** Kennedy Center website, http://www.kennedy-center.org/calendar/index.cfm?fuseaction=showIndividual&entitY_id=3798&source_type=A.

182 **"his humanistic and artistic work":** Quoted on the Pete Seeger appreciation page, http://www.peteseeger.net/.

182 **musicians jamming "kitchen style":** liner notes, Bruce Springsteen, *We Shall Overcome: The Seeger Sessions*, Columbia, 2006.

184 **"My father was the one":** Quoted in David King Dunaway, *How Can I Keep from Singing: Pete Seeger* (New York: McGraw Hill, 1981), p.39.

185 **"That guy Seeger":** Quoted in Ibid., p.65.

186 **"Pete went underground":** Quoted in Ibid., p.158.

186–87 **"I'd call up the local TV"** and **"The concert was like none I've ever seen":** Ibid., p.159.

187 **"Before my voice, memory, and sense of rhythm":** liner notes, *Pete Seeger Singalong*.

188 **"everyone's nose being buried":** This and other quotations, unless otherwise noted, come from the *Pete Seeger Singalong* liner notes.

190 **"Some critics sneer":** Pete Seeger, *The Incomplete Folksinger* (New York: Simon and Schuster, 1972), p.351.

191 **"There Was a Young Woman Who Swallowed a Lie":** is a parody composed by Meredith Tax.

191–92 **Other singers who have tried Seeger's approach:** Michael Cooney, personal communication.

192 **"It's a nice song":** transcribed from *Pete Seeger Singalong*.

192 **"Just make sure everyone agrees":** liner notes, *Pete Seeger Singalong*.

194–96 **"There was once a tribe"**: Pete Seeger interview, recorded by the author in Toronto, 1985.

CHAPTER 13 – THE RETRIBALIZATION OF THE WORLD?

197 **"Even when you find utopia"**: Richard Holloway, in the radio show "How to Read the Bible," *Ideas*, CBC Radio, July 9, 2008.

198 **"men acted as women"**: Quoted in Glenn Willmott, *McLuhan, or Modernism in Reverse* (Toronto: University of Toronto Press, 1996), p.119. Original is from Edmund Leach, *Rethinking Anthropology* (1966), p.135.

198 **"McLuhan always avowed"**: Willmott, *McLuhan*, p.120.

199 **"patron saint"**: *Wired Magazine*, http://www.wired.com/culture/lifestyle/news/2002/05/52441.

199 **"Electronic man is in desperate need of roots"**: Marshall McLuhan, "What Television Is Doing to Us—and Why," *The Washington Post*, May 15, 1977, p.H5.

201 **a rumour spread by the brothers**: Martin Loiperdinger, "Lumiere's Arrival of the Train: Cinema's Founding Myth," *The Moving Image*, 4,1 (Spring 2004), pp.89–118.

201 **seven thousand francs each day**: David Cook, *A History of Narrative Film*, 4th ed. (New York: W.W. Norton & Company, 2003), p.11.

202 **"The urban workers, the immigrants"**: Robert Sklar, *Moviemade America: A Cultural History of American Movies* (New York: Random House, 1975), p.4.

203 **often played by women**: Butsch, *Making of American Audiences*, pp.148–49.

203 **a live narrator filled in**: Sklar, *Moviemade America*, p.19.

203 **the keyboard players resisted these attempts**: Butsch, *Making of American Audiences*, p.149.

205–6 **"Cinema's 100 years"**: Susan Sontag, "The Decay of Cinema," *The New Yorker*, Feb. 25, 1996.

206 **"in the national interest"**: Quoted in Wade Rowland, *Spirit of the Web: The Age of Information from Telegraph to Internet* (Toronto: Somerville House, 1997), p.148.

207 **Westinghouse also set up a radio station**: Ibid., pp.154–55.

207 **stations as a "public service"**: Ibid., p.155.

207 **the number of radios in U.S. homes increased**: Butsch, *Making of American Audiences*, p.175.

208 **"The ether is a public medium"**: Quoted in Rowland, *Spirit of the Web*, pp.158–59.

208–9 **"For years the national advertiser and his agency"**: Quoted in ibid., p.167.

209 **the production of musical instruments . . . and sheet music sales**: Butsch, *Making of American Audiences*, p.221.

210 **television show genres reflected**: Joyce Nelson, *The Perfect Machine: TV in the Nuclear Age* (Toronto, Between the Lines, 1987), p.55.

211 **"social capital"**: Robert Putnam, *Bowling Alone: The Collapse and Revival of American Community* (New York: Simon and Schuster, 2000).

211 **By the 1980s viewing had climbed**: Butsch, *Making of American Audiences*, p.250. Obviously, people do lots of other things while watching, or rather listening to, television.

212 **"The television screen has throughout the world replaced"**: Adrienne Rich is quoted in Joyce Nelson, *The Perfect Machine*, pp.145–46. The original is in *On Lies, Secrets, and Silence* (1979).

212 **people employ video or small-scale television**: I witnessed this in a village in the state of Oaxaca, Mexico (see chapter 9). There are many other examples.

213–15 *La Commune (de Paris, 1971)*, **France, 1999**: Information on the production can be found on Peter Watkins's website, http://pwatkins.mnsi. net/commune.htm.

215 **the corrosion of character**: See Richard Sennett, *The Corrosion of Character: The Personal Consequences of Work in the New Capitalism* (New York: W.W. Norton, 1998).

216 **"we are inventing the goose that lays the golden egg"**: Thomas J. Jermoluk, President and CEO of Silicon Graphics, at Multimedia '94, Toronto, 1994.

216 **"I wrote an optimistic article"**: Clarke Mackey, "Transendent Technology: The Contradictory Promise of the Computer," *Queen's Quarterly*, Fall 1994.

217 **An article about it appeared**: "Let It Stream," *Forbes*, Summer 1998, pp.90–92.

219 **useful players in one's personal cybernetic fantasy**: This idea is developed more fully by Lee Siegel in *Against the Machine: Being Human in the Age of the Electronic Mob* (New York: Spiegel and Grau, 2008), p.174.

219 **pseudo-knowledge of the perpetual observer**: This idea is developed further in Siegel, *Against the Machine*; and Ursula Franklin, *The Real World of Technology*, rev. ed. (Toronto: House of Anansi Press, 1999).

266

219–20 **"cautious and derivative"**: Siegel, *Against the Machine*, p.54.

220 **"The wolf of unbridled appetite"**: Ibid., p.33.

220 **Wikipedia**: Stacy Schiff, "Know It All: Can Wikipedia Conquer Expertise?" *The New Yorker*, July 31, 2006.

220–21 **Asian sweatshops**: See, for example, Joseph Galante, Connie Guglielmo, and Mark Lee, "Apple Is 'All Over' Foxconn after Suicides, CEO Steve Jobs Says," *Bloomberg Businessweek*, June 2, 2010.

221 **poorer countries bear a disproportionate amount**: Elizabeth Grossman, *High Tech Trash: Digital Devices, Hidden Toxics, and Human Health* (Washington: Island Press/Shearwater Books, 2006), p.25.

221 **The manufacture of billions of silicon chips**: Ibid., p.4.

221 **"server farms"**: Ginger Strand, "Google's Addiction to Cheap Electricity," *Harpers Magazine*, March 2008, pp.64–65.

222 **electronic waste recycling**: Grossman, *High Tech Trash*, p.2.

CHAPTER 14 – THE POLITICS OF PLAY

224 **"This is the story of the Princess of the Stars"**: Quoted in R. Murray Schafer, *Patria: The Complete Cycle* (Toronto: Coach House Books, 2002), p.101.

225 **"structures where people can blow"**: John Fox, interview with the author, 1985.

226 **origin of Welfare State**: John Fox, *Eyes on Stalks* (London: Methuen, 2002), p.9.

228 **"The pictures and sculptures"**: David Cayley, "Puppet Uprising," *Ideas*, CBC Radio, 2003.

229–30 **"past its sell-by date"**: Baz Kershaw, *The Radical in Performance: Between Brecht and Baudrillard* (London: Routledge, 1999), inside front cover.

229 **"The performative quality of power"**: Ibid., p.5.

229 **"how radical performance can actually produce"**: Ibid., pp.18–19.

229 **"a lot of things in the past"**: R. Murray Schafer, interview with author, 1985.

230 **"You have to go to a particular lake"**: Ibid.

233 **"applied vernacular culture"**: John Fox, personal communication with the author, 2006.

233–34 **"The aims are to release creativity"**: John Fox, interview with the author, 1985.

239 **"We will never see this world again":** Paul Hogan, interview with the author, 1985.

240–41 **"Our economic role in this culture":** Thomas Homer-Dixon, *The Upside of Down: Catastrophe, Creativity, and the Renewal of Civilization* (Toronto: Random House of Canada, 2007), p.197.

241 **Ours is a time when notions of social and environmental justice:** See, for example, the widely popular blockbuster film *Avatar*, directed by James Cameron, released during the Christmas season of 2009. For more about this, read George Monbiot's article in *The Guardian*, Jan. 12, 2010, http://www.guardian.co.uk/commentisfree/cifamerica/2010/jan/11/mawkish-maybe-avatar-profound-important.

241 **the present is always a surprise to the past:** Ivan Illich said something similar in an article, "20th Anniversary Rendezvous," *The Whole Earth Review*, Winter 1988.

241 **"wisdom writing":** Harold Bloom, *Where Shall Wisdom Be Found?* (New York: Riverhead Books, 2004).

241 **the organization of musical performances:** Christopher Small develops this idea in *Musicking: The Meanings of Performing and Listening* (Hanover, N.H.: Wesleyan University Press, 1998).

242 **"time of punishment and ruin":** Wendell Berry, "A Few Words in Favor of Edward Abbey," in *What Are People For?* (New York: North Point Press,1990).

245 **recent emphasis on community arts**: For example, the Canada Council of the Arts now offers grants through its Artists and Community Collaboration Program. The Ontario Arts Council has a Community and Multidisciplinary Arts Office.

245 **"conspirato":** David Cayley, *The Rivers North of the Future: The Testament of Ivan Illich* (Toronto: House of Anansi Press, 2005), pp.215–19.

SUGGESTIONS FOR

FURTHER READING

Here are a number of key texts that inform the ideas in this book. They are a good place to start if you want to learn more about vernacular culture.

Berger, John. *Pig Earth*. New York: Pantheon Books, 1979.

Berger, John. *Keeping a Rendezvous*. New York: Pantheon Books, 1991.

Brody, Hugh. *The Other Side of Eden: Hunters, Farmers and the Shaping of the World*. Vancouver: Douglas and McIntyre, 2000.

Butsch, Richard. *The Making of American Audiences: From Stage to Television, 1750–1990*. Cambridge: Cambridge University Press, 2000.

Ehrenreich, Barbara. *Dancing in the Streets: A History of Collective Joy*. New York: Metropolitan Books, 2006.

Esteva, Gustavo and Suri Prakash. *Grassroots Post-Modernism: Remaking the Soil of Cultures*. London: Zed Books, 1998.

Franklin, Ursula. *The Real World of Technology*. Rev. ed. Toronto: House of Anansi Press, 1999.

Illich, Ivan. *Shadow Work*. London: Marion Boyars, 1981.

Illich, Ivan and Barry Saunders. *ABC: The Alphabetization of the Popular Mind*. New York: Vintage Books, 1989.

Johnson, James H. *Listening in Paris: A Cultural History*. Berkeley: University of California Press, 1995.

Kershaw, Baz. *The Radical in Performance: Between Brecht and Baudrillard*. London: Routledge, 1999.

Muchembled, Robert. *Popular Culture and Elite Culture in France 1400–1750*. Trans. Lydia Cochrane. Baton Rouge: Louisiana State University Press, 1985 [1978].

Sennett, Richard. *The Fall of Public Man: On the Social Psychology of Capitalism*. New York: W.W. Norton and Company, 1992 [1977].

Small, Christopher. *Music, Society, Education*. Middletown, Conn.: Wesleyan University Press, 1997 [1977].

INDEX

country dancing, 20–22; community and relationship in, 22
countryside, conversion of, 164–65
Covent Garden (London), 166
critical distance, experience of works at, 20
critics: emergence of in arts, 173; media, 8
Cro-Magnon. *See Homo sapiens*
cultural commons, 110–11
cultural evolution, 45, 112
cultural expression, elite control over, 143
"cultural guerrilla tactics," 186
culture: assumptions about, 8–9, 12; as bridge to renewal, 241; commercial, 18–24; commodification of, 141–43; consumer, 11, 53, 101, 108, 168, 187, 197, 209, 219, 243; as dominated by texts, 19; of elite minority, 72; etymology of, 9; folk, 10; high and low, 112, 154; historical organization of, 9, 50; of majority, 72; mass, 10, 11; as part of our evolutionary heritage, 1; popular, 10; prehistory and, 49–50; as product for sale, 9; transformation of, 154; Western, attack on, 13. *See also* vernacular culture
culture-making, 1–2; benefits of, 2
"Culture, Technologies, Convergence" conference, 216
cyberculture, 218–22; local vs. distant in, 218; virtual vs. real in, 218. *See also* World Wide Web

Daily Worker, 185
Dali, Salvador, 92
dancing, 18; hunter-gatherers and, 60; !Kung and, 61–63; prehistory and, 50; street, 10; trance, 62–63,113. *See also* contra dancing; country dancing
Davies, Samuel, 113
de Forest, Lee, 206
Déjeuner de bébé, 201
democracy, 20, 118, 154; direct, 241; representative, 104
democratic ideals, 13, 14; printing press and, 142, 144
developed world, 104–5
Diamond, Jared: *Guns, Germs, and Steel*, 55–56
Dickson, William, 200–201
DiFranco, Ani, 179
digital age, 71; vernacular culture and, 221–22
digital devices, 221–22; metals and, 221
digital media, 220
Dion-Buffalo, Yvonne, 110
discipline: applause as, 172; orchestras and,

174; physical and psychological, 154; sweatshop, 154
disconnectedness to the earth, reaction to, 31
"disenchantment of nature," 169
dissatisfaction, 241
dissent, 142
documentaries, 205
Domestic Resurrection Circus, 226–27
Doucet, Clive, 27
drama, home-made performances of, 158, 215. *See also* theatre
"Dreamtime," 61
drumming, 62
Dryden, John, 46
Dufferin Grove Park (Toronto), 35–38
Dylan, Bob, 181, 183

ecology, human ancestors and, 48
economic crash (2008), 240
economic exchange, 8
economic globalization, 104
economic insecurity, 240
Edison, Thomas Alva, 200–202
education, compulsory, 104, 105; inequality and, 142–43; literacy and, 142–43
egalitarianism, 56
Egypt, hieroglyphics from, 137–38
electronic technology, 14; as adjunct to vernacular culture, 212; *La Commune* as challenge to, 215; global village and, 198; mixing of with traditional ways, 133–34; people's use of, 212
elite minority, culture of, 72
elitism, 13
El Salvador, 190
email, 218
emotion, public suppression of, 170–71
emotional catharsis, 1
emotional discharge, 81–82
empire-building, language and, 144–50
Enciso, Fernando Díaz, 129–30
encores, 163
Endicott, Karen, 56
entertainment: assumptions about, 8–9; historical organization of, 9, 50; homemade, 209; as product for sale, 9; working-class solidarity and, 205
environmental destruction, 215; human ancestors and, 47–48
environmental justice, 241
equality, 13. *See also* egalitarianism
Eratosthenes of Cyrene, 145

275

277

281

282